# Presimetrics

# Presimetrics

What the Facts Tell Us
About How the Presidents
Measure Up On the
Issues We Care About

MIKE KIMEL and MICHAEL E. KANELL

Information Graphics by
**NIGEL HOLMES**

BLACK DOG
& LEVENTHAL
PUBLISHERS
NEW YORK

Published by

Black Dog & Leventhal Publishers, Inc.

151 West 19th Street

New York, NY 10011

Distributed by

Workman Publishing Company

225 Varick Street

New York, NY 10014

Manufactured in the United States of America

Interior design by Susi Oberhelman

Cover illustration by Nigel Holmes

ISBN-13: 978-1-57912-835-7

h g f e d c b a

Library of Congress Cataloging-in-Publication Data available upon request.

"Facts are stubborn things; and whatever
may be our wishes, our inclinations,
or the dictates of our passions, they cannot
alter the state of facts and evidence. . . ."

—JOHN ADAMS,
in his summation to the jury in defense of
British soldiers accused of murder during the
1770 trial after the Boston Massacre

# Contents

# Introduction

Turn on the television or radio, open a newspaper or magazine, and soon enough you are sure to come across an expert (or three) with an opinion on the hot political issue of the day. Most of these experts seem to have an answer to every problem, from dealing with the national debt to reducing the crime rate. Sometimes their opinions are supported by appeals to the past. An expert might say that President So-and-So's policies made an issue better (or worse), so if we implement these policies again, we will see similar results (making some allowance for how the world has changed in the interim). This might appear to be a reasonable assumption, except that it seems no two experts are ever in complete agreement about what actually happened in the past. Did President Reagan really produce the fastest economic growth, or was it President Clinton? Did Lyndon Johnson's war on poverty succeed or fail? You'll find opinions on both sides of these questions. And it's not just the experts; we bet you don't know the answer either, and neither did we when we started doing the research for this book.

Our goal in researching and writing the book was simple: to present quantifiable facts about how our modern presidents, from Eisenhower to George W. Bush, have performed on the issues that matter most to Americans. Who succeeded and who failed, and at what? We did not rely upon opinon or conventional wisdom. Instead, we mined dozens of government sources for data and statistics, and carefully and consistently compiled them to objectively measure how each administration performed on specific issues. And the numbers, as they say, don't lie.

What we discovered over and over again in the course of our research was surprising. It turns out that in many cases, what most people believe happened in the past didn't. In fact, the pundits and historians are often wrong. For example, it's commonly acknowledged that President Reagan was successful in cutting the size of the federal government. But this opinion is simply not borne out by the data. Of the eleven American presidents who served from the end of World War II to 2008, Reagan was the only one who *increased* both the size of the national debt as a percentage of Gross Domestic Product (GDP) and the percentage of Americans employed by the federal government.

Of course, sometimes public opinion is correct. For example, these days people remember the years of the Carter administration as a dismal period when most people's income fell and the crime rate exploded. Well, it turns out that during the Carter years, adjusting for inflation, most people's income did, in fact, fall; the murder rate rose; and consumer confidence took a pretty big dive.

We've focused our fact-finding efforts on the Office of the President because it is ultimately the president who sets and controls the policies that govern our nation—policies that affect us all to varying degrees. Every president has had his own policies, which are often quite different from those of his predecessor and his successor. Furthermore, every president has not only made promises during his campaign, but also, to some degree or other, claimed to have lived up to those promises and left the country better off than he found it.

But all these claims of success can't possibly be true. So our examination of the presidents takes a look at their policies, how those policies were implemented, and how those policies held up—or didn't—in the real world.

WHEN WE STARTED WRITING THIS INTRODUCTION, we thought it would be a good idea to visit the White House Web site in order to find a concise description of the job of president of the United States—perhaps something about the job requirements or what it takes to be a good president. Interestingly enough, while there is a biography of the president (and the vice president, and the First Lady), as well as photographs and transcripts of the president's speeches, we didn't find a description of the job there.

So let's step back and start with another question: What does it take to be president? According to the Constitution, the only job requirements are that the president has to be American-born, be thirty-five years of age or older, and have lived at least fourteen years in the United States. In terms of specific skills, the only thing a person has to be able to do in order to be president is take an oath of office, and truth be told, it's a pretty simple oath.

But the Constitution also says this: "The executive Power shall be vested in a President of the United States of America." This means that the president is in charge of the executive branch, which is the part of government that runs day-to-day operations and executes the laws of the land. The executive branch also includes the military, and the president is commander-in-chief of all U.S. armed forces.

The executive branch has about 2.6 million civilian employees, not counting the U.S. Postal Service, and about 1.4 million active-duty military personnel. Some civilian employees are career civil service personnel. Others are appointed by the president. Some of them report directly to the president, but most work for one of the many federal agencies that are part of the executive branch. We will talk about many of those agencies later on in the book.

Other powers given to the president include the right to veto laws that are passed by Congress (though Congress can over-ride the veto), and the right to make treaties with other countries (though Congress has to ratify treaties for them to take effect). The president also makes appointments to the federal judiciary, appointing judges and justices. (The federal courts are mostly outside the scope of this book.)

But let's put all that aside for a moment. What most of us expect from the president, what we want from him, is for him to help create the conditions that make daily life better for everyone. If, at the end of a president's term, most of us are doing worse than when he took office, that president is deemed a failure. Reagan told Americans to ask themselves, "Are you better off now than you were four years ago?" He may have finessed the distinction between individual and national well-being, but his question is still the best measure we've heard for how well a president has done his job.

Obviously, not everything that happens during a president's term is his fault. He must contend with Congress, the courts, the Federal Reserve, leaders of other countries, economic trends, and even forces of nature. But a successful president is one who deals well with problems, grasps opportunities, and manages to make us better off.

PRESIDENTIAL PERFORMANCE ON MOST ISSUES, from economic growth to health care, can be measured. It just takes data to do it. And the U.S. government is, among other things, a data-collecting machine. There are branches of the U.S. government that compile or generate high-quality, impartial data that can be trusted, and whose reliability extends beyond partisanship. We have collected most of our data from such federal agencies. In a small number of cases, we obtained data from private sources, but even then, we made an effort to ensure that those sources were highly reputable.

The scope of our research extends across more than a dozen major issues that matter most to Americans, from economic growth to employment to taxes. In each case, we tried to find the data that best explained the issue. And for each data series that we examined, we compute the annualized change over the length of each administration. That is, we looked at how things changed from the point right before that administration took office to right before that administration left office. We also tried to pick time frames that were both consistent and made sense for the data at hand. When we looked at the change in real GDP per capita over the length of the Eisenhower administration, for example, we compared the annual real GDP per capita in 1952 (the year before he became president) to that in 1960 (Ike's last full year in office), as most people are used to seeing GDP data yearly, even though it is available quarterly. However, when we looked at the change in the stock market value during the Reagan administration, we compared data from the last trading day of the year in 1980 to data from the last trading day of the year in 1988, as stock market data is generally looked at daily.

Two presidents in our series did not serve a full term. John F. Kennedy served less than three years. That was enough time for him to be confronted with the Bay of Pigs, the building of the Berlin Wall, and the Cuban Missile Crisis. Gerald Ford served less than two years, buffeting along on events that were somewhat less glorious and melodramatic than the Camelot years. During his short term, Ford pardoned Nixon, dodged several assassination attempts, mounted an abortive campaign against inflation and a modestly more successful—if bloodier—military rescue in Cambodia shortly after the fall of Saigon. He lost a close election to Carter in 1976, perhaps because *Saturday Night Live* had by then managed to avoid the serious stuff and tag him as a clumsy, earnest goof. However, we felt that neither JFK nor Ford served long enough to fairly judge his overall performance. After all, some decisions take a while to have an effect. In many ways, Lyndon Johnson continued Kennedy's legacy, and in many ways, Gerald Ford extended Nixon's policies. Therefore, we thought it made sense to look only at "complete" administrations, although some were two-termers and some served just one term.

Thus, throughout the book, we referred to the presidents as categorized in Figure I-1.

We don't go back any further than Eisenhower, except in a few special cases. This is for a number of reasons. First, many of the data sets we use in this book simply do not go back that far, and some others become less reliable the further back they go. Additionally, because the world changed dramatically over the decades leading up to 1952, we can find no strong

## PRESIDENTIAL ORGANIZATION

| FROM | TO | ADMINISTRATION(S) | OUR TITLE |
| --- | --- | --- | --- |
| January 1953 | January 1961 | Dwight D. Eisenhower | Ike |
| January 1961 | January 1969 | John F. Kennedy and Lyndon B. Johnson | JFK/LBJ |
| January 1969 | January 1977 | Richard M. Nixon and Gerald Ford | Nixon/Ford |
| January 1977 | January 1981 | Jimmy Carter | Carter |
| January 1981 | January 1989 | Ronald Reagan | Reagan |
| January 1989 | January 1993 | George Herbert Walker Bush | Bush Sr. |
| January 1993 | January 2001 | Bill Clinton | Clinton |
| January 2001 | January 2009 | George W. Bush | GW |

Figure I-1

parallels between the events prior to 1952 and those that came after. The Great Depression, World War II, and the post-War demobilization of forces, the Marshall Plan to rebuild Europe, followed by a global cold war that included the outbreak of potentially cataclysmic hostilities in Korea were all events that radically reshaped history. We don't include data beyond 2008 because, as of this writing, there simply is not enough available to judge the performance of Barack Obama's administration.

ABOVE ALL, WE HAVE MADE A CONCERTED EFFORT to follow where the data leads us. One of us is a career journalist—someone who has written for decades about business and government and politics, and has been expected to maintain political neutrality. That's part of the job; in the newspaper business, everyone (except opinion writers) is expected to approach issues without bias. Of course, biases inevitably creep in, but good journalists, regardless of their politics, will strive to be fair, listen to all sides, and gather all the information needed to make their stories reflect reality. But if neutrality for a journalist is a professional obligation, it also turns out to be something of a luxury. Good journalists don't need to "carry water" for one side or the other, and are therefore free to change their mind when the facts don't fit their preconceptions.

The other author is a business economist who has worked both as a consultant and for Fortune 500 corporations. And while there are many business economists who are little more than advocates for one cause or another, a good business economist, like a good journalist, collects as much information as possible to figure out what is actually happening (or what will really happen). After all, bad information or biased conclusions can lead to very unfortunate business decisions.

We believe that an informed electorate—make that a truly informed electorate—is more likely to make good choices. Our goal is to provide information on a range of issues we think are important, not just to us, but to most Americans. We were not, of course, able to cover everything *you* might think is important. We weren't even able to cover everything *we* think is important; in some cases, there simply was not enough trustworthy data to do an issue justice. Additionally, there are probably some important issues that simply never occurred to us. But we covered as many relevant areas as we could.

And if there's one thing about this book of which we are proud, it is the approach we followed. We started by picking the most important issues we could come up with, and then tried to find the data we needed to figure out what actually happened, and why. We tried to be consistent, and to treat each issue, data set, and administration the same way. And we never tossed out an answer because we didn't like it. Our philosophy was to ask questions and let the data answer.

There's a story about the economist John Maynard Keynes, who when asked by a critic what he did when faced with new information, replied, "I change my opinion. What do you do?" In the process of writing this book, each of us came across information that contradicted our beliefs. When that happened, we followed Keynes's example and changed our opinion. We hope you will do the same.

## CHAPTER 1

# Real GDP per Capita

And now to our troubles at home.
They're not all economic;
the primary problem is our economy.

GEORGE HERBERT WALKER BUSH
State of the Union Address, January 28, 1992[1]

Some people may argue that the measure of a country's wealth is summed up in one word, uh . . . make that an acronym: GDP. In fact, you might have overheard one or two of those people at a cocktail party, with a glass of pink zinfandel in one hand and a mini quiche in the other, expound with conviction: "It's all about GDP." So is it all about GDP? Well, not exactly. But if you're trying to figure out the state of the U.S. economy and you want to use only one number to describe it, then a good place to begin is with GDP.

GDP, which stands for "Gross Domestic Product," is more or less supposed to be a gauge of all the economic activity in the country in any given year. It measures the value (i.e., the price times the quantity) of just about all the stuff (goods and services) made in the country that year. But not everything gets counted in GDP. Goods and services that aren't marketed don't get counted. Criminal activity isn't counted. Volunteer work is also not counted. Cleaning your home is not counted—unless you hire someone to do it for you.

And then there are things like pollution. You might think a company that dumps a lot of pollutants into the water, causing harm to people and wildlife, would subtract from GDP, but you'd be wrong.

Consider that in 2008, the GDP for the United States was about $14.265 trillion,[2] give or take a few billion. That's the official figure computed by the Bureau of Economic Analysis (BEA), which is an agency in the Department of Commerce responsible for a lot of our country's national accounting. So even in the midst of a harsh and long recession, about fourteen and a quarter trillion dollars' worth of marketable goods and services were produced in the United States in 2008. Fourteen and a quarter trillion dollars! That's a huge number—and that's good, right? Well, $14 trillion and change doesn't actually mean anything. It lacks context.

GDP in 2008.

So what context should we use? Dollars per square mile of countryside? Dollars per pound of fish served in restaurants in Des Moines? We think the best way to put this huge number into context is to divide by the population, which gives us what's known as *GDP per capita*. The GDP per capita for the United States in 2008 was $46,841.[3] This means the average output of goods and services per person, made in the United States in 2008 was about $46,800. Now, that's a number most of us can understand.

GDP per capita also makes it possible to compare countries in some meaningful way. Consider Belgium and Malaysia. In 2008, both had a GDP a little shy of $400 billion, according to the Central Intelligence Agency (CIA).[4] But if we divide each country's GDP by its population, we find that the GDP per capita in Belgium is $38,300, much more than twice Malaysia's GDP per capita of $15,700.[5] In other words, comparing GDP figures shows that about the same amount of stuff was made in Belgium as Malaysia, but we need to look at GDP per capita to see that most Belgians are much better off than most Malays.

The U.S. GDP per capita, by the way, is the tenth-highest in the world. Yes, that's right . . . *tenth*-highest. Most of the countries that beat us out are oil-rich nations like Qatar, Kuwait, Norway, and Brunei or banking centers like Lichtenstein, Luxembourg, and Jersey. (Now we know what you're thinking: Jersey isn't a real country—you've been to Atlantic City, you should know. But even though the Jersey ranked ahead of us is not *New Jersey,* we agree with

you; Jersey is, after all, dependent on the United Kingdom for its defense, and from what we can tell, its laws are subject to approval by the representative of the queen of England or a "privy council" in London. Memo to the CIA: Even your own Factbook on the Net claims Jersey is not an independent country. Move us up to number nine!)

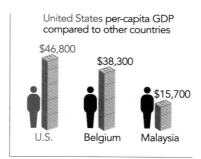

United States per-capita GDP compared to other countries

$46,800  U.S.
$38,300  Belgium
$15,700  Malaysia

Anyhow, GDP divided by population gives us a good, seat-of-the-pants notion of what's going on, economically speaking. But do we compare what's going on this year with what went on last year or ten years ago? Or take 1952, for that matter. In 1952, GDP per capita in the United States was $2,283. That's only about one-twentieth, or 5 percent, of $46,841, the GDP per capita in 2008.

It may appear odd to think that our national output was higher in 2008 than in 1952, considering that it seems as if everything is made in China these days. True, a smaller percentage of Americans are involved in manufacturing now, but what we manufacture—airliners, battle tanks, computer chips, and the like—tends to be high-end and high-margin. Americans also sell expensive services, such as financial engineering, energy exploration services, consulting, and marketing. And then there's research and development in a wide range of fields, from pharmaceuticals to physics.

But is it possible that even with all that, we only produced 5 percent as much stuff in 1952 as we did in 2008?

Actually, no. We can't just compare GDP per capita in 1952 to GDP per capita in 2008 because prices change over time. Just ask any senior citizen and he'll tell you: "Back in my day, it cost a nickel." It doesn't really matter if you're talking about loaves of bread, pieces of cheese, or even a car. OK, maybe not a car. But apparently, if the old folks we know are to be believed, a lot of things cost a nickel at one time. Since not much costs a nickel these days, we can conclude that not only do prices generally rise over time, given enough time prices can rise a lot. This general rise in the price of stuff is what economists call inflation. The fact that we've had inflation in the last few decades means that even if the same amount of stuff was produced in 1952 as in 2008, GDP per capita would still be higher in 2008 than in 1952.

So if we want to know if we really were *better* at making stuff in 2008 than in 1952, we need to adjust for the change in prices. Economists use the word *real* when they want you to know they have taken into account inflation, which means that if you see the phrase *real GDP per capita* you're dealing with GDP per capita, adjusted for inflation.

Adjusting for inflation may sound complicated, but it's not. Remember, GDP is the stuff produced multiplied by the price that stuff sells for. But if you multiply the amount of stuff made in 1952 by their prices in 2008, you end up with the GDP from 1952 adjusted for inflation into 2008. Economists would say you had computed real GDP for 1952 using 2008 as the *base year*. So to see how GDP per capita, for instance, has evolved over time, the first step is to put the GDP per capita from each year into the same base year.

As of this writing, when the BEA adjusts for inflation, it tends to use the year 2000 as its base year. The BEA updates its base year every few years, trying to keep prices relatively current. (It is scheduled to update its base year to 2005 just weeks after this book is due to be completed. Additionally, a number of series including GDP will be recalculated using a new methodology.) After all, most of us can relate to prices from the year 2000, but we'd have a harder time relating to prices from 1870.

According to the BEA's figures, the real GDP per capita (2000 base year) was $12,668 in 1952 and $38,265 in 2008. In other words, real GDP per capita

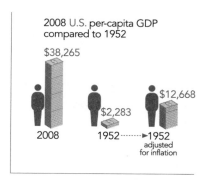

2008 U.S. per-capita GDP compared to 1952

$38,265

$2,283

$12,668

2008    1952········►1952
adjusted
for inflation

did increase from 1952 to 2008, but by three times, not the twenty times that GDP increased during the same period.

Before we take a more in-depth look at the numbers, there are a few more details about GDP to discuss. First, whenever possible, the base year we will use for any issue covered in this book is 2008. Also, to figure in inflation, we will use the Consumer Price Index (CPI) as a proxy for the price level.[6] The CPI, which is computed by the Bureau of Labor Statistics, keeps track of the monthly cost of a "representative basket of goods and services"—that is, it keeps track of the costs associated with a group of items that the average person consumes. To convert, say, the GDP per capita (or anything else) in 2000 dollars to the 2008 base year simply requires multiplying it by a conversion factor. In this case, the conversion factor is equal to the average CPI for 2008, divided by the average CPI for 2000. Or you can simply use the inflation calculator provided by the BLS, which uses the same methodology.[7]

# Real GDP per Capita—A Look at the Data

After all that discussion, let's get to the fun stuff, shall we? Figure 1-1 shows what the real GDP per capita looks like in 2008 dollars,[8] going back all the way to 1929, the first year for which the GDP was computed.

Notice that real GDP per capita has a tendency to rise over time. That is mostly a reflection of the fact that over time we develop better technology and methods of getting things done, which allows us in turn to make more stuff. We also have been steadily losing many low-value enterprises—and replacing,

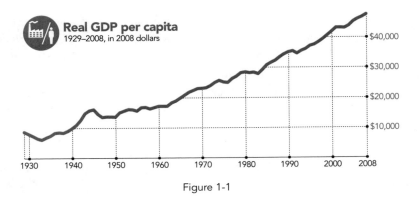

Figure 1-1

say, textiles production with a similar number of jobs making jets lifts GDP per capita.

You'll notice that real GDP per capita has had some bumps in the road, points where the economy slows down or even shrinks a bit. These points represent *recessions,* and we'll discuss that term a bit more later on. You'll also notice that there is a fairly big drop in GDP right at the beginning of the graph. That drop is known as the Great Depression, which began with the stock market crash of 1929.

That drop looks almost benign on Figure 1-1 because of the long time frame. But take a closer look in Figure 1-2 and see just how vicious that plunge was for America.

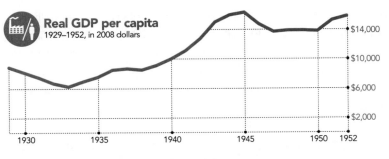

Figure 1-2

Real GDP per capita shrank about 25 percent from 1929 to 1933, the year FDR took office. The economy started getting back on track in 1933 or 1934 and had some years of extremely impressive growth through the rest of the decade, as well as one more short but sharp drop from 1937 to 1938. Real GDP per capita really took off during World War II, with massive amounts of deficit spending dedicated to the war effort. At the end of the war, there was another big drop in real GDP per capita as the country transitioned to a peacetime economy.

Figure 1-3 focuses in on the period from 1953, when Ike took office, to 2008.

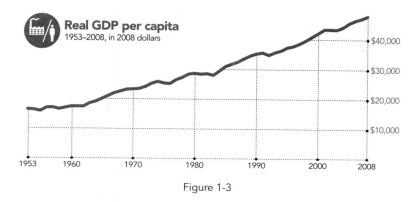

Figure 1-3

The line in Figure 1-3 is smoother than the previous two. There is no big downturn, as in the Great Depression, though we can still see some periods where real GDP per capita didn't grow much, or even declined slightly. For instance, real GDP per capita was mostly flat in the 1950s, dipped slightly in the mid-1970s, and dipped again in the late 1970s through the early 1980s. There were two more downturns since that time—one in the early 1990s and one after the year 2000. In a few years, we'll be able to look back and see another downturn, the one that began in 2007.

When all is said and done, the growth rate from 1952 (the year before Ike took office) to 2008, GW's last full year in office, was just a smidge under 2 percent a year, on average, and the real GDP per capita tripled in that time. But if we break this graph down further so that each section represents a different presidential administration, we'll see that some presidents did better than others when it came to making real GDP per capita grow. And some did worse. Some did much worse.

Figure 1-4 recasts Figure 1-3 as a bar graph to make it easier to see how real GDP per capita fared under each president.

Notice that while real GDP per capita has tended to trend upward during some administrations, it has been somewhat flat during others. So how do we compare the performance of each administration against that of other administrations? Well, if we wanted to compare the speed of different sprinters, even sprinters who have never raced against each other, we would compare their times over a specified distance. And a runner's time is measured from

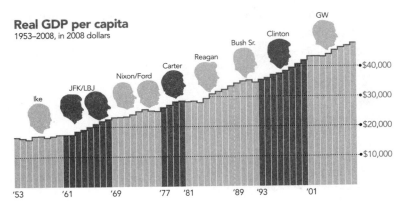

**Real GDP per capita**
1953–2008, in 2008 dollars

Ike

JFK/LBJ

Nixon/Ford

Carter

Reagan

Bush Sr.

Clinton

GW

$40,000

$30,000

$20,000

$10,000

'53    '61    '69    '77 '81    '89 '93    '01

Figure 1-4

when the starter's pistol goes off—which is right before she starts running—until the moment she crosses the finish line.

The analogous measurement when it comes to an administration's performance on making real GDP per capita grow is to look at the change in real GDP per capita from right before that administration took office to when it left office. Since we usually discuss the real GDP per capita by years (rather than by seconds, as we do with Olympic sprinters), that means we're going to measure the change in real GDP per capita from the year before an administration took office to its last full year in office.

To extend the metaphor, some sprinters get the advantage of a tailwind while some are hindered by a headwind. Similarly, some presidents come into office while the economy is humming; some face hard times from the start or run into hurdles along the way. So when we do our comparison, we will discuss some of those hurdles and hard times.

However, unlike sprinters, different presidents spend different amounts of time in the Oval Office, so a proper comparison requires us to determine the annualized growth rate in real GDP per capita. For example, consider Ike. Real GDP per capita in 2008 dollars was equal to $15,839 in 1952, the year before Ike took office, and $17,304 eight years later in 1960, his last full year in office. Thus the annualized rate of return for Ike's administration was $(\$17{,}304/\$15{,}839)^{1/8}-1 = 1.11\%$. Figure 1-5 shows the annualized growth in real GDP per capita over the span of each administration.

At the top of the heap, JFK and LBJ together presided over a 3.48 percent annualized growth rate in real GDP per capita. That result was a function of a number of things—some of it was luck, some of it was circumstance, and some of it may even have been due to the dawning of the Age of Aquarius. But,

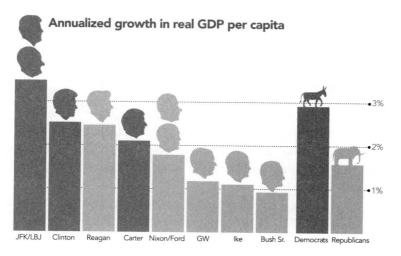

**Annualized growth in real GDP per capita**

Figure 1-5

as we will see elsewhere in the book, JFK/LBJ also focused on policies that produced rapid growth. Furthermore, as we can see from Figure 1-4, they were one of only two administrations to show year-after-year growth in real GDP per capita.

The second-fastest annualized increase in real GDP per capita—2.49 percent—occurred during the other administration that produced year-after-year growth in real GDP per capita, that of Bill Clinton. Fast growth is important, of course, but as we Americans learned to our detriment in 2007 and 2008, there are benefits to consistency as well.

Reagan comes in just behind Clinton, but with a growth rate in real GDP per capita of 2.45 percent, so close that you can think of him as tied for second. However, growth during the Reagan administration was more uneven; there was a short but nasty recession in 1982 followed by several years of rapid growth. Perhaps surprisingly, fourth place goes to Carter. He only served one term but it was infested with problems outside the president's control: inflation, the oil embargo, and crimes against nature like disco. But one thing is certain: A heck of a lot of leisure suits had to sell in order for the growth in real GDP per capita to be the 2.14 percent a year we saw during Carter's presidency.

Fashion aside, the rest of the presidents didn't do quite as well. At the bottom of the pile is another single-term president, Bush Sr., under whom real GDP per capita grew by a lackluster 0.93 percent a year. In terms of the two parties, the Democrats did quite a bit better than the Republicans, presiding over annualized increases in real GDP per capita of 2.82 percent, compared to the 1.54 percent observed during Republican administrations.

# Why the Difference between the Performance of Democrats and Republicans?

So those are the figures with regard to real GDP per capita. But do they mean anything? Do these rankings of economic growth reflect who did best on, or rather, who did best *for* the economy? And just as importantly, is the difference between the Democrats' performance and the Republicans' performance meaningful?

Well, yes and no. Consider Ike, who came in at second to last. At first glance that makes him look pretty pitiful. But Ike did a few things that laid the groundwork for future growth. For instance, as we will see in Chapter 3, his administration was the second most diligent when it came to paying down the real national debt per capita. And perhaps more importantly, as we will cover in Chapter 12, he had the vision for the nation's interstate highway system, something that still has a huge positive impact on the economy today.

So these rankings aren't perfect, but do we throw them out altogether? Well, no. Presidents often focus on the short term (when they, not their successors, get the credit or blame), and most of their decisions have their biggest effects in the short term.

But before we assign too much credit or too much blame, let's consider whether something else—something other than whether the president is a Democrat or a Republican—might affect growth rates in real GDP per capita.

For instance, pundits often point toward Congress as having just as much or more influence as the president. These pundits will often say one or another party has more of a tendency to spend money in inefficient ways or to act in ways that produce more growth. But is that true? Not according to Figure 1-6.

In fact, from 1952 to 2008, the average annualized growth rate in real GDP per capita—whether Congress was run by Democrats or Republicans—was 2.03 percent. While Democrats controlled Congress for three times as long as Republicans did (thirty-six years versus twelve years), the growth was exactly the same regardless of which party ran Congress. But what apparently mattered was that one party did run Congress—during the eight years of mixed congressional control, the annualized average growth rate was only 1.79 percent a year.

If it's not which party controls Congress, what else might it be? Another theory that is sometimes offered—and one that a president's supporters frequently give—is that their president would have done better if only his predecessor had left behind a better economy. For example, many supporters

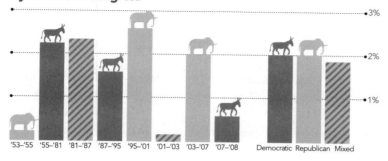

**Annualized growth in real GDP per capita, by control of Congress**

Figure 1-6

of GW Bush insist that the recession, which began several months after he took office, was Bill Clinton's fault.

It does make sense to posit that the administrations with the fastest increases in real GDP per capita were those that inherited better economies from their predecessors and those with the smallest increases in real GDP per capita inherited worse economies. So let's take a look and see if the data agrees. If we leave out the first year of growth for each administration, do those administrations that inherited poor economies look better, and those that inherited excellent conditions look worse? Figure 1-7 shows the growth rates in real GDP per capita, leaving out the first year's growth rate for each administration.[9]

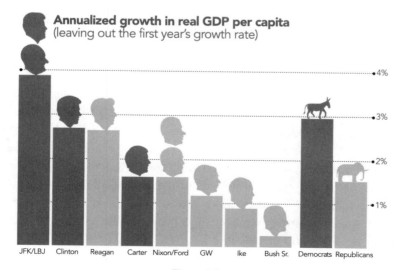

**Annualized growth in real GDP per capita**
(leaving out the first year's growth rate)

Figure 1-7

Leaving out the first year of each administration doesn't change the rankings at all, though it does affect the numbers. The two biggest losers, so to speak, are Bush Sr. and Jimmy Carter. Growth rates under Ike and Nixon/ Ford also are slower when the first year is left out. Clinton, Reagan, and GW all do a little better, but the big winner is the JFK/LBJ administration. This makes perfect sense, as there was a recession going on when the election for president took place in 1960 and the recession did not end until after JFK was sworn in as president.

In general, Democrats come off looking better when the first year is left out: The annualized average growth rate under Democrats actually increases to 2.99 percent a year. Conversely, the growth rate under Republicans is a smidge slower when the first year is left off. This indicates that since 1952, at least, Republican administrations were more likely to leave lousy economies to their successors than Democrats, as Barack Obama would likely attest.

And we did mention recessions, did we not? Recessions are periods in which the economic engine sputters. There's even an organization, the National Bureau of Economic Research (NBER), which has as one of its functions the job of determining (after the fact) when recessions started and ended. Contrary to popular opinion, a recession is not defined as two periods of declining GDP, but rather as "a significant decline in economic activity spread across the economy, lasting more than a few months, normally visible in real GDP, real income, employment, industrial production, and wholesale-retail sales."[10]

Figure 1-8 shows the number of months in each administration spent in recession as a percentage of the total months the president served.[11]

As Figure 1-8 shows, none of Clinton's term was spent in recession (although one began shortly after his departure). A recession was in progress when JFK was elected, and it ended in March 1961, a few months after he was inaugurated. At the other extreme, Nixon/Ford and Ike were saddled with recessions for 30 precent and just over 30 percent of their respective terms.

Not surprisingly, in general, the more time a given administration spent in recession, the slower the growth in real GDP per capita.[12] So perhaps recessions should be removed from our analysis. We think not. Going back to our analogy of the sprinters, that would be the equivalent of subtracting time from one of the sprinters who slowed down during a stretch of the race. If the president affects the economy at all—and while they are running for office most presidents promise they will do just that—removing recessions from our analysis would reward presidents who are bad stewards.

If the president is part of the reason that the economy is in recession— or part of the reason that the recession is deeper than it needs to be—then

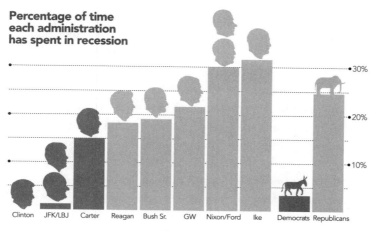

**Percentage of time each administration has spent in recession**

30%

20%

10%

Clinton    JFK/LBJ    Carter    Reagan    Bush Sr.    GW    Nixon/Ford    Ike    Democrats    Republicans

Figure 1-8

cutting it out of the calculation could be a way of excusing a president's own incompetence. And even if the president is merely the "victim" of a recession, it is still his job to find ways of ending it sooner and ensuring—if he can—that other recessions don't follow.

Consider, for instance, the argument we noted earlier made by many GW supporters—that his economic performance suffered due to a recession not of his own making. Such an argument would be easy to make for the JFK/LBJ administration; a recession that had begun in April of 1960—before they were elected—was still going on when JFK took the oath of office. Furthermore, that administration then went on to produce rapid, sustained growth for the remainder of its time in office..

That said, the recession that began a month and a half after GW became president may well have been brought on partly by the fact that GW arrived in office promising to dismantle many of the economic policies of the economically successful Clinton administration. For example, Bush promised to use the surplus that had been used to pay down debt to cut taxes, "strengthen" Social Security (which many people viewed as a plan to gut the program), and otherwise shrink the footprint of the federal government.

However, perhaps that recession would have happened regardless and GW bears no blame for its arrival. There is no way to know for certain. But we do know that the recovery from that recession was extremely anemic, and real GDP per capita growth was unimpressive during the rest of GW's term. Even leaving out his first year, GW still comes in only fifth out of the eight administrations. And then there's the Great Recession that began in 2007. None of that helps make the case that, if not for Bill Clinton, GW would have done a better job.

So what else can explain why Democrats outperform Republicans? Well, maybe it's just a function of the period we picked. Sadly, we don't have data from the future, so we can't measure the performance of the Obama administration. But we can go further back—all the way to 1929, the first year for which GDP was computed.[13]

By going back to 1929 we can add part of the Hoover administration, FDR's administration, and the Truman administration to our data. But before we do so, it is worth noting that many conservatives insist that FDR did a horrible job on the economy in the 1930s. These same people insist that FDR prolonged the Great Depression, which only ended because of World War II.[14] To accommodate that point of view, in Figure 1-9, we have separated FDR's administration into two: the last full year in office for "FDR 1" is 1940, and the last full year in office for "FDR 2" is 1944. (FDR died in April 1945.) Figure 1-9 also separates out the administrations of JFK and LBJ, and Nixon and Ford, looking at each president entirely on his own.

Figure 1-9 indicates that, if anything, going further back and looking at each president's performance separately only exacerbates the difference between Democrats and Republicans. As to those who criticize economic growth under FDR, they may want to take another look at growth in real GDP per capita during this time. Growth under FDR, even before the start of World War II, dwarfed that of other administrations. Furthermore, most of the top spots are not only occupied by Democrats, they are occupied by Democrats who, to some degree, sought to greatly expand the scope of the federal government in the same directions as FDR.

The only Democrat under whom the economy had a subpar performance was Harry Truman.[15] Truman was president when World War II came to an end, and the transition to peacetime was rocky. Strikes, shortages, stagnation, and scandal were all hallmarks of his administration. On the economic front, Truman was simply ineffective; he failed to push through most elements of his signature "Fair Deal" plan, and was forced to swallow tax cuts and the anti-union Taft-Hartley Act.

Another reason we might give for the difference in the performance between Democrats and Republicans is a variation of one we've seen earlier: Republicans generally do poorly because they inherit an economic structure from Democrats that tends to hinder growth, and the brakes on growth they inherit impact performance for a long time (i.e., for more than the one single year we checked earlier). Conversely, Democrats do well because they inherit a streamlined, growth-oriented machine from their Republican counterparts. However, as Figure 1-9 shows, Republican presidents that followed other

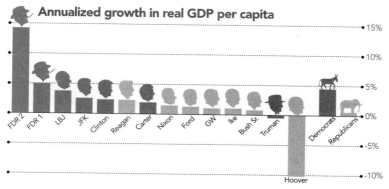

**Annualized growth in real GDP per capita**

Figure 1-9

Republican presidents (Hoover, Ford, and Bush Sr.) tended to post very poor growth numbers. On the other hand, Democratic presidents who followed other Democratic presidents included both Truman (with very slow growth) and LBJ (with very fast growth). Clearly, following a Republican president is no more a recipe for success than following a Democratic president is a recipe for failure.

# What about the Fed?

So what else is there? What else affects economic growth and might explain the difference between the performance of Republicans and Democrats? Well, there is the Federal Reserve, a.k.a. the Fed. The Fed is the nation's central bank. That means it is the Fed's job to decide how much money there is in the economy. The Fed does this by creating money out of thin air when it decides there should be more of it, and by making money disappear into the ether when it decides there should be less of it.

The main way the Fed creates money is by buying securities, usually U.S. Treasury bonds, notes, and bills. (Treasury bonds are U.S. debt instruments that mature in twenty to thirty years. Treasury notes have two- to ten-year maturity periods, and Treasury bills mature in a year or less.) So if the Fed wants to infuse $100 million into the economy one fine Tuesday morning, it credits the U.S. Treasury Department's accounts with $100 million (which did not exist until that moment) in exchange for securities worth $100 million. (This process actually adds $100 million into the economy immediately, but because of the way the banking system works, it will add well over $100 million into the economy over time. However, that mechanism is outside the scope of this book.)

But say the Fed wants to shrink the money supply by $100 million the following Tuesday; in that case, it sells someone (the Treasury or a large bank)

$100 million worth of securities. As to the $100 million it gets paid for those securities—that money simply vanishes into the ether. (Note: This process removes $100 million from the economy immediately, but a lot more than that over time.) We don't know about you, but we think being able to create a few hundred million bucks whenever we felt like it would be pretty cool.

So why does the Fed put money in and take money out of the economy? Well, consider this: When there's more money around—like anything else—it becomes cheaper. When money becomes cheaper, people use more of it—borrowing and lending it, creating new businesses, and buying lots of stuff. These things make the economy grow. But if money becomes too cheap, it loses value, resulting in too much inflation. So the Fed's job is—or should be, anyway—to put out enough money for the economy to grow, but not enough for inflation to become a problem.

So for the Fed to goose the economy, it has to increase the money supply per person. But that's not enough—it has to increase the amount of money per person faster than prices are rising (i.e., faster than inflation). If the money supply per person rises by 1 percent a year, but prices are increasing at 3 percent a year, there is less, not more, money "out there" lubricating the system, at least in real terms. But if the Fed increases the money supply per person by *too much,* well, as we said earlier, too much money causes it to lose its value, which means the Fed will be inadvertently accelerating inflation. So for the Fed the trick is to increase the money supply by *enough* but not by *too much*.

And if the Fed thinks the economy is growing too fast for its own good, that people are taking too many unsustainable risks, it may want to slow things down. It can do that by decreasing the real money supply per person.

There are a number of definitions of the money supply, but the narrowest, the one over which the Fed has the greatest control, is M1. M1 is made up of currency plus money in checkable deposits plus traveler checks. In other words, just about anything that is cash or would be accepted as cash in most parts of the country. Data on M1 is available online going back to 1959. The annualized change in real M1 per capita[16]—M1 adjusted for both inflation and population—over the span of each administration is represented in Figure 1-10.[17]

From Figure 1-10 we learn that the Fed has a tendency to keep the system lubricated just right when Republicans are in office—the only Republican administration for which we have data that saw a reduction in real M1 per capita was the Nixon/Ford administration. If any situation reflects the adage "The exception that proves the rule," it's the Nixon/Ford years. It was

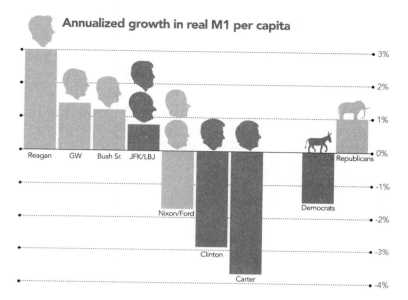

Figure 1-10

during the Nixon/Ford administration that the country abandoned the gold standard, at which point the Fed found itself in uncharted territory, and being in uncharted territory may have caused the Fed to make a mistake.

Conversely, only one Democratic administration, that of JFK/LBJ, got positive treatment from the Fed, and even then that treatment was a lot less favorable than that accorded to Reagan or either Bush administration. The Clinton and Carter administrations were positively hindered by the Fed's behavior. Greenspan's Fed would reduce real M1 per capita for seven straight years during the Clinton administration, an unprecedented span. Ironically, some of the smallest reductions came in the period from 1997 to 1999, the period in which Greenspan was warning us about "irrational exuberance." During the Carter administration, inflation was a major concern, and Paul Volcker was brought in as Fed chair in August of 1979 to deal with the problem. Unfortunately for Carter, he didn't get the prescription quite right until 1982, during Reagan's second year in office.

Thus, the growth in the Reagan administration was due in no small part to the Fed's help, and the poor showing by the two Bushes came despite plenty of help from the Fed. In all three instances, the Fed primed the pump enough to keep the economy moving, but not so much as to cause inflation. Furthermore, the Democrats outperformed the Republicans even though the latter generally got significant amounts of assistance from the Fed.

29

# One More Try to Explain the Difference between Democrats and Republicans

So we're back to our old question: Why did real GDP per capita increase so much faster under Democrats than under Republicans? We've seen that this difference isn't explained by which party controls Congress, nor can we blame it on conditions the president inherited, nor is the problem due to the sample of presidents we picked.

As we've already noted, the Fed has tended to be partial toward Republicans. Yet Alan Greenspan, a self-described "lifelong libertarian Republican,"[18] who chaired the Fed from the Reagan to the GW administrations, and who also worked for both Nixon and Ford, stated in his memoir: "I would say that he [Richard Nixon] and Clinton were by far the smartest presidents I've worked with."[19] In fact, Greenspan notes repeatedly that Clinton was very focused on economic growth.

The other Democratic administrations were also known for their economic focus: JFK/LBJ introduced the era of White House technocrats—eggheads, er, make that *numbers crunchers* who analyzed the economy as had never been done before and has been done few times since. Even Jimmy Carter, the worst-performing Democrat in our sample, was widely known as a micromanager. While that can't be confused with praise, it certainly doesn't indicate a lack of interest either.

By contrast, Alan Greenspan described how he tried in vain to brief then-presidential candidate Ronald Reagan on economic issues,[20] and how Reagan preferred to spend the allotted time telling jokes and folksy stories. He also wrote that Reagan told Paul Volcker, then the Fed's chairman, "I'm curious. People are asking why we need a Fed at all."[21] As to GW, Greenspan described his administration thusly, "Little value was placed on rigorous economic policy debate or the weighing of long-term consequences."[22]

So one reason that Democrats outperformed Republicans on the economy might simply be this: They cared more and they put more time, effort, and resources into making the economy grow.

But policies matter too, and we will be covering some of those policies later in the book. One policy that will come up again and again, however, is worth noting now: Democrats and Republicans have very different approaches toward taxes. As we shall see, those differing policies go a long way toward explaining some of the observed differences in the economic performance of the two parties.

## CHAPTER 2

# Fiscal Responsibility

I am not worried about the deficit.
It is big enough to take care of itself.

RONALD REAGAN
Joking at the Gridiron Club, March 24, 1984

I f your neighbor makes $30,000 a year, but spends $50,000, he is running a deficit. That's the opposite of running a surplus, which would require him to be spending less per year than he makes. But is running a deficit fiscally irresponsible? It depends.

If your neighbor runs a deficit because he throws weekly catered pool parties, takes the family twice a year to Bali, or insists on buying a new Lexus every year, most people would question whether he's spending his money wisely. After all, to run a deficit, your neighbor may be using up his savings, which means he won't have that money later on when he might really need it. Like many Americans, he might simply be borrowing to finance his spending habits. But every dime of borrowed money eventually has to be paid back. And not just paid back, paid back with interest, or "the vig," depending on where the money was borrowed from.

However, if your neighbor is running a deficit to pay for his degree in electrical engineering while subsisting on Ramen and canned peas, wearing threadbare clothes, and showering infrequently to save money, you might think he's being frugal and wise, if a bit aromatic. Even so, his behavior might not be frugal and wise if he never gets that degree and drops out of school. After all, running a deficit indefinitely means running down your savings and having to borrow more and more and more.

A lot of things are different about household and national budgets. But some things are similar for both the individual and the country. For example, the country finances its deficits the same way a person does: The money either comes out of past savings or from borrowing. And since the United States hasn't been saving for a long time, our deficits are financed by adding to our debt, which is a topic that we'll cover in more detail in the next chapter.

And, as with individuals, it's okay for the country to run a big deficit for a while, but eventually the costs pile up. A deficit that is very small relative to the size of the economy is not a big deal, and may be akin to a person using her credit card for day-to-day bills, but still paying off the credit card balance in full at the end of each month.

Whether the country runs a deficit or has a surplus comes down to two things: how much money the government receives, mostly through taxes, and how much the government spends. As we will see in this chapter, the president doesn't dictate the details, but he bears most of the responsibility for the budget. Whether the government has a surplus or a deficit is largely up to the person in the Oval Office. Not every deficit is bad, of course, and sometimes they're necessary, but barring extreme circumstances, such as a major war like World War II or some large catastrophe, a president who regularly runs large and increasing deficits is irresponsibly saddling the country with more debt. A president who year after year produces surpluses, avoiding the temptation to spend unnecessarily, is making the country better off.

## Government Spending

Outside of the most fervent libertarians, anarchists, and off-the-grid survivalists, there is general agreement that yes, we ought to have a government. But what should the government do? What are its limits? Just about everyone draws the line in a different place.

The Constitution says the federal government's role is to "provide for the general welfare." That's not too specific, but most people have taken it to mean that the government should provide services that the public needs and that the private sector cannot provide efficiently or should not be trusted with. These include services like building infrastructure, fighting epidemics, and protecting us from the Canadian hordes. It also includes whatever our leaders decide is "welfare," from bailing out bankrupt businesses to bombing the bejeezus out of other countries.

Which brings up the problem with government, or rather, for government—all those services cost money and somebody has to pay for them. It seems as if we're always part of that *somebody*—maybe you are, too—that ends up paying the bill through taxes. We the People who get government services, but also pay our taxes, hope that the government will be judicious about what it chooses to spend our money on.

Through the decades, the role of government has ebbed and swollen, doing more swelling than ebbing, if truth be told. But the federal tide has not always risen at the same rate. Needs change. For instance, we just might want a bigger military budget when we're fixing to defeat a couple of terrifying fascist states as in World War II. And sometimes we collectively decide that the government should do more. For example, until the Nixon administration, there was no Environmental Protection Agency, but nowadays most people accept that there is a role for the government in keeping the environment clean.

Some presidents are intent on "Doing Things," and Doing Things generally costs money. One president who wanted to Do Things was LBJ, and the things he did—from ramping up the Vietnam War to launching a war on poverty—were expensive. Some presidents at least talk about doing less—although it's a little tougher to find presidents who actually cut services to voters. Reagan came to office promising to be such a president, one who would reduce the footprint of the federal government. And then there are the presidents who, like Bill Clinton, promise to make the government more efficient.

Regardless of what the president intends to do, the process of actually Doing Things always begins the same way: The president submits a budget proposal to Congress. At the same time, the president unleashes his people; waves of economists and policy wonks who work for the Office of Management and Budget and the Treasury Department descend upon Congress and the Sunday talk shows to lobby, bribe, threaten, wheedle, and cajole. Members of Congress then do their own lobbying, bribing, threatening, wheedling, and cajoling on the Sunday talk shows and on the floor of the House of Representatives and the Senate. Eventually, a budget gets passed; a few of the items that the president put in get tossed out—some of those throwaways are put in for that very purpose—while powerful members of Congress add some new items (but not too many or the president will veto the whole thing and start the process all over!) and voilà, the final budget ends up looking a lot like the proposal the president submitted in the first place.

But what if an unanticipated disaster—like a hurricane, for instance—strikes after the budget is passed? When that happens, the president asks for "supplemental appropriations" and Congress usually gives him

exactly what he asked for. Nobody wants to be the one who voted against help-ing flood victims while CNN is showing the waters rising. Some presidents have used the fact that supplemental appropriations are not part of the budget to game the system, obtaining the spending they want using supplemental appro-priations and yet crowing to the public about limiting spending in the budget. George W. Bush raised this maneuver to an art form; toward the end of his administration, supplemental appropriations were funding not only the wars in Afghanistan and Iraq but also some of the costs of long-term military modern-ization. Were these unanticipated costs? We hope not.

However, while it might benefit a president politically to leave expenditures off the budget, spending that is left off the budget is still spending. Our focus in this section is on all the federal government's current expenditures; that is, every dime that has to be covered by the federal government either through its receipts or borrowing.[1]

Note that current expenditures are not exactly the same thing as "total expenditures." Current expenditures leave out purchases of structures and equipment, as well as expenditures on the government's own production of structures and software. However, while total expenditures have the advantage of being more complete than current expenditures, total expenditures are also an imperfect measure of government spending. For example, total expenditures also include investment expenditures by government enterprises—government-owned corporations like the Postal Service or the Tennessee Valley Authority—which have their own revenue streams and maintain separate accounts from the rest of the federal government. It is also worth noting that, unlike with government agencies, the president in theory has very little direct control over these government-initiated enterprises.

Thus, neither current expenditures nor total expenditures constitute a perfect measure of government spending in any given year. However, we opted to use current expenditures rather than total expenditures as our measure of government spending for several reasons. First and foremost, this is the measure the BEA considers most comparable to the White House's official federal budget.[2] Second, data on total expenditures is not available before 1960, but for most years, the difference between these two measures is small. The correlation between the two (from 1960 to 2008) is 99.98 percent, which means that, in general, the movement of the two measures is extremely similar.

Figure 2-1 shows this two ways: real federal expenditures per capita (i.e., how much the government spends per person, in inflation-adjusted terms) and federal expenditures as a percentage of GDP (i.e., spending by the federal government measured against the size of the overall economy).[3]

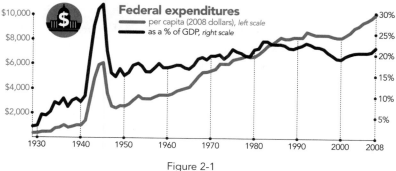

Figure 2-1

In 1929, the government spent $21.33 a person, which doesn't sound like much until you remember that back then almost everything cost a nickel. But seriously, even adjusted for inflation, it doesn't amount to all that much— $270 per person in 2008 dollars. By 2008, government spending per person had increased to about $10,160 per person, an average increase of about 4.7 percent a year.

A better measure of spending is a comparison of expenditures with GDP; after all, as the country gets wealthier, it can afford greater levels of spending. And since 1929, federal spending as a percentage of the economy has increased, rising from about 2.5 percent of GDP in 1929 to 21.7 percent of GDP in 2008. Federal expenditures as a share of GDP reached their peak during World War II. And though there have been a few (mostly) ups and (in the 1990s) downs in recent decades, since the late 1960s, government spending has never dipped below 18.5 percent of GDP.

Figure 2-2 shows spending as a percentage of GDP by president.

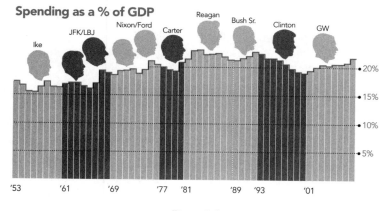

Figure 2-2

In the beginning of Ike's term, the Korean War was wrapping up and, partly as a result, spending ratcheted down, falling from 17.3 percent of GDP in 1952 to 15.6 percent of GDP in 1956. Then Ike decided he wanted to Do Things. First came the Federal-Aid Highway Act of 1956, which resulted in the interstate system we have today. And then came the wake-up call provided by *Sputnik,* which led to a burst of effort designed to allow our space program to catch up with that of the USSR. Nevertheless, it should be noted that while Ike Did Things, he did them on the cheap, relatively speaking; government spending equaled 16.5 percent of GDP when Ike left office, eight-tenths of a percent *lower* than it had been in 1952.

During the JFK/LBJ years, the federal government's spending as a share of the economy rose a bit at first, and then fell, dipping to a low of 16.4 percent in 1965. However, that was roughly the point at which LBJ decided he wanted to Do Things, the point at which the cost of the Great Society programs at home and the war in Vietnam began cranking up. By 1968, spending had risen to 19.1 percent of GDP, and LBJ was frantically looking for ways to reverse the tide. LBJ did manage to eke out a small victory of sorts at the end by dramatically reducing spending in his last few months in the White House. By the time he gave his final State of the Union Address shortly before leaving office, he could brag that spending for the year had already been restrained far more than forecast in the budget.[4]

The Nixon/Ford administration followed a pattern similar to that of its predecessor, with slight spending increases early on followed by a small dip, a big increase, and a last desperate push for restraint. Next came the Carter administration, which reversed the pattern. Despite his reputation today as a spendthrift, during Carter's first three years in office, he fought the congressional leadership of his own party when it came to spending, and managed to kill a number of big-ticket items he considered pork, such as the B-1 bomber that would famously be resurrected by Ronald Reagan. However, in his last year in office, perhaps with the upcoming election in mind, Carter's fist loosened up and spending rose.

Spending would continue rising during the first few years of the Reagan administration, reaching a post–World War II peak of 23.2 percent in 1983. As we noted earlier, borrowing has to be repaid with interest. Interest on the federal debt, equal to 2.5 percent of GDP in 1980, rose above 4 percent of GDP by 1985. In fact, by 1985, interest on the national debt consumed almost eighteen cents out of every dollar the federal government spent![5]

These expenses caught the eye of Congress, resulting in the Gramm-Rudman-Hollings Balanced Budget and Emergency Deficit Control Act of

1985. The act, designed to cut spending, was even more unwieldy than its clumsy name. Warren Rudman, one of its sponsors, declared it "a bad idea whose time has come." Like all bad ideas, it didn't quite work as advertised, but through threats and intimidation, it did lead to spending reductions. Still, the man who campaigned for the Oval Office complaining about Jimmy Carter's spending never lived up to his own promise to reduce expenses; in Jimmy Carter's last year in office, the federal government's expenditures were at 21 percent of GDP. In 1988, Reagan's last year in office, that figure had risen to 21.4 percent of GDP. Note that 1980 was the high-water mark of spending during the Carter administration, but 1988 was just about the low point for Reagan, as spending as a percentage of GDP exceeded that level for every year of his administration but the first one.

Spending rose again under his successor, George H. W. Bush. The burgeoning deficit, in fact, was a key factor in forcing Bush to renege—however modestly—on his "Read my lips" pledge of no new taxes. This was part of an agreement with Congress, an agreement snappily named Title XIII of the Omnibus Budget Reconciliation Act of 1990, known even more memorably as the Budget Enforcement Act of 1990. To go one more layer into the name game, the critical piece of that law was a cap on certain types of spending. That cap came to be known as PAYGO. What sounds like a Milton Bradley reject was actually meant as a rule forcing Congress to offset increases in spending for one area with decreases in spending in others—or, if Congress refused to make cuts, by increases in revenue. Or so the theory went; in the real world, spending by the federal government increased in 1991 and again in 1992.

Spending as a percentage of GDP did begin falling in 1993, when Clinton took office, and it fell every single year of the Clinton administration. The decline—from 22.8 percent of GDP to 19 percent of GDP—is only partly due to the rapidly growing economy. Among all the administrations in our sample, the Clinton administration was the only one to actually reduce real spending per capita, which fell about $373 (in 2008 dollars) while Clinton was in office.

Some people believe, or at least seem willing to tell others, that the relative frugality observed during Clinton's term owes more to Newt Gingrich and the Republican Revolution than it does to Clinton himself. However, spending as a share of GDP decreased faster between 1992 (the year before Clinton took office) and 1994 than from 1994 to 2000 (Republicans took over Congress in January of 1995).

Another theory offered for Clinton's ability to reduce spending is the aforementioned PAYGO of the Omnibus Budget Reconciliation Act of 1990 fame. But PAYGO was in effect from 1991 to 2002, and throughout that period spending decreased only during the years Clinton was in office.

Which leads us to conclude that, as much as his detractors don't like to admit it, a driving force of the spending reductions that occurred under Bill Clinton was, to put it simply, Bill Clinton. One big factor may have been Clinton's Reinventing Government initiative, which found ways of improving the efficiency of many government agencies and reducing their operating costs. Additionally, Clinton reduced the number of civilian employees on the federal payroll by 20 percent.[6]

Clinton's successor, GW, reversed many of Clinton's initiatives, and spending increased. A lot. Figure 2-3 summarizes spending changes during the administrations that have been in office since 1953.[7]

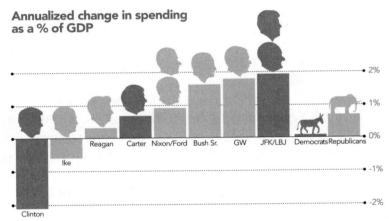

**Annualized change in spending as a % of GDP**

Figure 2-3

By far, the biggest annual drop in spending as a share of GDP came under Clinton. Ike was the only other president to cut spending as a percentage of GDP. Of administrations that increased spending, the smallest increases came under Reagan, followed by Jimmy Carter. The biggest increase came, not surprisingly, under JFK/LBJ: While the economy grew very quickly from 1960 to 1968, so did spending. The Vietnam War, the Great Society programs, putting a man on the moon—all expensive.

## Tax Receipts

None of us likes to pay taxes. But even a frugal government has to collect money in order to operate, and government revenues come mostly from taxes. Note that there is a difference between tax revenues and taxes. *Taxes* is generally shorthand for the rates people pay; that is to say, the percentage of their last dollar of income they are charged by the government. Tax revenues are the amount the government collects.

While people don't like paying taxes, tax revenue is vital for the government to operate, so taxes are a necessary evil. Oliver Wendell Holmes Jr. called taxes the price we pay for a civilized society. Taxes are also needed to pay down debt, and, as we will see in the next chapter, the United States is in debt. Reducing the amount the government collects in tax revenues at a time when the country is in hock is as wise as cutting an individual's income when that person owes money. Simply put, tax revenue is necessary to pay down that debt and the interest on that debt as well

But tax revenues also pay for other things—like infrastructure and maintaining the public order—things that we need for growth. Cutting taxes too low means we can't afford all these things, not to mention the interest on our debt, and growth slows. On the other hand, taxes may be too high. If the government takes away too much of people's income, they will be discouraged from working and investing; that slows growth. And if growth slows, tax revenues also decrease.

Tax policy, of course, can be stunningly complicated. It really isn't just a question of high or low taxes. There are myriad ways to raise revenue, targeting different tax brackets and economic activities—have we mentioned marginal tax rates?—but still, in a broad way, we can say that there is some level of taxation that is a kind of happy medium at which economic growth is maximized. There is also a happy medium where tax revenue collection is maximized. Sadly, the two happy mediums are usually not quite the same. We will be looking again at the happy medium in Chapter 6 and in the Interlude Chapter, but for now let's note that when people talk about the taxes they pay, they often mean the marginal tax rate, which varies with the amount of income people make. For example, in 2008, single people making less than $8,025 paid 10 percent of their income to the federal government, not counting deductions. If they made between $8,025 and $32,550, they still paid 10 percent on their first $8,025, and 15 percent on the part of their income that exceeded $8,025. (Again, we're excluding deductions.) The marginal tax rates gradually escalated on larger and larger amounts of income, reaching 35 percent on income above $357,700.

Figure 2-4 shows what the top marginal rate has looked like since 1913, the year the modern U.S. income tax was enacted, according to the IRS.[8]

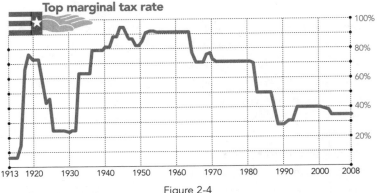

Figure 2-4

The top marginal tax rate on income has been as low as 7 percent, from 1913 to 1915, and as high as 94 percent, during World War II. After Ike took office, top tax rates stayed above 90 percent until 1963. They dropped as low as 28 percent from 1988 to 1990. And yet, despite all this variation in income tax rates, the share of the economy's total income collected in taxes has been relatively stable; as we see in Figure 2-5, from 1953 to 2008 current federal revenues (which are mostly made up of taxes, as well as a lot of "fees" that politicians try not to call taxes but which amount to the same thing) were between 16.3 percent and 20.9 percent of GDP every year.[9]

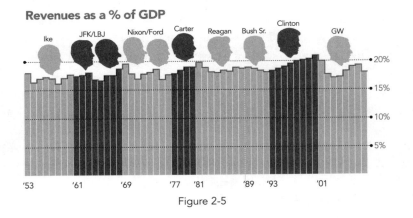

Figure 2-5

Changes in the tax rate do affect the government's revenues; for instance, tax revenues dropped (both as a percentage of GDP and in real per capita terms) after each of the major tax cuts between 1953 and 2008—the so-called Kennedy tax cuts in 1964, Reagan's tax cuts in 1982, and GW's tax cuts in 2001, 2002, and 2003. Conversely, tax revenues rose for eight years in a row beginning in 1993, the year of the biggest marginal tax rate increases in our sample.

So if there is a correlation between tax rates and revenues, why do revenues stay in a much narrower range than the marginal tax rates? The answer is that marginal rates, especially the top ones, are essentially a fiction; few people pay the top rate, and when they do, it's only on a portion of their income. This is partly because people with high incomes hire accountants to take advantage of exemptions and deductions.[10]

Of course, people with money *always* hire accountants, even when tax rates are at historic lows. Yet the amount that gets collected in taxes seems to behave very differently depending on who is president. Consider, for instance, that marginal tax rates were essentially unchanged between 1970 and 1980. And yet, during the Nixon/Ford administration, tax revenues as a share of GDP bounced up and down, generally trending south. Conversely, under Carter, tax revenues seemed to go in one direction: up.

Perhaps the difference lies in enforcement. Presidents appoint "their people" to positions in the executive branch. Those people decide how much to enforce—or not—existing regulations, and whether to impose new regulations. For the past few decades, Republicans have taken an anti-tax stance. And stealth tax cuts—tax cuts resulting not from changes in the law but rather from changes in enforcement that occur below everyone's radar—are just as real as tax cuts that get announced on television to much fanfare. So the data says Republican presidents have tended to appoint people to the IRS and the Treasury Department who are not fond of taxes, and who aren't particularly eager to collect them. The result is that, as we see in Figure 2-6, every single Republican administration reduced tax revenues as a percentage of GDP, and every single Democratic administration raised them.

The biggest reductions in revenues as a percentage of GDP came under GW Bush; when he said he'd cut taxes, he wasn't kidding. This isn't surprising since he made his intentions clear and repeated them often. He came to office promising tax cuts: During the campaign, the economy was booming and by cutting taxes he could give us back our money. By the time he took office the economy wasn't doing so well and tax cuts, he reasoned, were just what the doctor ordered to get the economy rolling again. And GW wasn't just cutting income tax rates. The estate tax rate was cut every year and because the economy still wasn't growing up to par, he instituted the American Jobs Creation Act of 2004, which cut taxes on income made by American corporations abroad.

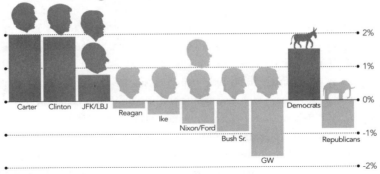

**Annualized change in revenues as a % of GDP**

Figure 2-6

Interestingly enough, three of the big tax cuts in the GW era had the word *Jobs* in their title: the Job Creation and Worker Assistant Act of 2002 (signed in March of 2002), the Jobs and Growth Tax Relief Reconciliation Act of 2003 (signed in May of 2003), and the aforementioned American Jobs Creation Act of 2004 (signed in November of 2004). None of these did as much as promised to put Americans to work, as we will see in Chapter 4.[11]

Of course, adding the word *Jobs* to the title of a bill is a great way to win support from the general public, but the "purpose" of those tax cuts to much of GW's base was something else altogether. For the first few years of his administration, the period when these tax cuts were getting passed, many of his supporters were advocating a novel political theory known as "Starve the Beast." In the widely quoted words of Grover Norquist, perhaps its most prominent advocate, the goal was to shrink the government "down to the size where we can drown it in the bathtub." The way to do so, of course, was by starving the government of funds; namely, taxes.

Much to many people's surprise, the second-biggest tax cutter (at least when measuring federal revenues as a percentage of GDP) was GW's father, Bush Sr. The man who reneged on the "read my lips" pledge (made at the behest of the aforementioned Grover Norquist!) may have raised marginal rates, but neither he nor his appointees at the IRS were particularly fond of collecting money, so for the most part they didn't.

Bush Sr. was followed by the Nixon/Ford administration. Nixon/Ford in turn were followed by Ike. Ike had a mixed relationship with taxes. He reduced some taxes (e.g., the Excise Tax Reduction Act of 1954), and he raised others (e.g., there were two separate highway bills, which both increased taxes on gasoline, and Ike signed legislation increasing the amount of income subject to Social

Security taxes), but by far the most important piece of tax legislation Ike signed was the Internal Revenue Code of 1954, the purpose of which was to increase the fairness of the system and ostensibly to make collection more efficient.

While Republicans typically point to Reagan's tax cutting as the approach all other Republican presidents should emulate, the Reagan administration came in last in terms of tax cutting by any Republican administration. Everyone remembers Reagan's big-ticket tax cuts; when he arrived in office, the top marginal tax rate was at 70 percent but by 1988 that figure had fallen to 28 percent, the lowest rate since 1933!

However, Reagan also signed a number of tax increases into law, the first of which, the Tax Equity and Fiscal Responsibility Act of 1982, came less than two years after he took office. That tax hike was followed by, among other things, an increase in Social Security taxes in 1983, the Deficit Reduction Act of 1984, and the Omnibus Budget Reconciliation Act of 1987. As we will see in the next section of this chapter, while Reagan reveled in his role as tax cutter, the massive deficits that resulted—despite assurances from advisors like Arthur Laffer and Robert Mundell (who would be awarded the Nobel Prize in economics in 1999)[12]—led him to reverse course to some degree. Still, his tax hikes were much more covert and were brought on with much less fanfare than his tax cuts. They also don't seem to be remembered by many of the Republican faithful.

The remaining three administrations—all Democrats—increased tax collections as a percentage of GDP. The smallest increase came under JFK/LBJ. This was in large part due to the massive tax reductions in 1964, often referred to as the Kennedy tax cuts, even though Kennedy died before they were muscled through Congress by LBJ.[13] Those tax cuts reduced the top marginal rate on income from 90 percent in 1963 to 77 percent in 1964 to 70 percent in 1965. However, JFK/LBJ didn't just lower income taxes; they raised tax rates as well, ranging from Social Security taxes (three times—once in 1961, once in 1965, and once in 1967) to income taxes (with a so-called "temporary surcharge") in 1968.

The biggest increases to federal government revenues as a percentage of GDP came under Carter and Clinton. Carter's best-known tax hikes were on Social Security (do you get the feeling by now that raising taxes on working people via Social Security is essentially fair game in American politics?) and on oil companies. Clinton famously raised marginal income tax rates in 1993; the top marginal rate rose from 31 percent to 39.6 percent of income. But he also cut tax rates on capital gains in 1997, just as the dot-com boom was starting, and still, revenues as a percentage of GDP rose every year he was in office.

Before we go on, we would like to point out one more thing—the notion that growth is hindered by taxes doesn't seem to be borne out by the data we've been using. In our sample of eight administrations, the three administrations that raised tax revenues, and the one that reduced them by the least, happened to be the four fastest-growing administrations in our sample. The four biggest tax-cutting administrations also produced the slowest growth by far. We will revisit this point in the Interlude Chapter.

## Surplus or Deficit?

In recent decades, the government has generally run budget deficits; that is, in most years it's spent more—sometimes far more—than it's gotten in revenue. One result of this is the growth of the national debt, as we will see in the next chapter. Polls often show that the public is in favor of taking steps to reduce the deficit, provided these steps don't involve raising taxes or cutting spending. This, of course, leaves Divine Intervention, the arrival of space aliens bearing fantastic new technologies, and taking Luxembourg hostage as the most viable remaining ways to get that budget down.

Sadly, none of these options is likely. However, as we've noted before, there are times when running a deficit makes sense—for example, when the country faces large, temporary problems. Nevertheless, in general, a fiscally responsible administration that inherits a deficit will try to reduce the deficit or even turn it into a surplus, and a fiscally responsible administration that inherits a surplus will try to prevent it from becoming a deficit.

Figure 2-7 shows the surplus (and deficit) from 1929 to 2008.[14]

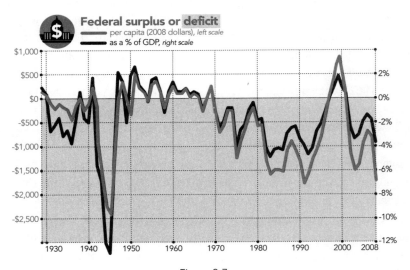

Figure 2-7

Figure 2-7 shows an enormous deficit during World War II. As we saw earlier, revenues went up a lot during World War II, but expenditures went up even more; as a result, by 1945 the government deficit—what it had to borrow—amounted to 13 percent of GDP! And this is just the deficit—not the burgeoning debt. But fighting a big war is an expensive proposition. At the end of World War II, the deficit shrank rapidly, and by 1947 the country was even running a surplus.

However, it seems that running a surplus is harder than it looks: From 1953 to 2008, the country ran a surplus only seventeen times. That is, the government had a surplus just 30 percent of the time; 70 percent of the time it was spending more than it was taking in. Figure 2-8 illustrates how that period looks, by administration.

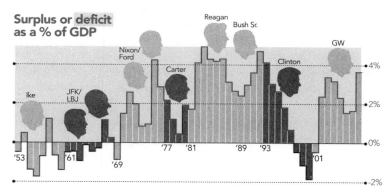

Figure 2-8

One of the most notable features of Figure 2-8 is the huge run-up of the deficit in Reagan's first few years, which reached a peak in 1983 of 4.9 percent of GDP (i.e., government borrowing was equal to 4.9 percent of the whole U.S. economy!). Reagan partly reversed course on tax cuts, but it wasn't enough, and he still left behind a substantial increase in the deficit.

Another notable feature of Figure 2-8 is the relentless, year-after-year reduction in the deficit under Bill Clinton. Simply put, raising tax revenues, cutting spending, and creating growth amount to a winning formula. Whatever you might say about Clinton's other policies and peccadilloes, we'd be in much stronger shape as a country had other presidents pulled off that particular trifecta.

Figure 2-9 summarizes the degree to which each administration was fiscally responsible or irresponsible by showing the annual percentage improvement or worsening of the country's fiscal position over the span of each administration.[15]

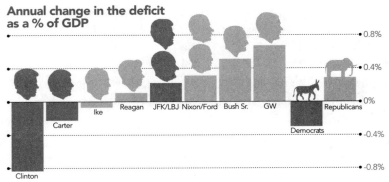

**Annual change in the deficit as a % of GDP**

Figure 2-9

Three administrations—those of Clinton, Carter, and Ike—left the country's books stronger than they found them. Each of them got there a different way. Clinton inherited a sizable deficit—equal to 4.7 percent of GDP in 1992—and turned it into a surplus of 1.9 percent, the biggest since 1951. Carter inherited a deficit of 2.8 percent of GDP and left office with a deficit of 1.9 percent. Ike inherited a surplus of about 1 percent of GDP, and grew it to 1.4 percent of GDP.

Of the remaining five administrations, the smallest increases came under Reagan and JFK/LBJ. Both produced rapid growth, which helped to make up for their profligate spending. Nixon/Ford followed, and Bush Sr. came in seventh. Last, and, as it happens, least when it came to fiscal discipline was GW Bush. He inherited a surplus of 1.9 percent of GDP, so the deficit of 3.7 percent of GDP in his last year represents a swing of 5.6 percent of GDP. In inflation-adjusted (2008) dollar terms, the 2000 surplus was equal to $839 per person, whereas the 2008 deficit was equal to $1,712 per capita. That's $1,712 that the government borrowed per person for a year on your behalf.

The data also shows that, in general, Democratic presidents were more fiscally responsible than their Republican counterparts. Part of the problem for Republicans was the reduction in tax revenues; the notion that cutting tax rates could somehow raise tax revenues seems to have had some credence among party members but that theory never quite intersected with reality. The other problem is that despite the brickbats Republicans often toss at Democrats when it comes to spending by the federal government, Republican administrations were far more likely to spend—and spend big—than Democratic administrations.

In the next chapter, we will look at the effect of surpluses and deficits on the national debt, and take a first pass at explaining what all that means for the economy.

## CHAPTER 3

# Debt: What Real GDP per Capita Leaves Out

You and I, as individuals, can, by borrowing,
live beyond our means, but for only
a limited period of time. Why, then, should
we think that collectively, as a nation,
we're not bound by that same limitation?

RONALD REAGAN
First Inaugural Address, January 20, 1981[1]

I n the previous chapter, we looked at real GDP per capita, how it grew under the various administrations and why. But we left out something important— debt. In this chapter, we will explain what debt is and how it matters to real GDP per capita. We will also show what happens to the economic performance of each presidential administration once debt is taken into account.

## The National Debt

Debt is as American as, well, spending. Maybe it wasn't always this way, but buying now and promising to pay later is how we do things these days. "Charge it!" is the American rallying cry. "Charge it!" is what we say when we're buying homes, cars, clothes, and groceries. And "Charge it!" is what we say when we're buying an aircraft carrier.

Now you may be thinking to yourself, "Wait a minute, I don't remember ever buying an aircraft carrier." But collectively, we, through the U.S. government, do purchase aircraft carriers . . . and roads and radio telescopes and mine-safety equipment. And whenever the government buys these things, ostensibly on our behalf, it usually says, "Charge it!"

When you say "Charge it!" you are incurring a debt. Maybe that debt is to a bank, maybe to a credit card company, or perhaps to the guy who sold you a mattress. But regardless of whom you owe that money to, you have to pay it back. And if you don't pay it back quickly, within some grace period, you will also have to pay interest on that debt.

Government debt works about the same way but with a few minor differences. The government doesn't borrow by putting things on its credit card, going to the bank, or asking a loan shark for money, as most people do. Instead, as we noted in Chapter 1, when it needs money, the Treasury Department issues (i.e., sells) "securities," which are just promises made by the Treasury on behalf of the rest of the government to repay whatever amount is being borrowed, without even having to put up any collateral. Some of those securities are very short-term, and get paid back after a few weeks. Some are longer-term; thirty-year bonds are not uncommon.

But sometimes when the Treasury sells debt on behalf of the government as a whole, the buyer is a government agency. In fact, a large chunk—over 40 percent—of what the government owes is owed to government agencies. That, in effect, is a situation where the government owes money to itself. For example, contrary to what most people believe, the Social Security Administration has accumulated a large war chest,[2] which it has lent to the U.S. Treasury. That doesn't mean the money doesn't have to be returned—the Social Security Administration also has obligations, and while it has generally run a surplus,[3] it is anticipated that it will need some of that money back to meet those obligations in the coming years. And if the Treasury doesn't have the money to pay back Social Security when Social Security needs that money—and we can safely forecast that it won't—it just means the Treasury will have to borrow that much more.

The Federal Reserve also holds significant amounts of Treasury debt. In fact, as we saw in Chapter 1, the way the Federal Reserve creates money is by buying up debt from the Treasury; when it buys debt, it essentially exchanges money it conjures (out of thin air!) for government bonds.[4] Neat trick, huh? Most of us dream of being able to create unlimited amounts of money, but unless you want to be incarcerated for fraud or counterfeiting, we suggest that you leave that trick to the Fed.

As of December 31, 2008, about 29 percent of that debt was held by foreigners, both investors and foreign central banks.[5] The breakdown of foreign ownership of U.S. debt is shown in Figure 3-1.

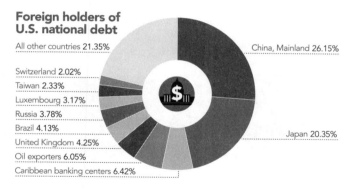

**Foreign holders of U.S. national debt**

China, Mainland 26.15%
All other countries 21.35%
Switzerland 2.02%
Taiwan 2.33%
Luxembourg 3.17%
Russia 3.78%
Brazil 4.13%
United Kingdom 4.25%
Oil exporters 6.05%
Caribbean banking centers 6.42%
Japan 20.35%

Figure 3-1

China and Japan account for about 46.5 percent of foreign holdings of our national debt.[6] Another way to look at it: About 13.5 percent of the total U.S. national debt is owed to these two countries.

On December 31, 2008, the federal government's debt amounted to precisely, and we do mean precisely, $10,699,804,864,612.13. That is, "just a few" bucks shy of $10.7 trillion. Put another way—on behalf of all of us the government owed about $35,000 for every man, woman, and child in the United States. Put yet one more way, at the end of 2008 the national debt was equal to 75 percent of the U.S. GDP, which means debt was equal to three-quarters of the country's total income in 2008.

The increase and decrease in the debt is closely tied to the surpluses and deficits we looked at in the last chapter; surpluses decrease the debt, and deficits increase it. However, the relationship is not one-to-one; minor accounting and timing issues mean that the change in the debt in any given year will be a little different from that year's surplus or deficit.

Figure 3-2 shows how debt has evolved since 1952.

When the United States entered World War II, the national debt increased dramatically; it would peak at 126 percent of GDP in 1946[7]—about 25 percent more than the country produced that year. After the war, debt shrank rapidly and by 1952, Truman's last year in office, debt had shrunk to 72 percent of GDP. Throughout the Eisenhower and JFK/LBJ years, debt shrank rapidly and pretty steadily, and by 1968, debt was down to 38 percent of GDP. The Nixon/Ford administration had a more complex relationship with debt; debt held steady in Nixon's first few years, then dropped to 32 percent of GDP by 1974. And though our primary focus is on debt as a percentage of GDP, it's worth noting that 1974 was the low point for the real debt per capita after World War II. That year, debt per capita in 2008 dollars was equal to just over $10,000 per person.

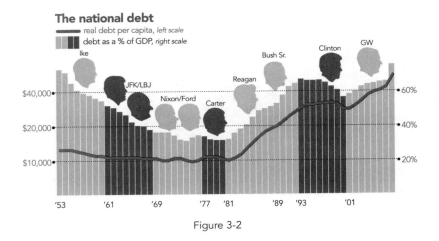

## The national debt

— real debt per capita, *left scale*
▮ debt as a % of GDP, *right scale*

Ike
JFK/LBJ
Nixon/Ford
Carter
Reagan
Bush Sr.
Clinton
GW

$40,000
$20,000
$10,000

60%
40%
20%

'53    '61    '69    '77  '81    '89  '93    '01

Figure 3-2

Nixon would be the last Republican president to pay down debt; from 1974 to 1976, when Gerald Ford left office, debt rose to 35 percent of GDP. The four Carter years saw a turn toward fiscal responsibility, but it would be all for naught. That's because Carter was followed by Reagan, who, less than a month after taking office, addressed a joint session of Congress this way:

> Our national debt is approaching $1 trillion. A few weeks ago I called such a figure, a trillion dollars, incomprehensible, and I've been trying ever since to think of a way to illustrate how big a trillion really is. And the best I could come up with is that if you had a stack of thousand-dollar bills in your hand only four inches high, you'd be a millionaire. A trillion dollars would be a stack of thousand-dollar bills sixty-seven miles high. The interest on the public debt this year we know will be over $90 billion, and unless we change the proposed spending for the fiscal year beginning October 1st, we'll add another almost $80 billion to the debt.[8]

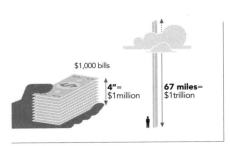

$1,000 bills

4" = $1 million

67 miles = $1 trillion

As we saw in the last chapter, whatever Reagan's plan was in theory, the reality was an enormous increase in the deficit during his first few years in office. By the time he left office, the national debt, which had been "approaching $1 trillion" had more than doubled to $2.7 trillion, and the stack of thousand-dollar bills that had been 67 miles high was now 193 miles high and rising fast. Interest payments on the debt—"over $90 billion" in 1981—were just shy of $200 billion in Reagan's last year in office.[9]

Using more relevant measures, real debt per capita (in 2008 dollars) grew from about $10,620 in 1980 to $19,860 in 1988, and from 32 percent of GDP to 51 percent of GDP over the same period. However you slice it, Reagan's profligacy bore no resemblance to his promises.

Bush Sr., Reagan's successor, continued Reagan's new tradition, pumping debt up even more to 64 percent of GDP. The run-up in the debt was halted by Bill Clinton; Clinton, as we noted in the last chapter, began cutting the deficit from his first year in office. However, the debt continued to rise for several years, eventually leveling off in the mid-1990s and then shrinking slightly at the tail end of Clinton's term.

But just as Carter's attempts to stem the tide of national debt were swamped by Reagan, Clinton's attempts to stem the tide of debt would be overwhelmed by his successor's spending. That successor, GW, viewed himself as the political heir to Ronald Reagan, and got Nancy Reagan's endorsement to boot. And he certainly was heir to Reagan's economic policies. However, as we saw in the last chapter, by his last year in office, in terms of both increases in spending and reductions in tax revenues, GW far outstripped his mentor. He also exceeded Reagan when it came to deficits. And yet, as we see in Figure 3-3, Reagan (and Bush Sr.) increased the debt as a percentage of GDP far more than GW did.

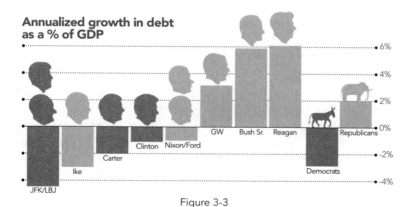

Figure 3-3

# Debt versus Deficit

So what gives? How is it that GW increased the annualized deficit by more than Reagan and Bush Sr., but under Reagan and Bush Sr. the debt increased by more than it did under GW? The answer is that debt is a stock, whereas the deficit is a flow. That is, the debt is the total accumulation of what the government owes on our behalf. The deficit, on the other hand, is merely the annual change in the amount the government spends less the amount the government takes in. So the difference between Reagan and GW is that Reagan borrowed a bigger sum of money during his eight years in office than GW did. However, Reagan started toning down his borrowing in his last few years in office, whereas GW's biggest borrowing bonanza came toward the end of his second term.

Another way to think about debts and deficits is to consider the plight of a cat owner. Such a person could tell you that at irregular intervals a cat will visit the litter box. Generally, that involves some sniffing around the box, a hop into it, a bit of rummaging around, and a not-insignificant amount of odor emanation. The process ends with kitty litter being scattered across the room in a parody of poop burying, followed by a hasty four-legged retreat.

That process is similar to the one that produces deficits. First, the president decides he wants to add a line to the budget. Some trial balloons are floated, some horse trading with prominent members of Congress takes place, a fair amount of trickery is employed to make things look better than they are, but no matter what, when all is said and done, something messy is usually left behind. That mess is the deficit. And cat owners know that while you don't have to clean up every time the cat uses the box, if you don't clean up every so often, you end up with a real problem. Letting the mess—er, deficits— accumulate results in a growing national debt.

As Figure 3-4 shows, Reagan, Bush Sr., and GW were like cat owners who never cleaned up the litter box. And while Reagan's cat learned to leave smaller poops over time (i.e., after a few years in office, his massive deficits began to shrink), it produced the most poop overall.

The remaining administrations were all, to some degree or other, responsible when it came to paying down the debt as a percentage of GDP. The most diligent at paying down debt were JFK/LBJ and Ike, followed by Clinton and Carter. Of the administrations that reduced the debt, the Nixon/Ford administration did so by the least. As noted earlier, our debt became less onerous while Nixon was in office but grew during the Ford years. Under Democratic administrations overall, debt as a percentage of GDP shrank, while on average under Republican administrations it rose.

But what is it about the last three Republican administrations (four, if you count Ford separately from Nixon) that resulted in all of them increasing the debt?

We think part of the reason for this is a structural shift that took place within the Republican Party during the 1960s and 1970s. The party built a winning base on several constituencies with not-always-congruent desires. They wanted their way on social issues, of course. They wanted a bigger military. They also wanted lower taxes. Promising everything has always been a good strategy for winning elections, even if many of the promises are contradictory. Moreover, much of the Republican base came to believe that the things Republicans want to see the government provide, such as the military, are virtually costless, while Democratic programs are filled with waste. Not that most Republican presidents managed to cut social spending, but still, the promise remained. As did the campaign posturing.

Nevertheless, while many Republicans might underestimate the costs of a more muscular military or overestimate the amount of fat available to be cut from social programs, most of them recognized that, overall, their spending plans required increases in spending, at least at first. The only way to round the square was to assert that tax cuts pay for themselves. For many in the Republican base, that notion has moved from "voodoo economics" to doctrine. That has made the Republicans the party not just of the free lunch, but free dinner and free breakfast the morning after.

Consider, for instance, that less than two months after taking office GW laid out a plan to aggressively pay down the debt while simultaneously cutting taxes and boosting military spending. The plan was titled: "A Blueprint for New Beginnings: A Responsible Budget for America's Priorities." One can only wonder what an *irresponsible* budget might have looked like to GW's advisors.

And yet this new breed of Republicans is also convinced that fiscal recklessness is the exclusive domain of their political opponents. This less-than-realistic view of the world may owe a lot to Reagan but it lives on today. Its effects are pernicious—as long as the television talking heads continue to perpetuate that myth, the most viable Republican candidates for president will be those promoting policies that will increase the debt. That doesn't work to the nation's benefit if Democrats who make it to the Oval Office realize that they are going to be tarred as fiscally irresponsible no matter what, so why make the tough decisions that Republican presidents have refused to make in recent decades?

## The Net Real GDP per Capita

As we noted in Chapter 1, it's all kinda sorta about GDP. Or rather, it's all kinda sorta about real GDP per capita. Except that we lied; it's not. Because real GDP per capita has a very big flaw. But before we tell you what it is, we want to bring up a hypothetical question.

Say your neighbor makes $40,000 a year. And say he has a $10,000 limit on his credit card. Now what if he maxes out his credit card, charging up $10,000 for a flat-screen TV, a digital camera, and some designer denim for his girlfriend? Would you say his income this year is $50,000? Good, because we wouldn't either.

Which brings us to the way GDP is calculated. See, one of the things that goes into GDP is government spending. That means that the government can boost GDP simply by spending money. And it can get more money to spend simply by borrowing. So if the government wants to boost GDP, and real GDP per capita for that matter, it can do it by borrowing a lot of money and spending it. And while this can help make the economy look "growthier," it also brings with it a big problem: Any debt has to be serviced eventually, and that's a cost that will have to be borne by the taxpayers at some point.

For many presidents, being able to boost growth at the cost of future tax increases or spending cuts is not a bad bargain. After all, what happens in the future happens on another president's watch but the growth it pays for happens now. As Alan Greenspan put it, "The hard truth was that Reagan had borrowed from Clinton, and Clinton was having to pay it back."[10]

So a more accurate measure of the size of economic growth would be GDP less the change in debt used to finance the government spending portion of GDP. By accounting for this change in debt, presidents who juiced GDP by borrowing and spending and foisting costs onto their successors (cough, cough, Reagan, cough) are penalized. For lack of a better term, we're going to call this measure—real GDP per capita less the change in real debt per capita—the net real GDP per capita.[11]

Let's go to the tape—Figure 3-4 shows what net real GDP per capita looks like going back to 1953, by administration.

Figure 3-5 shows the same measure broken down by administration.

Not surprisingly, the JFK/LBJ and Clinton administrations are in first place when it comes to net real GDP per capita; both produced rapid increases in real GDP per capita and did so while paying down debt. Third place goes to Reagan; his increases in real GDP per capita, already supercharged by a little "something-something" from the Fed, also benefited from massive increases in the debt. Once that obligation to future generations is removed, Reagan's growth looks less impressive; whereas real GDP per capita increased by 2.45 percent under Reagan, net real GDP per capita increased by only 1.7 percent a year.

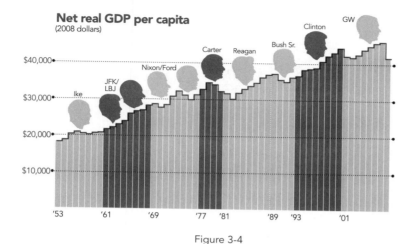

**Net real GDP per capita**
(2008 dollars)

Ike · JFK/LBJ · Nixon/Ford · Carter · Reagan · Bush Sr. · Clinton · GW

$40,000
$30,000
$20,000
$10,000

'53   '61   '69   '77   '81   '89   '93   '01

Figure 3-4

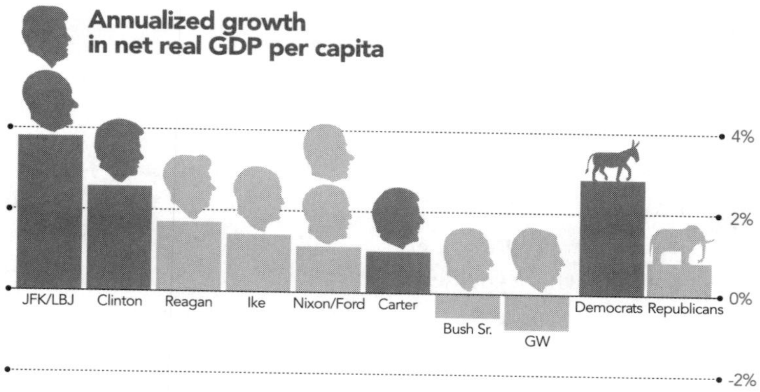

**Annualized growth in net real GDP per capita**

JFK/LBJ · Clinton · Reagan · Ike · Nixon/Ford · Carter · Bush Sr. · GW · Democrats · Republicans

4%
2%
0%
-2%

Figure 3-5

Ike, on the other hand, looks much better when you account for his fiscal diligence; he jumps from seventh place in real GDP per capita growth (1.11 percent a year) to fourth place in net real GDP per capita growth (1.39 percent a year). Nixon/Ford and Carter followed.

In last place were the two Bush presidents. Both of them produced decreases in net real GDP per capita. During their terms in office—GW's especially—mediocre growth was exacerbated by fiscal irresponsibility. The result was a national debt increasing faster than our collective national income.

Overall, Democrats produced faster growth rates in net real GDP per capita. Why? Perhaps the policies favored by Republicans—tax cuts, a focus on big business, and smaller government—may not be as amenable to economic growth as the policies favored by Democrats.

## CHAPTER 4

# Employment

But in terms of policy and the focus of
this administration, we're going to
do everything we can to increase jobs so
people can find work.

GEORGE W. BUSH
March 8, 2002[1]

e all need to eat. Unfortunately, food doesn't grow on trees or come out of the ground. It appears magically in markets, restaurants, and movie theaters where you need money if you want to buy it. Money is also used to pay for many more things we need to live, like housing, clothes, and most important, cable television. Ergo, we all need money.

For most of us, making money means having a job or a business. This chapter looks at issues relating to jobs over the past few decades, such as how easy they were to come by and how much they paid. We also look at the degree to which jobs provided an important benefit easily worth its weight in cash—health insurance.

## Do People Have Jobs? A Look at the Employment-to-Population Ratio

Being unemployed is, like many maladies, contagious. People who lose their jobs are beset with money worries. Because of those worries, they cut back on spending. If a bunch of people lose their jobs, especially if they live in the same area or buy from the same merchants, the effect can cascade throughout the economy. If a lumber mill closes down, the employees of that lumber mill aren't the only ones to get hurt. The restaurants, stores, and services that cater to the former employees of the lumber mill also lose money and shed jobs.

And when a lot of people lose their jobs (or are afraid they might lose their jobs), the effects spread widely. Businesses lose business. They too can start to lay off workers and the process feeds on itself. As a result, investors, economists, elected officials, and planners all pay a lot of attention every month when the Bureau of Labor Statistics releases the new unemployment rate figures.

But the way the unemployment rate is computed has a very serious flaw. It purports to show the percentage of Americans of working age who would like a job but cannot find one. (Running one's own business, by the way, is considered a job by the numbers crunchers at the Bureau of Labor Statistics.) However, what it really shows is the percentage of Americans of working age who want a job *but have not given up looking for one.*

See, unemployment figures do not count so-called "discouraged workers." Discouraged workers are people who want jobs but have stopped searching for them. Truth be told, some discouraged workers may be discouraged because they are unemployable. However, when economic conditions are tough and jobs are scarce, the number of people competing for a small pool of jobs can make it hard for even the very talented to find work. And when that happens, the number of discouraged workers can rise as people throw in the towel. And because discouraged workers are not counted in the unemployment rolls, as it gets harder to find a job, the unemployment rate can actually fall for a while. Nope, we're not kidding.

So a better measure of the job market's shape, that is, whether economic conditions allow people to find jobs or start businesses, is the employment-to-population ratio. It measures the percentage of noninstitutionalized civilians (i.e., folks who aren't in jail, in the military, or in nursing homes) sixteen years old and over who have jobs or businesses.[2]

The employment-to-population ratio figures, going back to 1948, the first year for which the data is available on the Bureau of Labor Statistics (BLS) Web site,[3] appear in graphic form in Figure 4-1.

Figure 4-1 shows that the employment-to-population ratio in the 1950s was in the neighborhood of 56 percent but it slowly rose in the 1980s; since then it has remained above 60 percent. A big part of this increase involves the changing role of women, who, perhaps to the surprise of 1950s-era patriarchs, are generally able to loaf at the office or goldbrick as well as any man.

Additionally, people live longer, healthier lives these days; it isn't uncommon to see people over sixty-five keeping their jobs or even getting

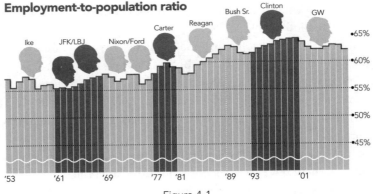

**Employment-to-population ratio**

Figure 4-1

new ones. Another factor that affects people's decisions about whether to get a job—and their ability to do so—is the economy. In bleak times, finding a job becomes harder. On the other hand, if jobs are plentiful and pay well, an otherwise-stay-at-home mom (or dad, in this liberated, twenty-first-century America) or retiree might find it advantageous to get a job.

In addition, some time in the last few decades the economy moved from a point where a single income could support a family to a point where it now seems to take two incomes to keep the average family afloat. The result is that a lot of women and elderly folks who in earlier times wouldn't want to be employed now work hard to keep those paychecks coming in.

The only eight-year stretch in the sample during which there were year-after-year gains in the employment-to-population ratio came during the Clinton administration. This was a time of rapid economic growth and prosperity. But as Figure 4-2 shows, despite the year-after-year gains from 1992 to 2000, the biggest annual increases in the percentage of the population with jobs came during the Carter years.

Carter was extremely concerned about the ability of Americans to get jobs. In his first communiqué to Congress, days after taking office, he lamented:

> The economy I found when I took office had 7.5 million Americans out of work, 1.4 million full-time workers forced to take part-time jobs, and still another 1 million workers who had dropped out of the labor force because jobs are so hard to find.[4]

(Notice the mention of discouraged workers!) Carter went on to propose job-training programs, works programs, and tax rebates to small businesses. He also proposed that Vietnam veterans be given extra opportunities—that program

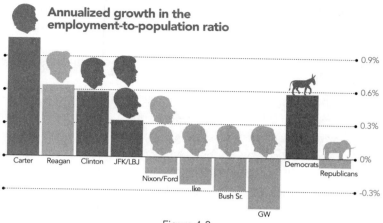

**Annualized growth in the employment-to-population ratio**

Figure 4-2

is still around today, as anyone who has filled out an employment application can attest. Carter would follow that up a few days later with a speech broadcast live on television and radio in which he affirmed to the American public:

[M]y primary concern is still jobs . . .[5]

Half a year later, the employment-to-population ratio had risen several points, and Carter could report that:

Since last November, we've had about a 3 million net increase in the number of jobs available in our country.[6]

Jobs remained a priority for Carter throughout his term. One of the highest-profile pieces of jobs-related legislation during his presidency was the Humphrey-Hawkins Full Employment Act of 1978. Carter endorsed the legislation in its early stages, then worked toward a compromise when the business community balked at some of the more ponderous, not to say inflexible and contradictory, goals of the original proposal. When finally completed, the watered-down version of the act set several targets for 1983; namely a 4 percent unemployment rate and 0 percent inflation rate. The federal government was also authorized to create new jobs (i.e., hire people directly) if the unemployment rate wasn't met.

None of these targets were achieved, but the act was an implicit declaration that the government was responsible for seeing to it that people find jobs. Not everyone believes such a thing, and that philosophical view doesn't seem to have outlived the Carter administration. Still, at least two provisions of the act have taken on a life of their own and continue to this day. One prevented discrimination in many jobs by gender, religion, ethnicity, age, or national origin. The other required the Federal Reserve to report to Congress twice a year on the state of the economy.

Despite his commitment to putting people to work, Carter's job-creation record was blemished during his last year in office. The economic downturn that began with the second oil crisis following the Iranian revolution also reduced job creation, cutting the employment-to-population ratio from 59.9 percent in 1979 to 59.2 percent in 1980.

The job downturn continued until 1983. Nevertheless, Ronald Reagan, who succeeded Carter, came in a close second when it came to employing Americans. Again, the main impetus for jobs was economic growth. But as we will see in the next section, for both Carter and Reagan the new jobs came at a price; they didn't pay very well. That was not true of the administrations that came in third and fourth place on job creation, those of Clinton and JFK/LBJ.

We've already noted that the Clinton administration was conspicuous for being the only administration in our sample under which the employment-to-population ratio rose every single year. Under JFK/LBJ, on the other hand, that employment-to-population level remained essentially flat until LBJ took office, at which point it marched steadily upward. The reason for this may depend on who you ask. Conservatives would point to the tax cuts in 1964. (We will look at the relationship between taxes and job creation in more detail later in the book.) Liberals tend to credit the massive increases in government spending that created opportunities for the poor through the war on poverty. They would also say that the Civil Rights Act, which made it easier for women and minorities to secure employment, probably helped as well.

The remaining administrations all oversaw job losses, with the biggest job losses occurring during the two Bush presidencies. Overall, Democratic administrations were better at creating jobs than their Republican counterparts. This is partly because Democrats do a better job at overall growth, but it doesn't hurt that Democrats also tend to focus more on responding to the needs of those seeking jobs, whereas for many Republicans, especially in recent years, the solution to every problem is a tax cut. (That isn't to say that the right approach may not be a tax cut at certain times, merely that reflexively relying on tax cuts to solve all the world's ills has proven to be naive. Or worse.) Recall, as noted in Chapter 2, that GW had three major tax cuts, each with some variation of the word *Jobs* in their name, and the results were weak, at least when it came to job growth.

# Real Wages

The job market isn't just about how many jobs are available. It's also about how much they pay. And most people don't make enough money. If you don't believe that, just ask around. You'll be hard-pressed to find a lot of people who will claim to be paid what they're worth, much less overpaid. But how badly are we Americans collectively underpaid? And how has that changed over time? Well, we don't know how much we're all getting underpaid, but we can tell you how much the average working American is making. Data for the real average weekly earnings "of production and nonsupervisory workers on private nonfarm payrolls" is available from the Bureau of Labor Statistics since 1964 as shown in Figure 4-3.[7] We advise those who are squeamish to avert their eyes—it is not a pretty picture.

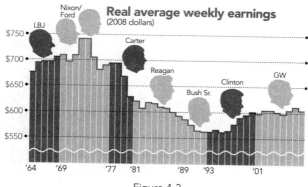

Figure 4-3

In 1964, the average real weekly wage (all wage figures in 2008 dollars) was about $676. That figure rose during the rest of the 1960s due in part to the rapidly growing economy. The real wage peaked in 1972 at about $741 a week. Since then, the real wage rate has mostly declined, with the only substantial period of rising real weekly wages occurring from 1995 to 2002, when the real wage rate rose from about $565 a week to over $600 a week. In 2008, the average real weekly wage was $608. Thus, in terms of buying power, the average worker made less per week in 2008 than his father did thirty-four years earlier.

The worst losses occurred from about 1973 until the early 1990s. In the early 1970s, inflation ratcheted up, the oil embargo began, and the gold standard became unsustainable and was abandoned. Inflation and expensive energy would continue to be an issue for a number of years, but so would

61

globalization. Globalization is good for people as consumers but as workers it often means they have to compete with less expensive labor in developing countries. By the mid-1980s, the general malaise of the 1970s had been replaced by a pervasive fear that the American century was over and the world would soon belong to the Japanese.

Yet by the mid-1990s, the Japanese economy had deteriorated, partly because the Japanese government refused—after the bursting of a real estate bubble—to make tough decisions and kill "zombie" banks. (Zombie banks are banks whose assets are worth less than their debts, but which continue to operate with a lot of government assistance. The concept may sound familiar to anyone who spent 2008 and 2009 in the United States.)

While the Japanese government was coddling the walking dead, the U.S. economy was back in ascendance; several years of deficit reduction, followed by displays of leadership in dealing with economic crises abroad (e.g., Mexico in 1994, the Asian contagion in 1997), convinced many Americans that the future was bright again. And nowhere was the future brighter than in the dot-com and telecom worlds, where American technology and know-how helped make the economy boom. The economic boom, in turn, resulted in the creation of many high-paying jobs.

The annualized change in real average weekly earnings over the span of each administration is summarized in Figure 4-4.

The fastest growth in real average wage rates occurred under JFK/LBJ and Clinton. During both of these administrations, the economy as a whole grew very quickly. Furthermore, both administrations stressed social policies geared more toward the little guy than big business. For example, when JFK/LBJ took office, the minimum wage was set at $1 an hour; when they left office, it was $1.60. In other words, during the JFK/LBJ administration the minimum wage rose by 60 percent, or about 36 percent after inflation was taken into account. This was, by far, the largest increase in the minimum wage over the span of any administration in our sample. Furthermore, Johnson's Great Society programs included job training for the poor and provisions in the 1964 Civil Rights Act prohibiting employment discrimination.

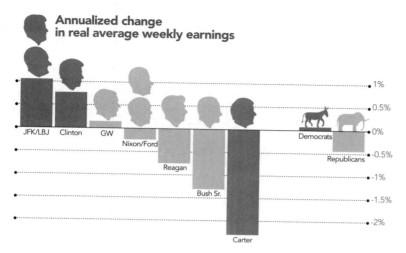

**Annualized change in real average weekly earnings**

1%
0.5%
JFK/LBJ    Clinton    GW                                    Democrats    0%
                      Nixon/Ford                            Republicans  -0.5%
                      Reagan                                             -1%
                      Bush Sr.                                           -1.5%
                      Carter                                             -2%

Figure 4-4

Other than JFK/LBJ and Clinton, only GW managed an increase in the real wage rate. However, it was an increase just a tiny smidge north of zero; the annualized growth rate of real wages was about 0.14 percent (i.e., zero point one four percent). Making matters worse, as we saw earlier in the chapter, a smaller percentage of Americans had jobs when GW left office than when he arrived on the scene. But even that doesn't tell the whole dismal story: Of the 3.5 million or so private sector jobs created during GW's administration, almost a quarter of them were in either construction or the financial sectors, both of which were pumped up by borrowed money, scandalously loose regulation, and even outright fraud, especially from 2004 to 2008.[8]

Looking at administrations under which there was a decline in real average wages, the smallest declines occurred under Nixon/Ford, despite the combination of relatively high inflation and price controls. Reagan had the next smallest declines: His administration produced job growth, but pay didn't "trickle down" to those at the bottom. Part of the problem was that the economy was trading relatively well-paid manufacturing jobs for service sector jobs that tend to pay employees less. That trend continued under Bush Sr., and was exacerbated by the mediocre economic growth during his term in office.

Bringing up the rear was Carter. While he produced decent economic growth, inflation was one of the banes of his presidency. In an attempt to combat inflation, he instituted a program of mandatory wage controls in the public sector, and the private sector was invited to participate on a voluntary basis. Put another way, Carter cleverly concluded that if only people's paychecks were prevented from keeping pace with inflation, eventually

63

inflation would come down. Naturally, many businesses found the logic of paying workers less money (in real terms) compelling and did what the president assured them was their patriotic duty. The end result, of course, was that workers who had been making, on average, about $691 a week in 1976 were making only about $630 a week in 1980 (figures in 2008 dollars), representing a 9 percent haircut.

## Employment-Based Health Insurance

As we noted earlier, adjusting for inflation the average American makes less money per week in wages now than in 1964. But money isn't the only compensation people get for working. Most of us get benefits too. Different employers offer different benefits to different employees. A CEO may get perks like paid country club memberships and free use of a corporate jet, while middle managers might get retirement plans or discounts on day care, and the lowest-paid employees may get few or no benefits. But it depends on the company.

The most expensive benefit many employers offer on a widespread basis is health insurance. So to get an idea about how Americans are being compensated above and beyond their take-home pay, we can look at the percentage of Americans covered by employment-based health insurance. Employment-based health care may be provided by the employer directly, or through a union, in which case it is still being paid for by the employer. The percentage of people covered by employment-based health insurance includes not only the worker, but also family members who are covered by policies provided by the worker's employer.

The practice of using health insurance as a benefit is really a quirk of history. Because wage controls during World War II kept employers from raising pay, they competed for workers by offering health insurance. In most other developed countries, health insurance is not a job-based benefit; it is paid for by the government through taxes.

The value of health insurance as a benefit is hard to quantify; usually, the employer or the union pays for part of that insurance, and the employee pays for the remainder. When companies are pressed, they often reduce their health insurance contributions or eliminate them altogether. We don't have data on the amount employers have contributed, but the Census Bureau has figures on the percentage of Americans covered by employment-based health insurance going back to 1987.[9]

Figure 4-5 shows what that looks like.

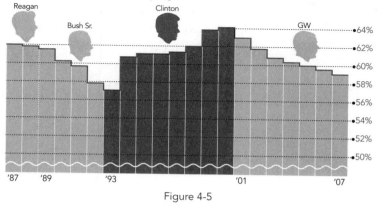

**% of Americans with employer-based health insurance**

Figure 4-5

Figure 4-6 summarizes the data from Figure 4-5 in a different form. Reagan is not included in the summary because there are only two years of data for his term.

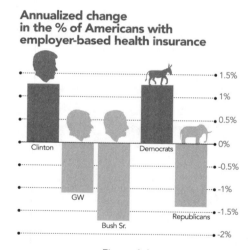

**Annualized change in the % of Americans with employer-based health insurance**

Figure 4-6

For both the Bush Sr. and the GW administrations, the percentage of Americans receiving health insurance through their employers declined. However, that percentage rose under Clinton.

Part of the increase observed under Clinton is probably due in part to the rapidly expanding economy; as growth picked up, so did competition for good employees, and more companies began offering health insurance to entice workers. But the increase in the percentage of people getting health insurance began even before the economy really started rolling. As we will see in Chapter 8, annualized health insurance costs rose by less under Clinton than under any other president. Perhaps part of the reason for this was the fear insurance companies felt about "Hillary-care"—Clinton's attempt to make health insurance more universal through government mandates. Perhaps it was a range of other factors, from cost-cutting through consolidation to health maintenance organizations to the demographics of having Boomers in their pre-breakdown years. Whatever the reason that costs were contained, while Clinton was in office, health insurance became a more attractive benefit for employers to provide.

## Employment Issues: Conclusion

In this chapter, we looked at three measures relating to the jobs that are important to the American public: the employment-to-population ratio, the average real rate of pay, and benefits (i.e., employer-based health insurance). To evaluate the presidents' performance on jobs, we developed an Overall Measure on Employment Issues. This measure is designed so that a president who was ranked first on each of three measures—percentage of people employed, average real wage rate, and benefits—would have a score of 100 percent, and a president ranked last on all three would have a score of 0 percent.

Figure 4-7 shows the overall score on jobs for each of the administrations.

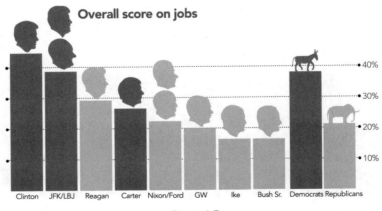

Figure 4-7

According to Figure 4-7, Clinton scored best, having come in first on employer-based health insurance, second on the increase in average weekly wages, and third on increasing the employment-to-population ratio. JFK/LBJ,

Reagan, and Carter round out the top four; the four final slots are taken up by Republicans, with Ike and Bush Sr. tied for last.

In terms of the two parties, when it comes to employment issues most Americans fared better when Democrats were in the White House. Most likely, this is partly due to the faster economic growth rates observed under Democrats than under Republicans. However, there is another factor that is equally important, which is that Democratic policies tend to be geared more toward workers than toward businesses, while Republican policies tend to be more favorable toward employers. This may have helped split the pie in ways that led to more jobs and better pay for middle class and blue collar workers under Democrats than under Republicans.

## CHAPTER 5

# Income and Wealth

★ ★ ★

Now the role of government is
not to create wealth.

GEORGE W. BUSH
Remarks to Small Investors in Alexandria, Virginia, February 12, 2003[1]

Ｗe Americans love television. On average, Americans age fifteen and over watch about 2.62 hours of TV a day.[2] That's more than 18 hours a week, and about 956 glorious hours per year. And while that television is on, it rewards us with all manner of wondrous things: poorly drawn cartoons, badly written sitcoms, and inane chatter about second-rate celebrities. But it also gives us news shows, some of which purportedly make an effort to tell us about, among other things, the economy.

In the U.S. people watch 2.6 HOURS of TV every day

(That's 5½ weeks of viewing a year)

Now, say the news tells us that the economy is booming, GDP (and no, we have yet to hear the words *real GDP per capita*—much less *real GDP per capita with the national debt netted out*—come from a TV news talking head) is growing rapidly, the deficit is shrinking, and unemployment is low. That's good, right?

Well, yes, it's good, but that doesn't mean you're better off. In fact, even with all that good news, a lot of people might still be suffering economically. Rising tides may lift all boats, but that only helps if you have a boat.

Which means that if you listen to only the big-ticket statistics you might wonder if what you're hearing relates to you. To paraphrase an old vaudeville joke: "Who ya gonna believe? The data or your own lying pocketbook?" If

GDP is growing, the deficit is shrinking, and unemployment is low but you're hurting financially, it might be just you. But it might be the data.

So while data on the economy as a whole is important, it also pays to look at data that reflects your pocketbook and that of most Americans. In this chapter we will look at data on income and wealth.

# Real Median Income

The first measure we'll examine of how well the average American's pocketbook is doing is *real median income*. Income is simply the amount of money people make, regardless of the source. Income includes a person's salary, but also other money coming in, like rent and transfer payments from the government such as Social Security. And remember: *Real* means that we're adjusting for inflation. The median is the halfway point in the sample, where half the folks are above and half are below. The median income for employed people fourteen years old and over in 2007, the last year for which we have data, was about $27,650; thus, half of all working Americans fourteen years and older had incomes above $27,650 and half of them had incomes below that.

So think of the median income as the income of the "middlest" of middle-income earners. This is different from the average income, which, because it includes the income of folks like Bill Gates, bears little resemblance to what most people make. So, as the cliché goes, when Bill Gates steps into a bar the average income of people in the room goes up over a billion dollars, but the median income, the income of the person with the "middle income" in the bar, doesn't change. Well, adding one more person to the bar may move the median, but so long as there's a decent-sized crowd that night, it won't move much.

Real median income is available from the Census for the years since 1947.[3] Figure 5-1 shows both the real median income, and, for comparison, the real GDP per capita.

Figure 5-1 indicates a few important facts. One is that the average person's income hasn't kept up with the increases in real GDP per capita. Most people's incomes have been shrinking compared to the average of the country's total income, at least since 1947. In other words, the share of the pie most of us get has been shrinking but the pie itself is growing. The middlest of the middle Americans, whose income in 1947 was 126 percent of the GDP per capita, was last seen slinking home with income equal to about 58 percent of GDP per capita in 2007. Clearly, the pie is getting bigger and bigger but some folks at the very top of the food chain are getting more and more of it. And as Figure 5-1 indicates, the rate at which the median has lost ground has only increased since 1973.

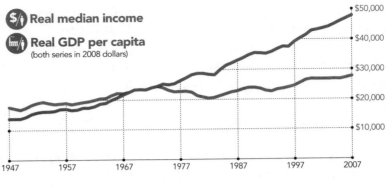

Figure 5-1

So what happened? Why did growth in real median income—not to mention its share of the total pie—slip so much beginning around 1973? The Arab oil embargo began in 1973, as did inflation. Forget about Altamont—this was the unofficial start of the 1970s; stagflation, disco, fat ties, custom vans, the works. The country staggered through several recessions and the once-dominant U.S. auto industry hit the skids, while both foreign competition and automation chopped away at American manufacturing. Joe Six-Pack took it in the gut during the 1970s, and never quite recovered.

Interestingly enough, 1973 was also the year that a patent was granted to "[a] currency dispenser [which] automatically delivers a medium of exchange in packets in response to a coded credit card presented thereto."[4] Yup, patent number 3,761,682 went to the ATM machine, which would make it much easier for Americans to spend, spend, spend, regardless of what was or wasn't happening to their income.

Figure 5-2 shows real median income by administration.

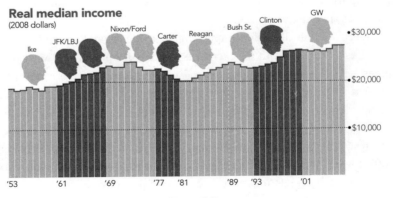

Figure 5-2

The annualized growth in real median income per capita over the span of each administration appear in Figure 5-3.

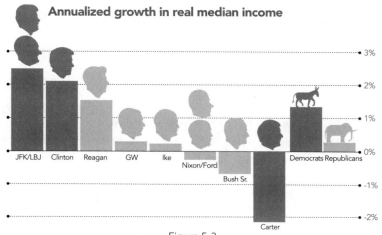

Figure 5-3

The biggest increase in real median income came under JFK/LBJ. That gain can be explained partly by the monster growth in the economy (a 3.48 percent annual increase in real GDP per capita and an even bigger increase in net real GDP per capita) and partly by their new social programs that increased participation in the economy for the poor. Under Clinton, the real median income also came in with respectable gains. Like JFK/LBJ, Clinton produced rapid economic growth (a 2.49 percent increase in real GDP per capita) and maintained a focus on the folks at the bottom of the social scale.

Reagan came in third place in terms of increasing real median income. Like JFK/LBJ and Clinton, Reagan presided over rapid economic growth (2.45 percent a year), but given that real median income increased by only 1.49 percent a year, it's clear that those supply-side programs had definite limitations when it came to trickling benefits down to the average American.

GW came in fourth place, barely on the positive side of the ledger. As of this writing, however, data on real median income was not available for 2008, GW's last year. And in general, GW's term didn't end on a positive economic note, so it's possible that with more complete data GW's ranking here might slip.

Also barely on the positive side was fifth-place finisher Ike; real median income increased 2.3 percent while he was in office, which amounts to an annualized growth rate of less than 0.3 percent a year. The West Point grad and World War II hero who warned us about the military-industrial complex continued and even expanded a number of New Deal programs. While economic growth was pretty weak during Ike's term—a 1.1 percent increase in real GDP per capita, combined with three recessions—he benefited from significant tailwinds when it came to real median income growth. One important tailwind was the fact that more than 2.4 million Americans (that is, about 2 percent of Americans fourteen years and older at the time) took advantage of the Veterans Readjustment Assistance Act of 1952. This act, which essentially updated the GI Bill for veterans of the Korean War, provided benefits like home loans, funding for education, "mustering out" services, and unemployment compensation for those who served in that conflict.

Under the remaining administrations, real incomes fell. They fell least under Nixon/Ford, followed by Bush Sr. The worst performance came under Carter. As we saw in the last chapter, Carter's wage control initiatives prevented many people's salaries from keeping up with inflation. In any given year the bulk of most Americans' income is their salary, so Carter's wage control schemes pretty much guaranteed that the majority of Americans would see their real income plummet.

One more thing Figure 5-3 tells us: Despite Carter's haplessness, Democrats easily outperformed Republicans when it came to increasing the real incomes of the most Americans. Rapid economic growth and a focus on the little guy tended to produce better results for people's pocketbooks than tax cuts.

It probably isn't a coincidence that the three presidents who ran for reelection and lost—Gerald Ford, Jimmy Carter, and George H. W. Bush—all served in administrations under which the real median income actually decreased. It should be noted that to some extent GW could be said to have broken the mold; in 2004, when he ran for reelection, the real median income was more than 1.5 percent below what it had been in 2000, the year before he took office. Then again, that may help explain how narrow his victory was in 2004.

## Net Real Disposable Income

We just looked at real median income, the inflation-adjusted income of the middlest American. If your real income goes up and not much else changes, the answer to Reagan's question, "Are you better off today than you were four years ago?" is yes. If it goes up by a lot, the answer is heck, yeah!

But wait. One thing that could change your answer is the amount you have to pay in taxes. If you make more money but pay more in taxes, are you still better off? And if your income falls but your tax obligations fall by more, aren't you bringing home more bacon?

As we've seen already, taxes are funny things. A president can affect the amount you pay in taxes not just this year or next, but even long after he leaves office. A president who drives the debt into the stratosphere may give you a tax cut today, but have you paying for that debt for a very, very long time. Sure, that's not what they tell you when they proudly proclaim that they're cutting your (current) taxes, but that's what they're doing nevertheless. Now, perhaps you might not mind that future tax hike, or you might at least consider it to be a fair trade—if your income increases by enough or you don't think you'll be around to pay it! A president who cuts the national debt, on the other hand, saves you from having to make interest and principal payments on that debt in the future, and therefore reduces your tax bill in later years.

Unfortunately, most people don't seem to make the connection between fiscal irresponsibility today and increased taxes later on, which is why so many presidents have been so happy to take the easy way out. So ideally, the real median income figure we just looked at could be adjusted to take into account both taxes paid and changes in the national debt that accrue to the median income earner. In other words, what is the real income of that middlest American, taking into account current and future tax obligations *that result directly from the economic policies of the current resident of the White House?* Bear in mind that the policies of the current resident of the White House include not only the new laws and regulations he puts into effect, but also how he enforces existing rules and regulations, and whether he expends the political capital to overturn them or strengthen them.

We weren't able to find any government agencies that reported that information, nor to locate the data we needed to calculate it ourselves, at least not precisely enough to have any confidence in our results. So instead we turned to the Bureau of Economic Analysis, which provides data on *average* real disposable income. That is, everyone's income less the cumulative taxes we all pay, all divided by the number of people in the country. We use end-of-year debt, and real disposable income for the last quarter of the year, for consistency.[5]

That little operation gives us the *real disposable income per capita less the yearly change in real debt per capita,* which we will refer to by the nifty acronym: RDIPCLTYCIRDPC. Just kidding. We're going to call this value the *real net average disposable income.* (Isn't that better? A little?) Think of it as the average amount of income Americans are getting in any given year that is free and clear of current and future taxes and adjusted for inflation. Don't forget, though, as we saw with the Bill Gates–walks-into-a-bar example, average income can be skewed upward (relative to median income) by people who make a lot of money, so it isn't directly comparable to median income. But

73

even if it doesn't tell us how the pie is sliced, it does tell us something about the size of the pie that is available to be split up.

Figure 5-4 shows what real net average disposable income looks like by administration.

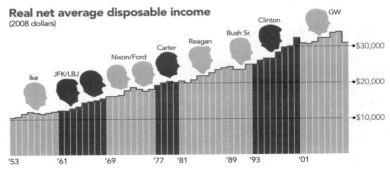

**Real net average disposable income**
(2008 dollars)

Figure 5-4

Fortunately, real net average disposable income has generally been rising. That's not surprising; since 1952, incomes have risen, and at the same time, the current tax rate has been falling; the top marginal tax rate when Ike was in office was over 90 percent; now it's about 35 percent. The only fly in the ointment when it comes to our net disposable income is the debt: Presidents from Ike to Nixon reduced the national debt, but since then Ford, Reagan, Bush Sr., and GW all increased it—so much so that by the end of GW's term in office, debt as a percentage of GDP was actually higher than it was in 1952. This run-up in the debt ensures that Americans will eventually have to pay more taxes.

What we can say now is that the money we have at our disposal has been—in general—going up. Figure 5-5 shows what it looks like in summary form.

The biggest increases—about 3.35 percent a year in real net average disposable income—came under JFK/LBJ and Clinton. This should come as no surprise. Both JFK/LBJ and Clinton also held the top two slots at economic growth (no matter how you measure it), reducing the debt and increasing real median income.

Carter came in third, with a not-too-shabby increase of 2.55 percent a year. Reagan followed at 2.17 percent a year, and he was followed by Nixon/Ford and Ike. The two Bush presidents came in last. Of the two, Bush Sr. at least turned in a positive performance. Under, GW, real net average disposable income was actually lower at the end of his two terms than at the start, a

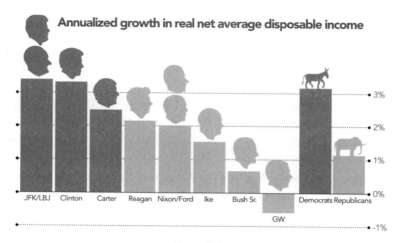

Figure 5-5

result of mediocre increases in real disposable income and uncomfortably large increases in the national debt.

One surprise on this list, given what happened to real median incomes during his term, was the third-place finish of Carter. How could Carter have toted up annual increases of 2.55 percent a year in real net average disposable income, yet have done so dismally when it came to real median income growth? Well, two reasons. One is that Carter diligently paid down the national debt, reducing real debt per capita at a rate of 1.5 percent a year. Thus, Americans didn't have to fear that whatever income growth might have occurred under Carter would later be taken away by a future tax-man.

The other reason has to do with the difference between medians and averages. As we saw in the chapter on jobs, Carter's wage control program hurt most Americans, but those wages that weren't paid out, coupled with a growth in real GDP per capita of about 2.1 percent a year had to go *somewhere*. Or rather, to someone. Many someones, in fact. But which someones?

Well, the someones that benefited while wage controls were in place had to be people for whom salary was not the primary form of income. That means one of two groups: either the very poor, who receive a large percentage of their income in the form of welfare, or the wealthy, for whom salaries—that is, other people's salaries—are considered expenses. But as we will see in Chapter 7, the percentage of people living in poverty under Carter increased, so the poor clearly were not the someones who were doing better. That leaves those whose income comes from being shareholders and company owners—those at the top of the heap.

Administrations that kept recessions to a minimum also tended to do well by this measure; the correlation between growth in net real disposable income and time spent in recession over the span of an administration is –61 percent. But being "people-friendly" also seems to have mattered. For instance, the economy spent more time in recession under both Ike and Nixon/Ford than under either Bush Sr. or GW. But Ike and Nixon/Ford continued many of the safety net programs of their predecessors, while in general, when it came to safety nets, the Bushes tended to be more the dismantling types.

Given that the three Democratic administrations came in in the top three slots, it's no surprise that Democrats easily outperformed Republicans.

## Real Net Worth

In the last two sections, we looked at income. And income, in the end, is just a means of getting stuff. In this section, we're going to look at how well people did at accumulating stuff over the span of each administration.

You've seen the bumper stickers: "The one who dies with the most stuff wins." Some of us quail at that attitude—after all, should the accounting wait until it's too late to do you any good? Plus it does seem excessively materialistic; by that metric, folks like Albert Einstein and Jonas Salk were losers.

Still, most of us accept the idea that stuff is a valid measure for *something*. Having a dishwasher, a closet full of lovely clothes, a car, and a nice house (plus another on the lake for good measure)—these things add to a household's standard of living. There are limits, of course, but in general, the more stuff you have, the better off you are.

True, some stuff doesn't add much in a functional way to your life. (Yeah, maybe we *are* talking about your collection of mint 1920s baseball cards. But if you had to, you could sell it, which, by the way, beats having your mother toss it). The sum of all your stuff is a measure of your wealth and, implicitly, your well-being.

The Federal Reserve keeps track of the stuff people own, though, and—this may surprise you—they don't call it stuff. Instead, their Web site has the net worth of households and nonprofits (and no, we have no idea why they bunched nonprofits with households).[6] Data can be adjusted for inflation and divided by population, as with data in previous chapters. Figure 5-6 shows what real net worth per capita looks like.

As Figure 5-6 shows, real net worth per capita has been rising. This increase is due to a host of reasons, including better productivity, the advance

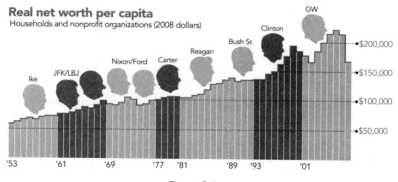

**Real net worth per capita**
Households and nonprofit organizations (2008 dollars)

Figure 5-6

of technology, a better-educated population, more international trade, and a trend toward borrowing in service of consumption.

That said, people always encounter some investment setbacks—businesses, stocks, bonds, mortgage-backed securities, and even houses sometimes lose value. But the value of the stuff we all own has tended to rise over time. In 1952, the total value of all the stuff in the United States owned by households (and, sigh, nonprofits) was about $1.18 trillion. In 2008 dollars, that's about $9.6 trillion, or about $60,600 per capita. In 2008, by contrast, that amount had grown to $51.5 trillion, or about $168,500 per person.

The annualized growth over the span of each administration is graphically represented in Figure 5-7.

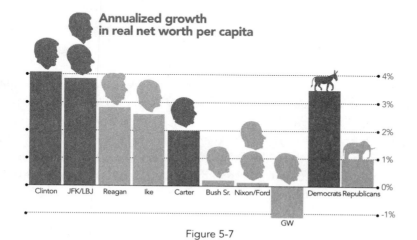

Figure 5-7

The biggest increase in real net worth per capita—about 4 percent per year—occurred during the administration of Bill Clinton, despite the big drop in the stock market in 2000, his last year in office. That means that the late 1990s' bubble in stocks was so huge that even the decline of 2000 left most shareholders better off than they'd been before.

The JFK/LBJ administration turned in the second-best performance when it came to creating conditions for Americans to accumulate wealth. From 1960 to 1968, real wealth per capita grew at an annualized rate of 3.8 percent per year. The twin engines of rapid economic growth and rapid income growth made it possible for Americans to accumulate lots and lots of stuff.

Reagan came in third, with increases of 2.8 percent per year; he too produced good growth in the economy and in people's pocketbooks, albeit not as good as Clinton or JFK/LBJ. Ike came in fourth—this was the era of the GI Bill and Levittown, and most Americans were accumulating stuff even if the economy as a whole wasn't growing very rapidly. Carter came in fifth; during his presidency, real net worth per capita increased at just under 2 percent a year. Sadly, among the assets accumulated during the Carter years were lava lamps and eight-track tapes of the Carpenters.

Under Bush Sr. and Nixon/Ford, real net worth per capita barely increased but at least it *did* increase. Which brings us back to GW. Under GW, it shrank . . . at about 1.2 percent a year. Even he seemed to recognize that when it came to real net assets, he presided over a train wreck. During his first few years in office, he talked a lot about an "ownership society." That talk slowly wound down, eventually petering out completely around 2005 or 2006. One of his post-reelection hopes was to privatize Social Security or otherwise make individuals entirely responsible for controlling the income they would receive at retirement. Given the performance of many assets, including the stock market, had GW gotten his way on privatizing Social Security, most Americans would have lost even more during his administration than they did.

It should be noted, however, that under GW, Americans did enjoy four years of extremely rapid increases in real net worth per capita. From 2002 until 2006, real net worth per capita increased at a blistering pace of 7.2 percent a year. (Sadly, as is evident from Figure 5-6, the decline from 2006 to 2008 was even faster, explaining how GW could post a negative growth in real net worth capita over the length of his entire administration.) What's so special about 2002? Well, the bubble that popped in the year 2000 led to declines in real wealth per capita during Clinton's last year in office. But the decline of 2000 continued into 2001. . . and 2002, which was a factor in explaining GW's dismal performance.

Of course, that wasn't the only reason that GW's performance could be described as dismal—he was, after all, president in 2007 and 2008. Still, it raises the question: Should Clinton get the blame for the declines in real net worth we saw in 2001 and 2002? Conversely, should GW get a pass on those declines? (Not that it would change his rankings: Even if we considered Clinton's term as running through 2002, GW would still come in last place in terms of growth in real wealth per capita because of the bubble collapse in 2007 and 2008.)

Let's start with the first question first—should Clinton get dinged for the declines in real net worth per capita that occurred in 2001 and 2002? We believe not. Sure, as we've stated a number of times a president can affect things long after he leaves office. (Think of Ike's highways still benefiting us today.) So actions taken by Clinton may well have had some part in creating the problem. However, once he left office there wasn't much he could do to *change* the course of events.

And whatever else anyone might say about him, Clinton reacted to problems that arose. And he managed to do so in ways that prevented the problems from getting worse, at least for Americans. Be it a large and growing deficit, tax policy, the Peso crisis, the Asian contagion, or even noneconomic issues like negotiating peace treaties in the Middle East, the Great Triangulator was rarely dogmatic when it came to finding a solution.

By contrast, GW's solution to just about every problem until mid-2008 was "stay the course"—which for him, in economic parlance, at least, amounted to tax cuts (or rather, deferring taxes into the future since there were no accompanying decreases in spending) and reducing regulatory oversight. For instance, while GW was campaigning for office, "tax cuts" were promoted as a way to give people back their money during a booming economy. By the time he took office, they were billed as a way to stave off a recession. Later still, GW was telling us "tax cuts" would get the economy back on its feet. Toward the end of his term, GW insisted that his tax cuts had to be made permanent; somehow, in GW's view, the possibility that his signature tax cuts would expire a few years after he left office was the cause of the sluggish economy.

GW's claim to being an innocent bystander to a collapse already in motion is defensible. But starting in 2001, it was his hand on the wheel. It was his job to make things better. His supporters might even argue (and many did) that were it not for the various rounds of tax cuts, the economy—and most people's real net worth—would have taken an even bigger hit. But why then was there a second, much larger collapse in people's real net worth so soon after the first?

So all in all we feel it's best to remain consistent, to continue using the same methodology we have used so far throughout the book. With real net worth per capita, as with other measures, we grade each administration on its performance during its term in office.

## Home Ownership

Among the most important assets many families will own is their own home. In fact, owning one's home is an integral part of the American dream. Home ownership is a function of several big things—mainly incomes, home price appreciation, and interest rates. But there is an often-ignored factor: demographics. People in their thirties are likelier to be net buyers of homes than people in their twenties (or eighties) so the age distribution of the population makes a difference. Moreover, immigration tends to move the meter, perhaps decreasing the percentage of people who own their own home at first, then adding to home buying as the new residents settle in for the long haul.

Quarterly data on home ownership rates—the percentage of Americans living in their own home—is available from the Census Bureau beginning in 1965. Figure 5-8 shows the home ownership rate for the fourth quarter of the year, by administration.[7]

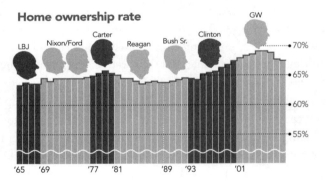

Figure 5-8

Figure 5-8 indicates that home ownership rates have tended to increase, although there have been several waves. For example, during the Carter administration, home ownership rates got within spitting distance of 66 percent, a rate they didn't reach again until the late 1990s.

The most notable feature in Figure 5-8 is the steady rise from 1994 to 2005. This trend may have begun with the booming 1990s economy. However, home ownership continued to increase even after the economy slowed down in 2001. That home-buying boom was like a stew concocted by a number of chefs. For starters, a surging economy does tend to boost home purchases, and the economy was surging in the mid- and late 1990s.

Then there were the ingredients added by the Federal Reserve, which responded to the economy's protracted weakness by cutting the benchmark interest rate starting in 2001 and keeping it extremely low for a long time. This in turn affected other rates and resulted in very low rates on mortgages and home equity lines of credit, all of which added to home sales, home building, and rising home prices.

There were also the new tools; adjustable rate mortgages (ARMs), for instance, let buyers start out with a lower-than-market rate. ARMs became stunningly popular, especially among first-time home buyers. If that weren't enough to send home ownership soaring, Wall Street began bundling and repackaging mortgages into increasingly sophisticated (and opaque) financial products that were bought and sold all over the globe. Then there was the use (and misuse) of subprime mortgages, offered to millions of people who had blemished credit.

"Stated income" loans were like the spice sprinkled into the bubbling concoction. Borrowers could qualify for these loans simply by stating that they made an appropriate level of income without having to provide any proof whatsoever. As a result, the economy sprouted a surprisingly large number of people applying for mortgages whose stated income was well into six figures, even if they worked at jobs that typically paid a fraction of the claimed amount. Not surprisingly, these stated income loans came to be referred to in the industry as "liar loans."

Taken together, these factors (very low interest rates, increased use of ARMs, the packaging of many mortgages together, and lax lending standards) helped crank up the heat by keeping demand for homes high. These tools also made it all too easy to make loans with that old guaranteed-money feeling. The higher rate of home purchases was pushing prices up, further fueling demand.

The question was this: Where and how would it end? The optimists and Kool-Aid vendors argued that this time it was different (isn't it always?)—all those immigrant home buyers, all those low interest rates, and all that talk about the "ownership economy" from the president meant we had reached a sparkling new paradigm of higher home ownership. But like the Beanie Baby bubble before it, not to mention every other craze, it would have to come to an end. And so it came to pass. And lo, even the most exuberant prophets of the promised market paradise began to realize that something was amiss in 2008, even if some of them managed to ignore the obvious until it reared up and bit them in the behind.

The data tells the story—warts, bubbles, and all. Figure 5-9 shows the annualized change in home ownership rates over the span of each administration since JFK took office.

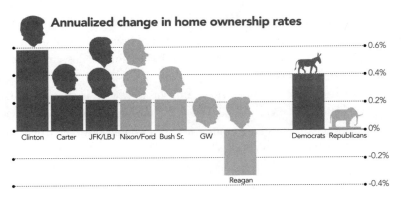

**Annualized change in home ownership rates**

Figure 5-9

The fastest increases in home ownership occurred under Clinton. Though the rise in home ownership would one day become a speculative bubble, while Clinton was in office it was still something different. Home prices in the 1990s would not rise anywhere near their frothy 2006 levels. But as any real estate agent will tell you, part of the value of a home is its location. A home in an area with good jobs and where future prospects are good, all else being equal, is worth more than a home in an area with no jobs and where future prospects are poor. And if there is such a thing as a location in time, while Clinton was in office in most of the country the economy was booming, jobs were good and plentiful, and home prices still had a long way to appreciate. Under those circumstances, buying a home made perfect sense.

Ranking behind Clinton was Carter, who has spent part of his post-presidency period building homes for Habitat for Humanity. One of the more significant pieces of home ownership–related legislation during Carter's term was the Community Redevelopment Act (CRA). The CRA required FDIC-insured institutions to provide loans in some of the same areas where they took deposits, whenever possible, subject to sound banking practices. The Carter administration also went on an urban renewal spree, with particular emphasis on urban centers.

Third place was a three-way tie between JFK/LBJ, Nixon/Ford, and Bush Sr. GW, the ownership society guy, came in second to last. He often bragged about how many new homeowners there were since he took office. But by 2007, he was reduced to looking for ways to keep homeowners from being foreclosed upon. Not surprisingly, GW's plan to help homeowners involved (wait for it!) tax relief of various sorts.[8] About a year later the tax cuts hadn't solved the problem, so GW signed into law the Housing and Economic Recovery Act of 2008. We decided to see how many times the word *tax* appeared in that law and gave up when our count hit 100.[9]

The only administration under which home ownership declined was Reagan's. Despite a fairly strong economy, and (as we saw in the last chapter) increases in real net worth, the gains in the economy were generally concentrated at the top. But it seems that it's not the top income layers that propel home ownership rates. From the looks of the data, home ownership gets its biggest push when first-time home buyers are pouring into the market, not when Old Money contemplates purchasing its fourth vacation home.

# Owner's Equity

Home ownership rates tell us the percentage of people who own their own home. However, as many people have discovered in recent years, you don't really, truly, absolutely own your home until it is paid off free and clear. Before that, you kind of own your own home, but you also kind of don't. And if you find yourself unable to keep making the payments on the house, the kind of don't part starts to outweigh the kind of do part, and if you don't make up what you owe, you lose your home. Thus, in some way "owning" a house that hasn't been paid off is not much different than being a renter, though it has better tax advantages.

But how many people who aren't pro basketball players or partners at some Wall Street firm that got bailed out by the government are able to pay cash for a house? Taking out a mortgage is a financial necessity for most people. And the more homeowners can borrow, the better the home they can afford. Then they can pay off their mortgage little by little—except when they don't.

Loss of a job, interest rates resetting higher (on an adjustable-rate mortgage), a debilitating sickness, plain old bad luck, or, in some cases, even irresponsibility, can make paying off a mortgage difficult or impossible. This in turn can lead to the loss of a home.

The degree to which we own our home is usually not all or nothing. Most people own part of their homes since they have paid off a portion of the mortgage principal. The portion you own is the "owner's equity." Your owner's equity increases as you pay down the mortgage and as the value of the house increases.

In general, higher equity is a good thing for the economy and the nation—as well as the family. It solidifies household balance sheets, provides a reserve for unexpected trouble, and becomes an investment in the future. Yet when average equity drops, that too can be a good thing under the right circumstances. For example, average equity can decrease over a period when many new home buyers enter the market (new home buyers generally have less equity in their homes than people who have been in their homes for many years), assuming those new home buyers have the wherewithal to make their mortgage payments for the duration of their mortgage.

And while stocks and bonds are a huge part of the national wealth picture, it is said that for most Americans, equity in their home is the biggest piece of their net worth. Economists talk about the "wealth effect" in stocks—the fatter your portfolio, the more you are likely to spend in your daily life—and the same principle can also be pegged to homes. So if you've got a lot of equity in a home that is becoming ever more valuable, you feel richer and you'll likely act like someone who's a bit richer.

Before we get into the data, a warning: The information we use in this section comes from the Federal Reserve, which, as we noted earlier in the chapter, likes to bunch together numbers from households and nonprofits. But we did manage to find data on owner's equity for households by themselves, which the Fed, in its wisdom, has titled "households and nonprofit organizations owners' equity in real estate excluding nonprofits." We're not kidding. We've divided that by "households and nonprofit organizations real estate *excluding nonprofits*." (Our emphasis.) The result is owner's equity as a percentage of real estate owned by households, though presumably the Fed would throw in the words "and nonprofit" and "excluding nonprofits" for good measure. Figure 5-10 shows what that data looks like by administration.[10]

In 1952, on average, about 80 percent of the total value of real estate holdings by households was actually owned by those households. Only 20 percent was owned by creditors in the form of mortgages, loans, or liens. This was probably not as much a function of people paying cash for their homes as it was the result of people living in the same home for their entire lives. Back in the day, when the price of just about everything cost a nickel and people didn't move around much, it wasn't uncommon for three or four generations from the same family to live under the same roof.

In the postwar expansion—aided in large part by the GI Bill—millions of people became first-time home buyers. Those new homeowners were, naturally, just starting to pay down their mortgages. Thus, as the percentage of people owning homes increased, the average time a homeowner had been

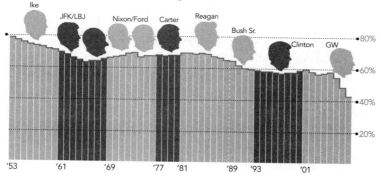

**Owner's equity
as a % of real estate owned by household**

Ike
JFK/LBJ
Nixon/Ford
Carter
Reagan
Bush Sr.
Clinton
GW

80%
60%
40%
20%

'53    '61    '69    '77  '81    '89  '93    '01

Figure 5-10

making mortgage payments went down and the amount of equity that was held in a home also decreased.

That changed after 1965, when owner's equity as a percentage of household real estate holdings began to rise. One reason for this may have been the booming economy, which also raised many people's incomes; that might have helped many people pay off their mortgages sooner than they otherwise would have. Another reason: 1965 is the year the Department of Housing and Urban Development was created. HUD's purpose was to make it easier for people, particularly those with low incomes, to become homeowners, often by providing low-cost loans. But HUD also regulates corporations like Fannie Mae and Freddie Mac, and engages in other activities that help middle-class and high-income people as well. To a greater or lesser extent, HUD helped shine a light on some of the practices associated with home buying, and as the old cliché goes, sunlight is the best disinfectant. Taking out financing ceased to mean being forced to sign over your first-born child, and sometimes you got to keep your less valuable second- and third-born children as well.

Other than a drop in the early 1970s—brought on by that pesky oil embargo we mentioned earlier—equity as a percentage of household real estate holdings rose until the 1980s. And then two things happened. One was that HUD had, over the years, become riddled with corruption; as a result, a lot of the home-buyer benefits HUD provided went by the wayside as the dollars needed to supply them were vacuumed up by corrupt politicians and administrators.

Another thing that affected household equity patterns was a change in tax law: Interest payments on most forms of debt stopped being tax deductible. However, interest payments on mortgages were not affected; they remained tax deductible. As a result, the attractiveness of taking out mortgages, and of not paying those mortgages off, increased relative to other forms of debt. After all, if you have to borrow you might as well borrow in ways that are tax deductible.

Take the corruption at HUD and the change in tax law, throw in some not-so-impressive real net disposable income growth under Reagan (and downright awful real net disposable income growth under Bush Sr.), and you have a recipe for consumers borrowing more and more. The pattern would change again in the mid-1990s. The decline leveled off and the owner's equity as a percentage of real estate holdings began to rise ever so slightly; the increasing prosperity of the Clinton era made it possible for more people to buy homes and make relatively large down payments.

However, since 2000 it's been a different story. The economy soured, then expanded slowly while home prices surged. With real incomes stagnant but interest rates at record lows, homeowners began using their homes as ATM machines. They cashed in equity (i.e., taking out second mortgages or homeowners' lines of credit) to fund the levels of consumption to which they had become accustomed but which their no-longer-rising incomes could not finance any more. Furthermore, adjustable-rate mortgages became extremely popular; some mortgages allowed individuals to put nothing (or less than nothing) down, and pay nothing but the interest. The kicker was that interest rates would reset quite a bit higher after several years. Another thing popularized during the GW era were liar's loans, mentioned earlier in this chapter, whose attractiveness was propelled by the fact that after 9/11, the FBI moved many of its agents in charge of investigating mortgage fraud into terrorism investigation.[11]

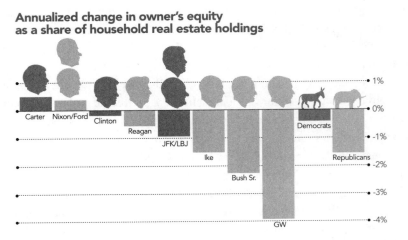

**Annualized change in owner's equity as a share of household real estate holdings**

Figure 5-11

Figure 5-11 offers a graphic summary of the change in owner's equity as a share of household real estate holdings.

Owner's equity as a percentage of household real estate holdings increased while Carter was in office, as well as during the Nixon/Ford administration. It decreased under the remaining administrations. The smallest decreases came under Clinton, Reagan, and JFK/LBJ, all of whom presided over relatively strong economies. The drops were bigger under Ike and Bush Sr., and biggest of all under GW.

# Income and Wealth: Conclusion

In the last five sections, we looked at issues involving income and wealth: real median income, real net average disposable income, net assets, home ownership rates, and owner's equity as a percentage of real estate holdings. Using these five issues, we calculated an Overall Score on Income and Wealth. This variable is constructed so that a president ranked first on all the income and wealth issues would have a score of 100 percent, and a president ranked last on all of these issues would have a score of 0 percent.

Figure 5-12 shows how the presidents scored.

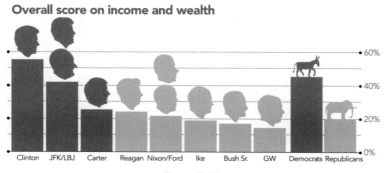

**Overall score on income and wealth**

Figure 5-12

Clinton has the best score; he was ranked first in three areas, second in another, and third on the fifth issue. He was followed by JFK/LBJ and Carter. Reagan came in fourth, followed by Nixon/Ford and Ike. The two Bush presidents came in last, with father outperforming son.

While our goal is to avoid partisanship, we're starting to see a pattern in the data: On most of the issues we've covered so far—and they've all been economic issues—Democrats have outperformed Republicans. This difference may be particularly galling here, when it comes to income and wealth. After all, creating conditions needed to increase people's income and make them wealthier is something Republicans pride themselves on, and the public perception is that they do it better than Democrats. How is it then that Republican administrations did so poorly relative to Democratic administrations?

The answer can't be derived from the data. But in part it looks to be because Democratic administrations have presided over faster economic growth on average and done so without adding as much to the national debt as Republican administrations. It goes the other way as well; increasing people's income and wealth can also lead to faster economic growth. And the policies Democrats have pursued have increased income and wealth more quickly than the policies Republicans have pursued.

Democratic policies typically call for more inclusion, more focus on those at the bottom of the economic spectrum. By contrast, Republican policies have been more of a "trickle-down" variety, the idea being that if the wealthy are made better off through lower tax burdens and less regulation, they will invest more in new ventures, expand existing businesses, and just generally toss more money into the economy, thereby helping to create jobs and improve the lives of everyone else. But perhaps the strategy of inclusion not only benefits those who would otherwise get a smaller piece of the pie but also increases the size of the whole pie for everyone. That is, a trickle-up economy seems to beat a trickle-down economy. So sayeth the data.

## CHAPTER 6

# Republican Issues

But remember one thing—it came from the West,
I know, but I'm still singing it—the greatest
thing that's happened for the Republican Party is, when
the chips are down and the decisions
are made as to who the candidates
will be, then the eleventh commandment prevails, and
everybody goes to work, and that is:
Thou shalt not speak ill of another Republican.

RONALD REAGAN[1]
Remarks in New York City at a Reception for
Delegates to the State Republican Convention, June 17, 1982

Some issues matter to everyone. We all want the economy to grow. We want more jobs and rising incomes. And we prefer a smaller national debt to a larger one.

But on some important issues there is disagreement and that disagreement can define your political identity. There are some issues that don't necessarily matter to Democrats or Independents, but matter to just about all Republicans. What's more, Republicans tend to find themselves in near-unanimous agreement on these issues.

Consider national defense. Republicans pride themselves on being strong on defense. And while there are also some Democrats and Independents who would characterize themselves that way, most people who are not Republicans don't make national defense a top priority. Furthermore, many non-Republicans might feel that we as a

nation spend too much on national defense and that such spending should be scaled back dramatically. Such a view is anathema to most Republicans.

In this chapter, we will look at so-called "Republican issues." We will avoid issues for which there is not widespread agreement among Republicans. There are, after all, some fault lines in the Republican party. For example, many Republicans, particularly social conservatives, vehemently oppose allowing people to live an openly homosexual lifestyle and have likened homosexuality to child molestation or bestiality. However, to a lot of other Republicans it is not the government's place to dictate whether a person should live a homosexual or a heterosexual lifestyle. We'll stay away from that one.

In this chapter, we will also avoid issues for which there is widespread agreement across party lines. For instance, while most Republicans want abortions to be illegal and most non-Republicans do not, almost all Americans would agree that fewer abortions would be a good thing. The disagreement lies with how best to make that happen.

We will also try our best to measure Republican issues the way many Republicans would measure them. In a few instances, this means measuring in ways that are somewhat misleading or inappropriate. When that happens, we will point out why those measures don't make sense. However, since this chapter is intended to measure the performance of each administration from the Republican point of view, we will proceed with the Republican way of measuring that.

We begin the chapter by looking at national defense, which we will measure two ways: first, by the number of military personnel on active duty and second, by the amount of spending that goes toward national defense. Then we'll move on to other Republican concerns. Republicans believe in tax cuts and that the "the most effective, responsible and responsive government is government closest to the people," to quote the Republican Party's Web site in 2008. Republicans also have a dislike for the federal bureaucracy, welfare, and a little agency called the National Endowment for the Arts.

## The Military and National Defense

Republicans love a strong military. Despite Ike's warning about the "military-industrial complex" and various bouts of isolationism that spread through the party (such as the years leading up to both world wars and the 1990s), the view that the country should carry a "big stick" has hardly wavered.

There are several ways to measure an administration's interest in defense. One is to look at the size of the military as measured by active-duty personnel.[2] Figure 6-1 shows that information by administration.

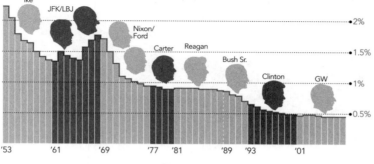

**% of the population serving in the active-duty military**

Figure 6-1

In 1952, there were about 3.6 million personnel on active duty with the U.S. armed forces, amounting to about 2.3 percent of the U.S. population. In 2008, with a much more populous United States fighting two wars, the size of the armed forces was just 1.4 million, or less than 0.5 percent of the population.

The large drawdown in military forces began in the early 1950s with the end of the Korean War. The number (and percentage) of active-duty personnel stabilized in the early 1960s and then rose as the Vietnam War heated up. However, after the Tet Offensive in 1968, and with the arrival of a new president, Nixon, *de-escalation* became the watchword in Vietnam, and American forces shrank rapidly until 1973 or 1974. In 1973, the drawdown of American forces in Vietnam began in earnest, reducing the need for keeping vast numbers of Americans in the service. At the same time, Nixon ended the draft, creating the all-volunteer professional military we have today. After the Vietnam War, there were a few periods in which the size of the armed forces increased marginally, but for the most part, the conflicts the United States has been involved in have not required greater numbers.

Figure 6-2 shows the annualized change in the size of the active-duty military by administration, from highest to lowest.

The biggest increase in the size of the active-duty military occurred during the JFK/LBJ administration. In 1960, there were just under 2.5 million (mostly) men in uniform; by 1968, that figure had increased by more than a million. As a result, the percentage of the population made up of active-duty military personnel increased from 1.37 percent to 1.77 percent. Much of the ramp-up under JFK/LBJ came via the draft, which proved to be an unpopular way to staff what became a highly unpopular war.

Under all the other administrations, the percentage of Americans serving in the active-duty armed forces decreased. Even when there were increases in

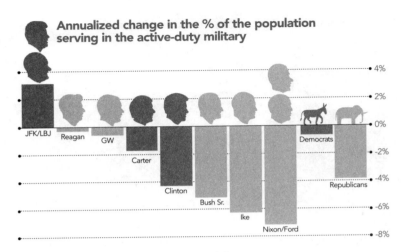

**Annualized change in the % of the population serving in the active-duty military**

Figure 6-2

personnel, as there were under Reagan and GW, the boosts (by 87,000 under Reagan, by 18,000 under GW) were smaller than the growth in population. However, both Reagan and GW sought to project a muscular image—Reagan with the Strategic Defense Initiative (colloquially known as "Star Wars") and GW with twin wars in Afghanistan and Iraq.

Under GW, the initial euphoria of success in Afghanistan and Iraq gave way to a realization that things were not going quite as advertised. Much of Afghanistan was in the hands of warlords, thugs, and fanatics with whom we were nominally allied but who each ran their own corner of the country as a fiefdom, often complete with customs duties! Making matters worse, in parts of the country the Taliban was untamed. And while Osama bin Laden's whereabouts were unknown, he apparently remained more alive than dead. In Iraq the situation was even worse; for years the regime we backed was not able to provide security for the Iraqi people. Over time the situation seemed to stabilize but the cost in blood was high. The results were not good for morale. Despite lowered standards for new recruits, the armed forces started to have trouble meeting recruitment goals. However, by the end of GW's administration, officials at the Pentagon were announcing that the poor economy and lack of civilian job prospects were making the military look much more attractive for young Americans.[3] Mission Accomplished, we guess.

It is worth noting that as of this writing, the wars in Afghanistan and Iraq are ongoing. President Obama has set a date for cashing in the chips in Iraq, while doubling down in Afghanistan, but as we write it's too early to judge how either will turn out.

Carter and Clinton came next on our chart, reducing the size of the armed forces both in absolute numbers and as a percentage of the population. Three Republican administrations came at the bottom in terms of expanding the size of the military: Bush Sr., Ike, and Nixon/Ford. Each presided over the winding-down period following the end of a major mobilization, whether "hot" (the Korean War and Vietnam) or not (the Cold War).

The percentage of Americans on active-duty service in the U.S. military decreased under both Democratic administrations, but it decreased by more when Republicans were in office. Yet the size of the military is not a very precise measure of military strength. For instance, while JFK/LBJ relied heavily on draftees, the current military is a professional force made up entirely of volunteers. Under many circumstances a smaller professional force of volunteers is more effective than a much larger force of conscripts.

Another factor has been the recent rise in the military's reliance on contractors. These contractors, however, aren't counted as members of the military at all. This tendency to rely on contractors for everything from truckers to rifle-toting security increased dramatically under GW, motivated in part by GW's faith in the private sector as well as the military's aforementioned difficulty in recruiting.

The military has also changed in other ways. Today's smaller, professional military relies more heavily on automation, specialized equipment, and sophisticated systems for C3I (command, communication, control, and intelligence). These things cost money. A lot of money.

So another way to look at military strength is by examining defense spending, a catchall that includes payroll expenses, money spent on contractors, the costs of buying and maintaining equipment, rent, military assistance, and just about all other defense-related expenditures. As with all measures of spending, it is important to put this in context. Presumably, the ideal context for such spending would involve the country's need for it. For example, in recent years, GW argued that Islamic terrorism constituted a threat to U.S. survival. Was terrorism truly more of a threat to the United States than the Soviet Union used to be, what with the USSR's thousands of nuclear weapons? Probably not. But if GW was right, a pretty high level of spending would be justified.

It is certainly fair to say that our spending is at a pretty high level. The United States spends far more on defense than any other country—in 2006, for instance, about 45 percent of the entire world's total expenditure on defense was spent by the United States.[4] No other country comes anywhere close. Which, of course, raises a question: Does all this money spent on defense—

dollars that could be used on other things—defend us? To be honest, we don't know. We have not figured out a way to measure that.

But we can look at defense spending itself. And whether we look at defense spending as a share of the budget or in real dollars per capita, the pattern looks about the same, as Figure 6-3 shows.[5]

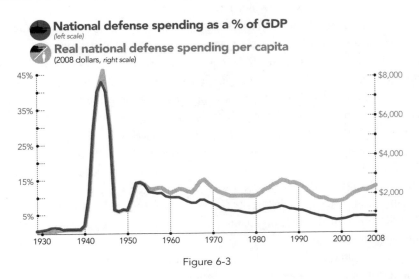

Figure 6-3

Military spending's economic importance surely peaked during World War II, reaching a stunning 43 percent of GDP, or $8,356 per person in 1944.

More than seven years later, as Ike took office during the Korean War, military expenditures were about 14 percent of GDP and dropping fast. What about defense spending as a share of the budget? That is shown in Figure 6-4.

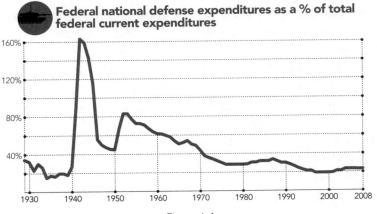

Figure 6-4

Now just a sec, you may be saying to yourself. I know defense spending went way up during World War II, but defense spending couldn't be 160 percent of total federal expenditures. So what gives?

What gives is that, as we noted in Chapter 2, the government computes expenditures in a number of different ways, and for reasons of completeness and precision,[6] we have chosen to use "current expenditures" as our measure of federal government spending. However, as we also noted in Chapter 2, that measure leaves out a number of items, including some of the government's purchases and its own infrastructure construction. Most years those amount to small potatoes, but during World War II, in the pre-contract era, the government was building infrastructure—airports, seaports, roads, dams, barracks, and the like—at a frenzied pace. These expenditures add up, but they aren't counted as current expenditures.

However, as noted in Chapter 2, total expenditures and current expenditures generally move in tandem.[7] So while the magnitude of the military expenditures/current federal expenditures may be overstated, the patterns and rate of change in the data should be the same regardless of the federal expenditure data used. Figure 6-5 shows the change in the share of military expenditures as a percentage of total current federal expenditures, by administration.

## Total federal national defense expenditures as a share of total current federal expenditures

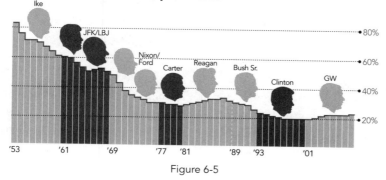

Figure 6-5

A summary of annualized changes in defense spending as a share of federal expenditures is shown in Figure 6-6.

The biggest increase in defense spending as a share of the budget—an increase of about 2 percent a year—came under GW. Furthermore, the magnitude of the increase is so big in part because these expenditures followed two administrations that cut military spending as part of the so-called "peace

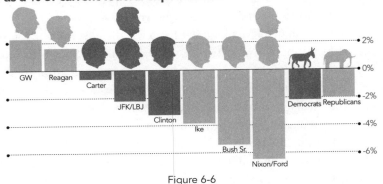

**Annualized change in national defense expenditures as a % of current federal expenditures**

GW  Reagan  Carter  JFK/LBJ  Clinton  Ike  Bush Sr.  Nixon/Ford  Democrats  Republicans

2%  0%  -2%  -4%  -6%

Figure 6-6

dividend" following the collapse of the Soviet Union. All this expenditure was necessary because GW launched two wars—one in Afghanistan and one in Iraq. Even though neither enemy was formidable in conventional terms, they were not easily suppressed. Both wars—and the expenses—dragged on.[8]

Reagan produced the second-largest increase in spending (and the second-largest increase in the size of the active-duty military) in our sample. When Reagan became president, the American military was demoralized. The 1970s were punctuated at one end by the bloody and divisive Vietnam War and at the other end by the failed attempts to rescue the American hostages in Iran.

But Reagan believed that it was "morning in America" and his faith extended to military affairs. He wanted a larger navy and more muscular ground forces, and he pushed for a series of high-tech, high-cost weapons. The techiest and costliest, of course, was known as Star Wars. Some of his supporters believe Star Wars, or the Soviet attempt to match that spending, was what did in the USSR. Nonsupporters might point to a host of other issues, from the growing costs of maintaining a long border with China to the burden of managing Eastern Europe. Probably the biggest economic shift was the collapse in energy prices, which had been a critical source of cash for the Soviet Union.

There is evidence that the Soviet military was rattled by U.S. spending, but not much evidence that the USSR actually tried to keep up with U.S. spending or to replicate the more outlandish imaginary capabilities of the Reagan military. But if the collapse of a hollow, bankrupt empire was inevitable, Reagan deserves credit for moving the process along.

The remaining administrations all oversaw decreases in spending as a percentage of GDP. The smallest decreases occurred under Carter, who—despite his reputation—put a lot of money into modernizing the military.

Funding development of the MX nuclear-tipped missile (called, naturally, the Peacekeeper) and the Advanced Technology Bomber (ATB) project, the precursor to the B-2 Stealth bomber, are among the best-known examples of Carter's efforts.

Ranking behind Carter were JFK/LBJ and Clinton, and they in turn were followed by Ike and Bush Sr. The biggest declines occurred under Nixon/Ford, who found that the military could be maintained at a much lower cost once American involvement in Vietnam ended.

Neither military spending nor the size of the armed forces is a perfect measure of an administration's commitment to national defense. We constructed a third, overall measure by averaging each administration's rank on military size and military expenditure, providing the scores on military issues for each as shown in Figure 6-7.

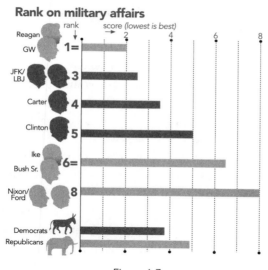

Figure 6-7

Reagan and GW tied for top honors. Reagan averaged a score of 2, coming in second on both the size of the military and military expenditures. GW got the same score by coming in first on military expenditures and third in terms of expanding the military.

JFK/LBJ followed close behind, with a third-place finish on expenditures and a top rank when it came to expanding the size of the military. Next came Carter, Clinton, and a tie between Ike and Bush Sr. Bringing up the rear was Nixon/Ford, having decreased the size of the military the most, both in terms of the number of personnel and in terms of expenditures.

# The Size of Government

A common refrain for Republicans is that government is too big, too intrusive, and in need of downsizing. As we saw earlier, some Republicans advocate privatizing some services that government employees provide. Unfortunately, when government jobs are privatized, the process often doesn't result in the savings many Republicans envision. The war in Iraq provided a good test case, given the extensive use of contractors in the conflict. Using contractors sometimes cost the military significantly more than it would have to do the job itself. Whether delivering unsafe water to troops in the field, providing shoddy electrical work at military bases, or overcharging for food, many contractors found it was more profitable to rip off the taxpayer than to provide high quality of service. (And let's not even get into the way some contractors stoked antagonism for Americans—thus adding to the risks borne by U.S. military personnel—by acting like lawless, well-armed bullies.)

But outsourcing government functions is not the only way to reduce the number of government employees. Another way is simply to lower the level of services. To many Republicans this is actually the point. However, whether the goal is to produce the same services more efficiently or simply fewer services, one constant for Republicans is the need to reduce the number of government employees. Teachers, postal workers, welfare caseworkers, IRS agents—Republicans tend to view these government employees as overpaid loafers doing jobs that either should not exist or that could be done more efficiently by the private sector.

The general Republican contempt for government workers extends only to the *civilian* employees of the federal government; members of the military are generally lauded as highly as their civilian counterparts are derided. We can measure the number of civilian federal employees of the executive branch from 1962 to 2007.[9]

The data does contain one ambiguity as far as we are concerned—it includes civilian employees who work for the Department of Defense. However, it isn't entirely clear that rank-and-file Republicans are united in their appreciation of this group of civilians so it wouldn't make sense to subtract them (even assuming we had the data needed to do so). Additionally, we note that the data does not include employees of other branches of the federal government (e.g., the legislative and the judicial) or state governments. While many Republicans would consider some of these folks parasites as well, the president doesn't have much control over those sectors.

So how many of these federal employees lurk in the executive branch? Figure 6-8 shows civilian federal executive branch employees as a percentage of the population, by administration.

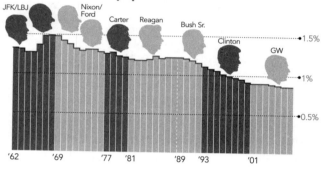

Figure 6-8

As Figure 6-8 shows, in the early 1960s civilian federal executive branch employees made up about 1.3 percent of the population. The figure declined slightly for a few years and then increased markedly, peaking at 1.5 percent of the population at the height of the Vietnam War and the war on poverty.

From then on, the executive branch's workforce shrank—more or less steadily—until the early 1980s. During the 1980s, the percentage of the population working for the government began to rise again. However, once Reagan left, office federal employees shrank as a percentage of the population in every year through 2007 but one (2003). By 2007, less than nine-tenths of a percent of the population was employed as civilian members of the executive branch.

Figure 6-9 summarizes the annualized changes in the number of civilian federal employees as a percentage of the population over the span of each administration.

As we saw in earlier chapters, the Clinton administration produced the biggest decreases in spending among all administrations. Part of this spending decrease came from aggressively reducing the size of the federal workforce, resulting in the biggest cut—proportionally—in the civilian executive branch workforce. Just as the fastest annualized decreases in spending under Clinton came before the Republican Revolution, the biggest annualized reductions in the federal workforce also preceded Newt's rise to power.[10]

This decrease in the size of the federal workforce was achieved in part through automation and the National Partnership for Reinventing Government.

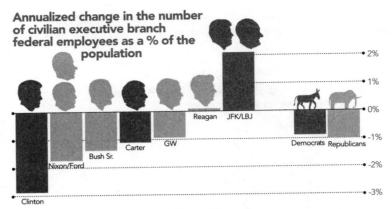

Annualized change in the number of civilian executive branch federal employees as a % of the population

Reagan  JFK/LBJ

Carter  GW

Bush Sr.

Nixon/Ford

Clinton

Democrats  Republicans

2%
1%
0%
-1%
-2%
-3%

Figure 6-9

That program, launched just weeks after Clinton took office and spearheaded by Vice President Al Gore, was intended to make the government more responsive to the needs of ordinary Americans while, at the same time, cutting costs. We do not have data on how responsive the government is to its citizens' needs, but Reinventing Government did succeed in cutting costs.

Coming in second was the Nixon/Ford administration. A big part of the reduction during that administration, as noted before, came as the Vietnam War ratcheted down, which suggests that many of the reductions came among the staff that supported the prosecution of that war. Reductions in the federal workforce as a share of the population also occurred under Bush Sr, Carter, and GW.

Two administrations increased the relative size of the civilian executive branch workforce: Reagan (yes, Reagan) and JFK/LBJ. The latter did it by the most, a combination of social programs like the War on Poverty and the administrative support for the buildup in the Vietnam War. As for the former, well, you wouldn't know it from listening to either his rhetoric or his self-appointed image makers who came around later.

## Taxes

Tax cuts. If any two words embody the Republican Party, it's these two. That said, as we noted in Chapter 3, a president who cuts taxes while at the same time driving up the debt is not really "cutting taxes." He is merely transferring taxes from now until some later date. Still, when Republicans say "tax cuts," they mean cutting the amount people pay right now, so in this chapter we're going to focus on current taxes.

There are two ways to reduce the amount people pay in taxes right now—one is to cut tax rates and the other is to cut back on enforcement of tax laws. Cutting tax rates is the obvious way. Presidents who do so generally beat their chest and trumpet their tax (rate) cuts to all corners of the land. Cutting enforcement is done more quietly; it involves putting people in charge of the IRS who interpret tax rules and regulations just so, putting less pressure on alleged violators or even cutting the budget at the IRS and firing auditors. After that, it's just a matter of letting the public do its thing.

And the thing that many people do when they're allowed to do it is cheat on their taxes. The IRS has estimated that the "overall gross tax gap for Tax Year 2001—the difference between what taxpayers should have paid and what they actually paid on a timely basis—comes to $345 billion."[11] To put this in perspective, the federal government's current revenue in 2001 was a little over $2 trillion. Thus, the IRS estimate means that tax evasion cost the federal government somewhere in the neighborhood of *15 percent* of its income. And that figure understates the true effect of tax evasion, since it was based on statistical sampling of 46,000 tax returns and thus ignores the effect of people simply not reporting anything at all to the IRS. It also "does not include taxes that should have been paid on income from the illegal sector of the economy."[12]

As a result, it is important to consider the overall *tax burden* (i.e., the percentage of their income people pay in taxes) that people actually do pay, not just what the law or the tax tables say they're supposed to pay. But people aren't supposed to pay just federal taxes, they are also supposed to pay taxes to state and local governments. And those taxes sometimes go up when federal taxes go down; after all, when the federal government cuts services because it doesn't have the revenue to pay for those services, state or local governments often pick up the slack. Contrariwise, when the government subsidizes local government—as it did as part of the 2009 stimulus package—state taxes do not rise, while federal obligations do. Thus, however indirectly, the president affects not just how much people pay Uncle Sam, but also the tax collectors closer to home.

So Figure 6-10 shows not only the top marginal tax rate on income, but also the actual tax burden.[13] Note that the tax burden tells us nothing about how the taxes are apportioned among different segments of the population. However, Figure 6-10 does show us, on average, what percentage of income is paid in taxes.

Between 1929 and 2008, the top marginal rate ranged between 24 percent and 92 percent. At the same time, the tax burden ranged between

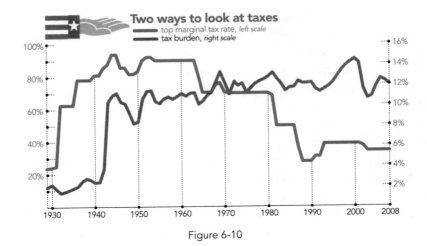

Figure 6-10

1.4 percent and 14.7 percent. As Figure 6-10 shows, the marginal income tax rates that presidents and TV pundits keep talking about bear little resemblance to the tax rates we pay in the real world. Clearly, the marginal tax rate is not in the driver's seat or, to mix a metaphor, even in the same ballpark when it comes to determining how much people actually pay in taxes. So we're going to ignore the marginal income tax rates and focus on the tax burden, which is graphed by administration in Figure 6-11.

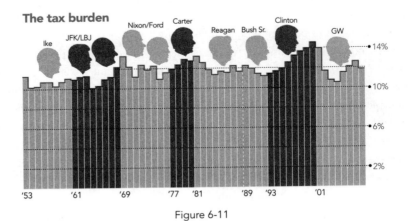

Figure 6-11

The changes over the span of each administration are summarized in Figure 6-12.

Here's confirmation of at least one stereotype: All five Republican administrations cut taxes, and all three Democratic administrations raised

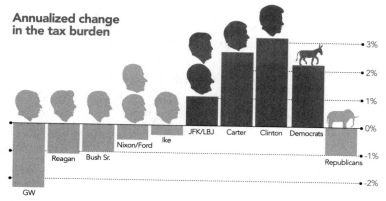

**Annualized change in the tax burden**

3%
2%
1%
0%
-1%
-2%

JFK/LBJ  Carter  Clinton  Democrats

Ike

Nixon/Ford

Reagan  Bush Sr.

Republicans

GW

Figure 6-12

taxes. The biggest tax cuts came under GW—easily twice those under Reagan, who came in second. As we've seen elsewhere in the book, GW tended to view cutting taxes as something of a panacea.

Reagan cut tax rates by more than any other president, and he did so with great fanfare. The top rate was reduced from 70 percent in 1980 all the way down to 28 percent in 1988. However, Reagan realized that the resulting debt was untenable, so he quietly raised other taxes on income—primarily Social Security taxes and payroll taxes. Most of his well-publicized tax cuts went to the folks at the top of the income scale, while the stealth tax hikes had their biggest impact on everyone else.

Which brings us to Bush Sr., the third biggest tax-cutter in the sample. What's this? Bush Sr. comes in third when it comes to cutting taxes? Wasn't he the one who went back on his "Read my lips" pledge? Didn't he raise taxes? Well, he raised some tax rates, but at the same time the folks he placed at the IRS made sure that less of people's income was going to Washington. Bush Sr.'s administration provides a nice illustration of the difference between cutting marginal tax rates and cutting the amount people actually pay in taxes.

Nixon/Ford came in fourth. Ike followed in fifth place, having cut the top marginal rate from 92 percent to 91 percent (no, these are not typos!!) and trimming the bottom marginal rate from 22 percent to 20 percent in 1954. (And you thought marginal tax rates were high now!) It should be noted that on a number of occasions, Ike actually recommended that various excise and corporate taxes be extended beyond their original expiration dates. (What are the odds he could get through the Republican primaries with proposals like that now?)

Among Democrats, the smallest tax increase occurred under JFK/LBJ. This administration often receives kudos from Republicans for cutting taxes—and JFK/LBJ did cut marginal tax rates in 1964. But Republicans would be very disappointed with the stated goals of the administration when it came to taxes, as laid out by President Kennedy in a letter delivered to Congress on April 20, 1961. Kennedy noted the need for more tax equity, which he felt required more "uniform and vigorous enforcement" of the existing tax law, particularly targeted to ensure more "compliance, largely in the high income group subject to a higher tax rate."[14] His approach to achieving compliance included ensuring that each taxpayer, be it an individual or a corporation, was identified by a single tax ID number, which together with automation would make it easier to tell if someone was cheating on their taxes. There was also an increased focus on the kind of income that tends to be the province of the wealthy, such as capital gains and dividends. Glory be, with added enforcement, marginal tax rates fell but collections actually rose.

The remaining two Democratic administrations collected an even greater percentage of the national income in taxes. On an annualized basis, Carter increased collections more than twice as quickly as JFK/LBJ and Clinton increased them almost three as times as quickly. In fact, collections as a percentage of personal income increased every single year of Bill Clinton's presidency, including after the well-publicized cuts in capital gains tax rates.

In the Interlude chapter we will examine two claims that many Republicans make about taxes, namely that reducing current taxes will boost economic growth rates and that it will also lead to increased tax revenues.

## Washington versus the States

The ascendancy of the Goldwater wing of the Republican Party, capped by Reagan's landslide election in 1980, brought with it a tougher line on some core issues: taxes, military spending, and the size of government. That tougher line eventually had its moment of triumph in the arena of public discourse. Even a supposedly liberal president would proudly announce that the era of big government was over.

But Republicans don't just want big government to become small (or insignificant) government; they usually want the federal government to shrink relative to state and local government. This view is based on the notion that state and local government is closer—and more responsive—to the American people.

The president can move toward this goal by taking power (i.e., money) and responsibility from the federal government and transferring them to state and local governments. Typically, this is done by providing the state and local governments with grants. Figure 6-13 shows data on federal grants to the state and local governments, going back to 1929, the first year for which we have data.[15]

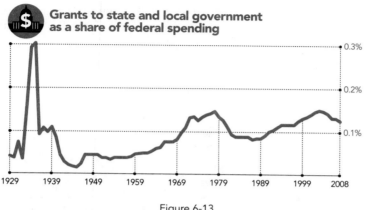

**Grants to state and local government as a share of federal spending**

Figure 6-13

At first glance it might not look like it, but Figure 6-13 shows that beginning in the late 1930s the federal government followed two distinct approaches to sharing power with state and local government. The approach followed by most administrations seems to have been simple: When the country faces a perceived external threat, the share of the spending decisions made in Washington increases; the opposite is generally true at other times. Since the late 1930s, the big reductions in federal grants to state and local government as a share of current federal expenditures fell around the time of World War II, the Berlin blockade, the Korean War, the 1973 oil embargo, the 1979 oil crisis, and the second Gulf War.

The big outlier on the list is the second Gulf War. While the other events on that list involved battling major powers or economic catastrophes that threatened the country's way of life, the second Gulf War was a relatively minor affair against enemies that most Americans agree—at least in retrospect—were not truly a danger to America. Nevertheless, the aftershock of 9/11 gave GW the momentum needed to win support for the war, as well as for expansion of his powers, whether by moving spending decisions to Washington or pushing through laws with flag-and-country–type labels. These included the USA Patriot Act and the Protect America Act.

Be that as it may, it is not surprising—nor necessarily a bad thing—that the federal government tries to increase its power during times of external threat. However well-intentioned it might have been, the city government of say, White

Sulfur Springs, Montana, just wasn't in a position to do much about the threat represented by the Nazis or the Empire of the Rising Sun during World War II. Ditto the mayor of Cuyahoga Falls, Ohio. To fight a war of that magnitude takes a central government and central planning, and that in turn takes money—money that therefore cannot be sent to the states, counties, and cities.

But as we mentioned, this pattern—moving power away from Washington when there are few threats, and bringing power back to Washington when there are external threats had one exception which can easily be spotted in Figure 6-14.

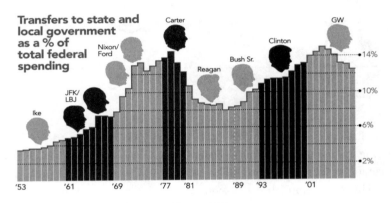

Figure 6-14

As Figure 6-14 shows, the normal trend (i.e., granting more power to state and local governments) reversed itself in the last two years of the Carter administration with the 1979 oil crisis. This was a period of national emergency. Carter declared the oil crisis to be the "moral equivalent of war" and proceeded to fight that war, albeit as ineptly as GW would fight the wars in Afghanistan and Iraq almost thirty years later. He imposed a complicated system of oil rationing, conservation, and even import quotas, all of which required the powers of the federal government.

However, the devolution of money (and power) from state and local governments to the federal government continued and even accelerated during Reagan's first two years in office, although by then the oil crisis had ended and the epic battle against Grenada was still not on anyone's radar screen. From 1980, the year before Reagan took office, to 1983 the percentage of the federal budget being transferred to state and local governments dropped from 12.3 percent to 8.8 percent, and while this trend slowed beginning in 1984, in Reagan's last year in office that figure was down to 8.4 percent.

The annualized changes in such grants, by administration, are summarized in Figure 6-15.

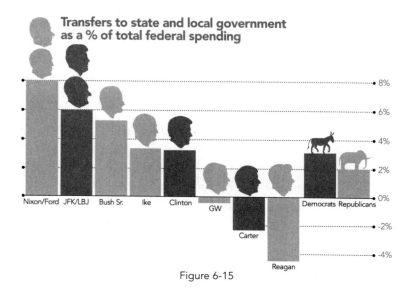

**Transfers to state and local government as a % of total federal spending**

Figure 6-15

The Nixon/Ford administration, which straddled the wind-down of a major war, did the most to turn over spending from the federal government to the states, almost doubling the percentage of federal spending made up of grants to state and local government.

One of the most important tools the Nixon/Ford administration used to funnel money to state and local governments was the State and Local Fiscal Assistance Act of 1972, which provided matching funds to state and local municipalities. That act grew out of a recognition by the president and Congress that

> there was need for a new aid program to give the State and local governments the flexibility that they need to use the funds for the most vital purposes in their particular circumstances.[16]

The act provided funding—more than $30 billion in the first five years[17]—to the states with very few strings attached. It is worth noting that in 1972, the year before the act was passed, total federal transfers to the states equaled to $64.4 billion.

Even on smaller issues, Nixon worked to shift assets from federal to state and local control. For example, he asked Congress for and received a bill "to permit states and localities to receive title to surplus Federal structures of historic and architectural interest."[18]

JFK/LBJ followed Nixon/Ford in the rankings, occupying second place. Despite the ramp-up of the Vietnam War and high-profile federal initiatives like the war on poverty and the race to the moon, they moved a lot of spending out of Washington's hands and into the hands of state and local governments. Third and fourth place went to Bush Sr. and Ike, two presidents who, like Nixon, enjoyed a peace dividend. Clinton was the final president who moved power away from Washington.

Three administrations would centralize more power in Washington. One was that of GW Bush—no surprise to anyone who ever read the USA Patriot Act. He was followed by Jimmy Carter. However, the president who did the most to move power—at least the kind controlled by the purse strings—away from the state and local governments and to the federal government, was Reagan. Reagan talked a good game about taking power away from Washington but he didn't walk the walk. Reagan even went so far as to kill Nixon's State and Local Fiscal Assistance Act of 1972.

Out of all the administrations in our sample, Ike and Clinton deserve special notice. As noted in Chapter 2, both of them decreased current federal spending as a percentage of GDP, and yet both of them managed to increase the share of that reduced federal spending going to state and local governments. And since of these two only Ike also cut taxes as well, perhaps Ike is the true conservative in a crowd of pretenders. The architect of victory in Europe backed a strong military but as president mostly passed on foreign adventures. The highway-builder-in-chief poured federal asphalt from sea to shining sea because doing so would help commerce, but he turned back power from the feds to the states.

# Welfare

Visions of welfare queens driving Cadillacs and freeloading on society drive the average Republican crazy. But what is welfare? We went rummaging around spreadsheets and files and documents at a number of government agencies and never quite came up with either a formal definition of *welfare* or a line item for it. But we did locate federal government spending on "social benefits." These include Social Security, Medicare, veterans' benefits, unemployment insurance, food stamps, black lung benefits, direct relief, payment to nonprofit institutions, student aid, and the earned income tax credit. Looking at all that, we concluded that Republicans tend to favor benefits for veterans, but otherwise consider the rest of the list to be welfare. Figure 6-16 shows how that spending has changed over time.[19]

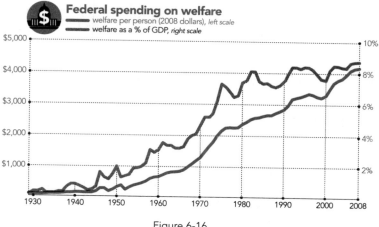

Figure 6-16

In 1929, the government spent about $100 million on welfare—about eighty-two cents per person, or about $10.30 in 2008 dollars. By 2007, overall spending in 2008 dollars had grown to over $1.2 trillion, and real spending per person had increased by over $4,000!

We can look at how important welfare spending was to the government by looking at such spending as a share of the budget (see Figure 6-17).

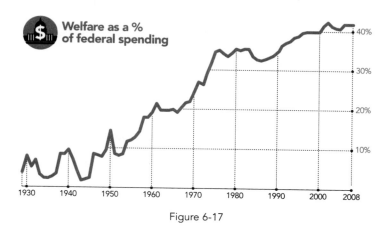

Figure 6-17

Welfare spending grew from 3.8 percent of the budget in 1929, the first year of the Hoover administration, to 6.7 percent in 1932, Hoover's last full year in office. During 1929 the stock market crashed and the Great

Depression started. However, during FDR's first few years in office, welfare shrank again, dropping to less than 2 percent of the budget in 1934 and 1935. While the FDR administration's measures were enough to get the economy moving again, the public was still hurting and FDR began putting more into welfare; the share of the budget going into welfare rose to 9.4 percent of the budget by 1940.

And then came World War II, when the country found itself with other priorities, namely survival. Spending on welfare dropped to 1.3 percent of total federal spending in 1943 and 1944. At the end of the war, it rose rapidly to 14.3 percent of the budget in 1950, and then dropped again with the arrival of another major war, the Korean War.

Figure 6-18 shows what federal spending on welfare has looked like, by administration, since 1953.

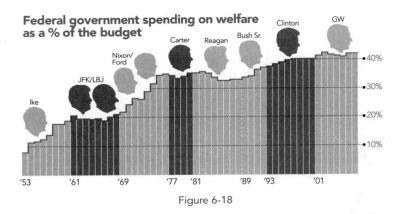

Figure 6-18

Spending on welfare as a percentage of total budget increased under Ike; just a couple months after taking office, Ike formed the new Department of Health, Education, and Welfare, telling Congress:

> The purpose of this plan is to improve the administration of the vital health, education, and social security functions now being carried on in the Federal Security Agency by giving them departmental rank. Such action is demanded by the importance and magnitude of these functions, which affect the well-being of millions of our citizens. [20]

While always wary of "creeping socialism," Ike would expand a number of New Deal programs. Whether that was because he believed in those programs or was being pragmatic about the public's views has been debated.

Interestingly enough, welfare spending as a percentage of total spending did not increase much during the JFK/LBJ years, at least until 1966. Clearly, many of the early skirmishes in the war on poverty were fought along other fronts.

However, it was a different story under the Nixon/Ford administration, when spending on welfare as a share of the budget once again began increasing rapidly, finally leveling off when Ford assumed the presidency. The slow growth started again under Carter, but welfare's share of the budget decreased under Reagan. Welfare spending once again began expanding faster than overall federal spending under Bush Sr. as the "peace dividend" allowed money to be redirected from military affairs. It would continue to rise under Clinton until welfare reform, after which it flattened out. That relative flatness continued under the compassionate conservative president, GW Bush.

Figure 6-19 shows a summary of the annualized changes in welfare spending as a share of the budget.

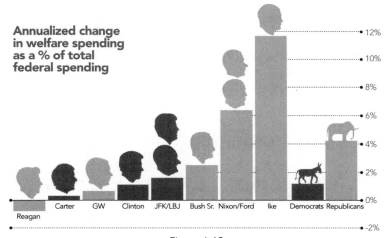

Figure 6-19

The Reagan administration was the only one to shrink welfare as a share of the budget. The smallest increases came under Carter, followed by GW Bush, Clinton, and JFK/LBJ. The biggest annualized increases in welfare spending as a share of total spending came under three Republican administrations—Bush Sr., Nixon/Ford, and Ike. So Reagan's data confirms this part of his image. But overall, Republicans had a tendency to increase the percentage of total spending that went toward welfare almost four times more quickly than Democrats. We're willing to bet that's not what you expected to read when you started this chapter.

# The National Endowment
# for the Arts

The National Endowment for the Arts (NEA) holds a special place in the heart of Republican rhetoric. With very few exceptions, Republicans wish to see the agency eviscerated if not eliminated altogether.

It's not that the NEA is a big or even a growing part of the federal budget. Its total budget in 2008 was less than $145 million[21]—a lot of money to me and you (assuming you're not Bill Gates), but the federal government as a whole spent that much (on current expenditures) every twenty-six minutes or so during the 2008 calendar year. At its high-water mark in 1979, the NEA received 0.0297 percent of the federal budget—that is, less than one-third of one-tenth of 1 percent of the federal budget. The NEA is closer to a rounding error than a budget-buster.

But the Republican dislike—if not outright disdain—for the agency is not so much about the numbers, but rather the symbolism: Most Republicans don't believe in government funding for the arts and certainly not the sort of arts that are funded by the NEA. The NEA has often served nicely as a kind of poster child for waste of a particularly pernicious kind: Pouring taxpayer money into work that many people view as sacrilegious, anti-American, even obscene.

Figure 6-20 shows the NEA's budget as a percentage of total federal spending beginning in 1966, the year it was created by LBJ.

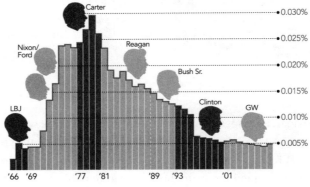

**The NEA's budget as a % of total federal spending**

Figure 6-20

The high-water mark for NEA funding came in 1979, and since then, the agency's funding has shrunk in size relative to the federal budget. As we stated earlier, the NEA got one-third of one-tenth of 1 percent of the federal budget in 1979, but that was six times the share of the budget the agency received in 2008.

Figure 6-21 summarizes the annualized change in funding to the NEA over the span of each administration for presidents since LBJ. (LBJ was not included because the agency was around for only three years during his administration, which would provide only two years' worth of data.)

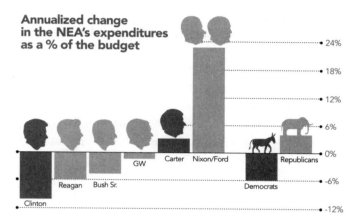

Figure 6-21

The biggest cutter of NEA funding was . . . Bill Clinton. While he cut NEA funding from the beginning of his term, this is one issue on which the Republican Congress got its way. After all, the biggest annual drop in funding during his term, a reduction in excess of 40 percent, occurred from 1995 to 1996.

Clinton was followed by Reagan, Bush Sr., and GW Bush. Carter produced a small increase in the NEA's funding as a share of the budget, but Nixon/Ford really increased it by a lot. It may not be fair to group Ford and Nixon on this one topic. Nixon increased funding to the NEA, and Ford cut that funding. So what was Nixon thinking, increasing spending for an agency so despised by most Republicans? Perhaps Nixon was simply a supporter of risk-taking, iconoclastic art. Or perhaps, like Clinton, Nixon also triangulated. In a time of government subsidies and more liberal domestic policies, Nixon could undermine his critics by supporting the NEA, opening up relations with China, supporting the creation of the Environmental Protection Agency and the Occupational Safety and Health Administration, and, for that matter, declaring that "We are all Keynesians now." Or maybe that was all just a cynical play for votes.

# Republican Issues: Conclusion

In the last few chapters, we looked at how each administration performed on various distinctly Republican issues: military preparedness, the size of government (as measured by the number of civilian employees), the federal tax burden, the degree to which the federal government delegated responsibility and funding to state and local governments, welfare, and funding for the National Endowment of the Arts as a share of the federal budget.

Because all these issues capture a different aspect of what is important specifically to Republicans, the ideal measure might be one that takes them all into account. At least, it would give us a rough summary of what is going on. Something like what the Consumer Price Index is intended to do.

Therefore, we have constructed our own index—an overall score on Republican issues illustrating how each administration performed on each of the Republican issues. The index was constructed so that an administration that was ranked first on all Republican issues would have a score of 100 percent, and an administration that was ranked last on all Republican issues would have a score of 0 percent.

Figure 6-22 shows each administration's score and ranking on Republican issues.

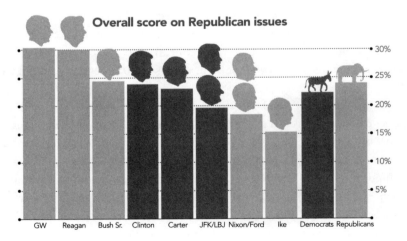

Figure 6-22

As Figure 6-22 shows, there is no breakout winner on Republican issues, though overall the best performance was turned in by GW on the strength of a first-place finish in military preparedness and a third-place finish on welfare.

However, he scored in the bottom half when it came to decreasing the size of government, devolving power back to the states, and cutting the NEA's budget.

Reagan followed close behind; the man most Republicans today consider to be the quintessential Republican president did well when it came to cutting welfare (first place), the strength of the military (tied for first), cutting taxes (second place), and cutting the NEA's budget (second place). However, despite his rhetoric, he increased the federal workforce and was singularly uninterested in sharing power with state and local governments.

In third place was Bush Sr., who was followed by the three Democratic administrations. It's worth noting that Bill Clinton even managed two first-place finishes on Republican issues: for reducing the size of government and trimming the NEA budget.

In seventh on Republican issues were Nixon/Ford, and last place went to Ike. Clearly, what seem to be Republican issues today were not as important to Republicans prior to the 1980s. That said, it's not surprising to note that, in general, Republican administrations did a better job at what we today think of as quintessential Republican goals than Democrats did.

# On Taxes

Raising taxes won't balance the budget; it will encourage more government spending and less private investment. Raising taxes will slow economic growth, reduce production, and destroy future jobs, making it more difficult for those without jobs to find them and more likely that those who now have jobs could lose them.

RONALD REAGAN
Address Before a Joint Session of the Congress Reporting
on the State of the Union, January 26, 1982[1]

At the risk of oversimplification, the Republican view of government is that it's too big, too intrusive, and too inefficient. Worse, government funds itself by taking people's hard-earned money—money that its rightful owners would have used more productively. And taxes also harm the economy, discouraging people from working; after all, why put in the work needed to make an extra dollar (or million, for that matter) if the government is going to tax it away?

Nevertheless, most Republicans will admit that the government is more than a simple pie-eating mooch. Many of the things the government does—from building roads to enforcing patents—are necessary for the economy to be efficient and to grow. And all these things have to be paid for, which means that all these things require some form of revenue. And the government's revenue—the revenue that pays for all this good stuff and a whole lot more—has a name: taxes.[2]

That means that cutting taxes could shortchange these essential services, and if it does it will make us all poorer. So under ideal circumstances the government will straddle the line, staying small enough to be (relatively) nimble and efficient but large enough to provide the level of services we need for the economy to grow; put another way, taxes shouldn't be so high that they strangle economic growth and hurt our living standards, nor should they be so low that we don't get the services we need for growth.

In this interlude chapter, we're going to examine whether lower tax burdens (or cuts in the tax burden) have been associated with improvements in the economy.

# Taxes—In Practice

As we saw in Chapter 6, though marginal tax rates can remain unchanged for a long time, the tax burden—the share of their income Americans actually pay in taxes—moves up or down every year. Similarly, the growth rate in real GDP per capita is constantly changing. If lower taxes are better for growth, we should generally expect to see faster growth in real GDP per capita when the tax burden is lower and slower increases in real GDP per capita when the tax burden is higher.

So let's see if that's true, shall we? Figure I-1 below shows the tax burden and the one-year change in real GDP per capita for every year from 1953 to 2008.[3]

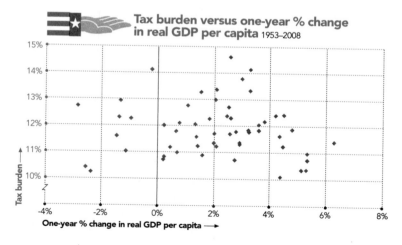

Figure I-1

Figure I-1 looks too scattershot to show much of a relationship between the tax burden and economic growth. But we can measure the correlation of the two measures. The correlation between two variables tells you the degree to which the variables move together, and it can range between –100 percent and 100 percent.

If the correlation between two variables is 100 percent, it means that every time one variable moves, the other variable makes a proportional move in the same direction. For example, the correlation between the number of cats a person has and the amount of waste that has to be cleaned out of the litter box is pretty close to 100 percent. A correlation of –100 percent, however, means that the two variables move opposite each other in mirrored lockstep. For example, the correlation between the amount of your paycheck your spouse spends and the amount you manage to put away is going to be pretty close to –100 percent. Finally, if the correlation is close to zero, the two variables don't move together at all. That is, if they do, it's just a random occurrence.

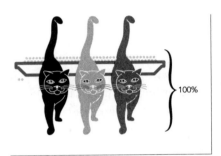

100%

The correlation between the tax burden and the one-year percentage growth in real GDP is –5 percent, meaning that as taxes go up, growth rates have a tendency to be lower, as many Republicans would expect. But –5 percent is close to zero, so it seems like a pretty weak relationship between the two things.

How weak, you ask? To answer that, consider Rondônia, which is a small, remote state in northwestern Brazil, best known for, um, come to think of it, it isn't all that well known for anything. In 2007, Rondônia had a population of less than 1.5 million people.[4] Rondônia is mostly rural, though it does have a grand total of fifty-two towns, villages, and other assorted municipalities. Closer to home, the state of Ohio has eighty-eight counties, with a total population of 11.5 million in 2007.[5] The correlation between the population of the fifty-two municipalities in Rondônia (arranged in alphabetical order) with the population of the first fifty-two counties in Ohio (also arranged in alphabetical order) is –6 percent; that is, there is a slightly stronger negative correlation between these two measures that have nothing at all to do with each other than there is between taxes and growth in real GDP per capita.

But perhaps we're looking at this the wrong way. Maybe the tax burden takes a little time to do its nefarious work. Figure I-2 shows the tax burden in each year from 1952 to 2007 against the one-year percentage growth in real GDP per capita the following year.

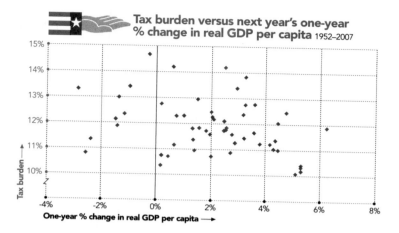

Figure I-2

It's still hard to see much of a relationship with the naked eye. Nevertheless, the correlation is still negative, and a bit stronger: –29 percent. Though it's still not a compelling correlation, it does at least suggest that lower growth rates occur in the year following a higher tax burden and that, conversely, lower tax burdens tend to be followed by years in which the growth in real GDP per capita is faster.

So we're done, right? We've seen that—even if the relationship is weak—higher taxes correlate with slower growth. So that means we should also expect to see that administrations that imposed a lower average tax burden also produced the fastest growth rates in real GDP per capita. But that's not what happened, as we see in Figure I-3.[6]

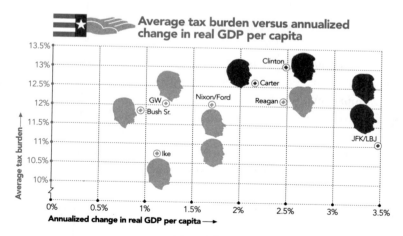

Figure I-3

In Chapter 1, we saw that when it comes to growth in real GDP per capita, only one Republican administration (that of Ronald Reagan) finished in the top four. On the other hand, the bottom four administrations were all Republican. As Figure I-3 shows, if there is a correlation between the average tax burden and the annual change in real GDP per capita over the span of each administration, it is weakly positive (i.e., the correlation is 10 percent). But, looking only at administrations beginning with Nixon/Ford produces a very strong positive relationship (almost 74 percent!) between the tax burden and growth rates; that is, in recent decades, higher tax burdens have been associated with faster, not slower, economic growth.

So what's going on here? Why is it that there is a slight tendency for lower taxes to be associated with faster growth on a year-by-year basis, but *not* over the span of entire administrations? And whatever the relationship between the growth in real GDP per capita and the tax burden, Democrats on average produce much faster growth than Republicans. Why?

Several possibilities come to mind, including these:

1. Democratic policies produce faster growth. The increases in tax collections observed under many Democrats is a by-product of people becoming wealthier and moving into higher tax brackets.
2. Democratic policies produce faster growth. However, they also have a tendency to increase the tax burden on the public, which does not in any way impact growth.
3. Perhaps lower taxes really do produce the conditions that would ordinarily lead to slower growth, but even so, overall Democrats follow better economic policies by focusing on other things that matter even more than lower taxes.
4. The range in which the tax burden moved from 1953 to 2008, from a low of 10.1 percent to a high of 14.7 percent, is simply too low or too narrow for changes to have had any significant impact on growth.
5. Lower taxes may boost growth in the short run, but have more deleterious effects in the long run. This may be because the decreased revenues from lower taxes over time force a cutback in services or an increase in debt and interest payments on that debt.

The first of these explanations—that increased tax collections are a result of people getting wealthier and moving into higher tax brackets—is unlikely. After all, growth in real GDP per capita (and income) was similar under both Reagan and Clinton, but the tax burden decreased under the former and increased under the latter. Likewise, the fastest growth rates in real GDP per capita came during the JFK/LBJ administration, which also had the second-lowest average tax burden. Additionally, consider that four administrations—those of Nixon/Ford, Reagan, and the two Bushes—all had similar average tax burdens and all cut the tax burden during their time in office. However, annualized growth in real GDP per capita was very different in all four of these administrations. The change in real net disposable income under each one varied even more.

While the first explanation does not work, the others cannot be ruled out by any of the facts we have presented in the book so far or will present in the rest of this chapter. Alan Greenspan described one of his meetings with Bill Clinton early in Clinton's presidency, which also applies to the above scenarios:

> But I was impressed that he was not trying to fudge reality to the extent politicians ordinarily do. He was forcing himself to live in the real world on the economic outlook and monetary policy. His subsequent decision to go ahead and fight for the deficit cuts was an act of political courage. It would have been very easy to go the other way. *Not many people would have been the wiser for a year or two or even three.* [Emphasis added.] [7]

Clinton would pay a political price for this act of courage: His party would lose control of Congress in 1995 and his failure, or rather his refusal, to bring home the bacon can't have helped. It certainly angered many politicians from his own party. But it put the United States on a path to rapid economic growth that likely would not have happened otherwise.

Another issue worth pondering: Why is the correlation between the tax burden and growth in real GDP per capita stronger when the first two administrations are left out? In other words, an increase in the tax burden was associated with an increase in real GDP per capita growth and this relationship was stronger when the Ike and JFK/LBJ administrations were left out. Why?

One possible reason: The average tax burden was lower under Ike and JFK/LBJ than under the other administrations, even though the tax burden increased under JFK/LBJ. Perhaps if the tax burden is low enough, what matters more are changes in the tax burden—tax cuts or tax hikes. We will look at the effect of such changes later in this chapter.

But for now let's look at the effect of the average tax burden on other variables. For example, Figure I-4 shows the relationship between the tax burden and net real GDP per capita.

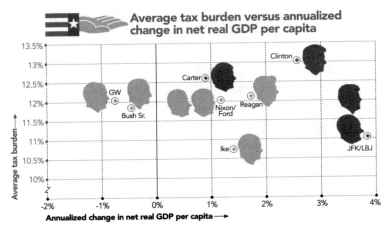

Figure I-4

Once again, the Ike and JFK/LBJ administrations are kind of outliers (leaving them out produces a positive correlation between the average tax burden and the annual change in net real GDP per capita of over 70 percent). However, whether those two administrations are included or not, what we aren't seeing in Figure I-4 is much evidence that lower taxes produce faster growth.

What about increased tax collections? This has been an article of faith among many Republicans since Ronald Reagan's meeting with Arthur Laffer and his famous napkin: Lower taxes bring in more revenue. Inspired by lower taxes, people work harder and make more money, so they actually end up paying more taxes. Faith, in this case, gets no support from the data. Look at tax collections as a percentage of GDP, as seen in Figure I-5.

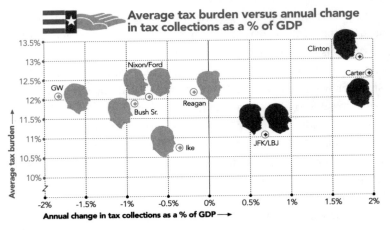

Figure I-5

Figure I-5 seems to indicate that tax revenues as a percentage of GDP are higher, not lower, in administrations that had higher average tax burdens. The correlation between the tax burden and tax collections as a percentage of GDP is above 40 percent, and above 88 percent if only the last six administrations are counted. An 88 percent correlation, it should be noted, is pretty high.

The lower taxes = higher tax revenue story also doesn't work with real tax revenues per capita, as noted in Figure I-6.

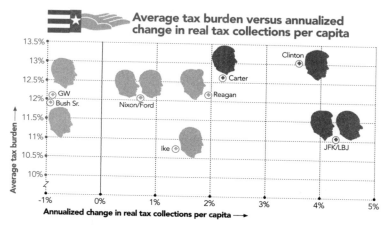

Figure I-6

There is a slight positive correlation between the tax burden and the annualized change in real tax collections per capita over the span of each administration (5 percent for all eight administrations, 88 percent for the last six administrations). Clearly, the expectation among some that tax cuts could lead to increased tax revenues is, at best, faith in a free lunch.

But since the whole purpose of the government is to serve us, it's worth asking—what about our own incomes? Does what's in our pocketbook increase faster when tax rates are lower? Figure I-7 shows the average tax burden and the annualized change in the real median income, by administration.

Eyeballing Figure I-7, the results are somewhat ambiguous. (The correlation between the two series is −16 percent; it's a positive 25 percent when Ike and JFK/LBJ are left out.) In other words, there is no clear relationship between the average tax burden imposed by an administration and the growth in real median income that occurs while that administration is in office. Administrations with low tax burdens were no more likely to produce faster growth rates in real median income than administrations with higher tax burdens.

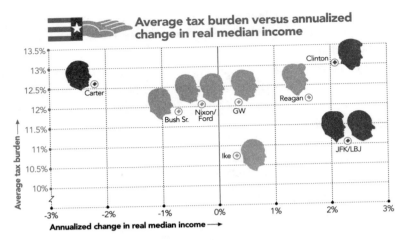

Figure I-7

The story is a bit different when we look at the relationship between the average tax burden and the annualized change in real net disposable income (see Figure I-8).

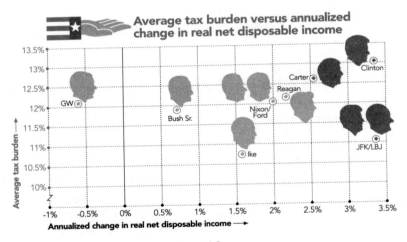

Figure I-8

The correlation between the average tax burden and the annualized change in the real net disposable income over the span of each administration is about 14 percent, or about 74 percent when the Ike and JFK/LBJ administrations are not included. Whichever measure we use, there doesn't seem to be any evidence here for the proposition that lower taxes result in

P R E S I M E T R I C S

higher incomes. Again—we may not be able to say definitively that higher taxes *lead to* faster growth in real net disposable income, but it is pretty evident that higher taxes were not exactly hurting people's pocketbooks, as Republicans tell us.

What about jobs? As we noted earlier, GW pushed for and signed three major tax cut bills that had some variation of the word *Jobs* in their title. And most Republicans believe the relationship between jobs and taxes is clear: Lower taxes encourage entrepreneurs to work harder, start more businesses, expand more aggressively, and thus create more jobs. But the data says that has not been true in recent decades, as seen in Figure I-9.

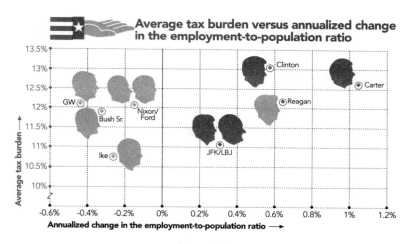

Figure I-9

The correlation between the average tax burden during the span of an administration and the annualized change in the employment-to-population ratio over that same period was about 52 percent, or about 71 percent for the six most recent administrations. In other words, the administrations that imposed higher average tax burdens also happened to be the ones that created the most jobs. That doesn't mean higher taxes create jobs, but it certainly throws cold water on the idea that lower taxes lead to job creation.

So it seems that, within the range of tax burdens we have experienced since 1953, lower taxes—at least by themselves—are not the way to increase economic growth, increase tax collections, put money in our pockets, or create jobs. In fact, a few of these desirable outcomes seem to happen more frequently when the tax burden is higher, not lower.

# What about Tax Cuts?

If lower tax burdens don't stimulate the economy, what about tax cuts? Maybe people adapt to a certain level of taxation and only react when taxes are cut from that level. That's a reasonable possibility, but the data is not particularly cooperative here either. Figure I-10 shows the change in the tax burden over the span of each administration against the change in real GDP per capita.

In Figure I-10, administrations that cut the tax burden are those for which the change in the tax burden is negative. Conversely, a positive change in the tax burden is an increase. It's fairly clear from Figure I-10 that administrations that cut taxes tended to see slower growth rates in real GDP per capita than admin-

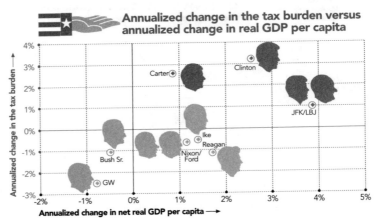

Figure I-10

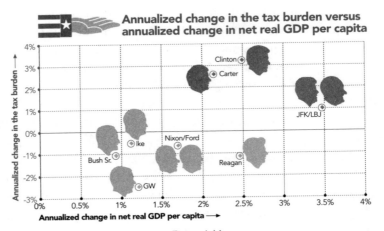

Figure I-11

istrations that raised taxes. (The correlation between the two measures was 57 percent, or about 65 percent for the final six administrations.) That doesn't imply that raising taxes necessarily produces faster growth in real GDP per capita, but it sure makes it harder to argue that cutting taxes leads to faster growth.

It's even harder to argue that cutting taxes leads to faster growth in real net GDP per capita, as is obvious in Figure I-11.

The relationship between tax collections and the tax burden is also unambiguous; administrations that cut taxes also collected less in taxes than administrations that raised taxes (see Figure I-12), and they also collected less in real, per capita terms, (see Figure I-13).

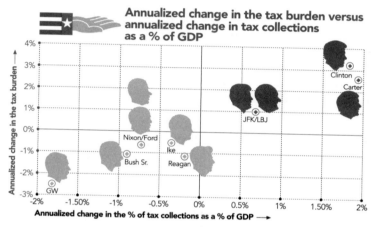

Figure I-12

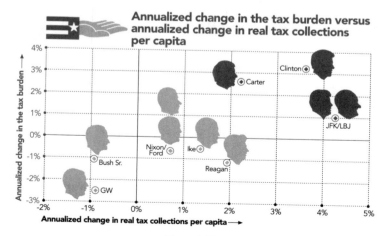

Figure I-13

However, there doesn't seem to be much of a correlation between changes in the tax burden and changes in real median income. The correlation between those two measures is very close to zero, as seen in Figure I-14.

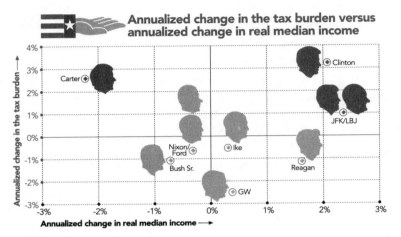

Figure I-14

But those administrations that raised the tax burden the most also happened to be the ones that produced the fastest increases in real net disposable income, as seen in Figure I-15.

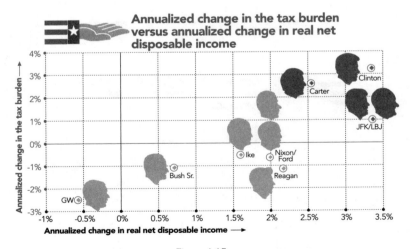

Figure I-15

That is, administrations that increased the amount they collected from your paycheck also happened to be the ones in which you found yourself with more in your wallet after taxes (present and future) were taken out. Okay, this probably isn't what you've been told, but the correlation between changes in the tax burden and changes in real net disposable income is well over 80 percent.

Finally, we look at the relationship between tax cuts and jobs (see Figure I-16).

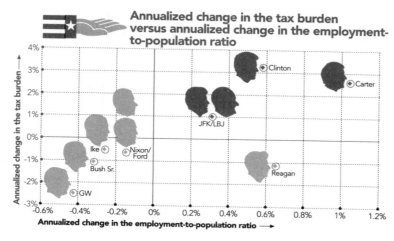

Figure I-16

Figure I-16, like several of the others, is pretty clear in its repudiation of standard Republican dogma: Administrations that reduced the tax burden tended to do poorly on job creation and those that raised the tax burden generally did pretty well at putting Americans to work.

# Taxes: Conclusion

Both parties have blind spots and sacred cows, convictions at odds with the facts. Republican beliefs about taxes—that lower taxes lead to faster economic and income growth as well as increases in real tax collections—are among the strongest tenets of the Republican faith. Yet we see that these firm beliefs don't get much support from the data. In fact, they are somewhat contradicted by the experience of presidents from Ike to GW.

The numbers are pretty compelling. Lower average tax burdens do not produce faster economic growth, faster income growth, or more jobs, or bring in more tax revenues. Similarly, tax cuts also do not produce faster economic growth, faster income growth, or more jobs, or bring in more tax revenues.

Often, the presidents under whom taxes were highest or who raised taxes were the ones under whom the economy worked best for most of us.

Unexamined faith in a principle that is demonstrably false is no way to run a country. It leads to policies that at best aren't helpful and at worst produce the opposite results of what is intended. This may help explain why, in general, Democrats have outperformed Republicans on the economy.

Unfortunately, this is not a topic where being wrong is an academic issue. Slower economic growth reduces real incomes for many people with jobs, consigns more workers to unemployment, creates financial hardships, and makes it more difficult for people to pay their bills. This in turn creates other problems. Job losses and financial insecurity put families at risk—money problems are sometimes a catalyst of divorce and can even be bad for one's health.[8]

Thus, it is ironic that this belief in the awesome power of tax cuts not only is wrong and does not help produce faster economic growth, but it may also contribute to many of the problems that Republicans and non-Republicans alike so fervently want eliminated.

## CHAPTER 7

# Democratic Issues

Today, we pledge a return to core
moral principles like stewardship, service
to others, personal responsibility,
shared sacrifice and a fair shot for all . . .

2008 Democratic Party Platform[1]

As we saw in Chapter 6, Republicans have issues. So do Democrats. Republicans claim to prefer shrinking the government (while increasing the size of the military) and trusting the marketplace. On the other hand, Democrats feel markets can go awry and they seek a role for government in mitigating the damage of an erratic market.

One way to correct for markets run amok, say Democrats, is to spend money on social issues. Another is to reduce poverty and income disparity. Furthermore, Democrats want to make sure the wealthy pay their "fair share" of taxes, and they believe in protecting the environment. Each of these issues will be covered in this chapter.

There are other issues important to Democrats as well. Democrats often talk about equality of opportunity (though Republicans might counter that the policies Democrats favor act against equality of opportunity) and regulation to prevent the market's excesses. We won't be covering these issues since we did not find the data necessary to measure them properly.

# Social Benefits

Democratic voters want the government to spend money on social benefits. These include Social Security, Medicare, unemployment insurance, food stamps, and the earned income tax credit. This also includes benefits provided to our nation's service personnel and veterans, including medical care, pensions, disability payments, and funds to help our service personnel adjust to the civilian world upon their discharge. If all this sounds familiar to you, it should; it is very similar to welfare that Republicans want cut, which we covered in Chapter 6. The only real difference is that most expenditures that are intended to benefit veterans and their families are not included as part of welfare that Republicans want to see cut, but are included in social benefits that Democrats want to see increased.

Spending on social benefits has increased over time, as Figure 7-1 shows.[2]

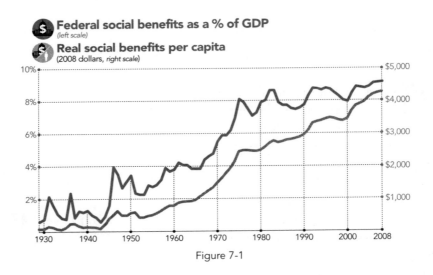

Figure 7-1

Let's look at some numbers to put this all in perspective. In 1929, the government spent roughly $62 per person on social benefits (in 2008 dollars). That amount grew slowly, reaching $4,300 per person in 2007. Looking at it another way, back in 1929 federal spending on social benefits amounted to less than six-tenths of 1 percent of GDP. By 2007, it was more than 9 percent of GDP.

But perhaps a better measure of the government's commitment is how big a share of the total *budget* that spending is. The question is this: Where does it rank as a priority?

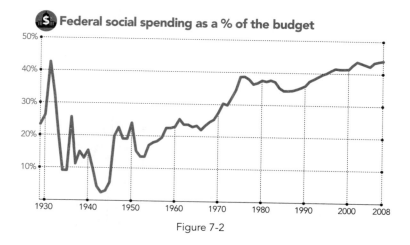

**Federal social spending as a % of the budget**

Figure 7-2

As we can see in Figure 7-2, social spending increased rapidly during the Great Depression, but not as dramatically as is often believed. And the first shift happened under Herbert Hoover. As a percentage of the budget, social spending rose from 23 percent to 30 percent between 1929 and 1932.

FDR is usually blamed by Republicans for bloating the welfare state. Yet in terms of priorities, the data tells a more nuanced story. From 1932 to 1940 (the year before he took office to the year before U.S. entry into World War II), spending on social benefits *decreased* as a share of the budget, from 30 percent to 15 percent. That may have been due to federal expenditures increasing rapidly on other things. For example, even before the attack on Pearl Harbor, military expenditures began to rise. Similarly, putting people to work with programs like the Works Progress Administration (WPA) or the Civilian Conservation Corps (CCC) also reduced the need for some other social spending: If you take young men out to the woods to build roads and trails and you feed them as part of their work, you don't have to spend money feeding them at home as part of social spending.[3]

Once World War II began, social spending's share of the budget decreased even further, reaching as low as 2 percent in 1943. By then, of course, the government was feeding, clothing, and caring for a sizable chunk of the population whose costs were listed under defense spending, not welfare.

After the war, millions of people stepped out of uniform and started looking for work just as factories stopped churning out military hardware. Unemployment rose and social spending increased quickly, with some ups and downs, until the start of the Korean War, at which point there was another drop. Spending on social issues began rising again after the Korean War ended. The clear lesson: Social spending takes a back seat to wars. A second lesson:

Wars also soak up some surplus workers and production, reducing the need for social spending. Figure 7-3 graphically illustrates social spending as a percentage of the federal budget, by administration.

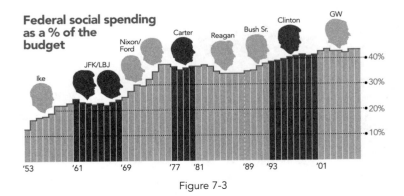

Figure 7-3

Growth rates, by administration, are summarized in Figure 7-4.

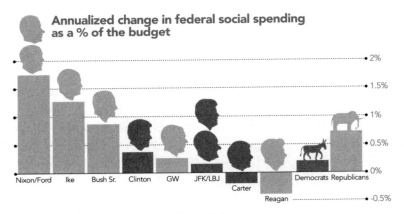

Figure 7-4

Organizing the data this way reveals a few very unexpected results. For one thing, the top three slots are held by Republican administrations: The biggest expansions in spending on social issues as a share of the budget took place under Nixon/Ford, Ike, and Bush Sr. Nixon/Ford continued many programs begun during the previous administration's war on poverty, at least for a while. Ike operated at a different time, a time when Americans believed we were somehow "all in this together." Spending on those in need was less abhorrent to Republicans in the 1950s than it is to many Republicans today.

Bush Sr., on the other hand, didn't need to spend the more modern Republican way—at least on defense. With the collapse of the Soviet Union came the peace dividend, which meant less had to be spent on the military and more could be spent on "feel good" items. Additionally, Bush Sr. followed two administrations under whom the share of the budget going to social issues had been cut, which potentially meant those programs had more of a need than they otherwise would have.

Bush Sr. was followed by Clinton, the Great Triangulator. Clinton was a Democratic president, a child of the 1960s, whether he inhaled or not. But he won a three-way race to the White House in an era dominated by conservative ideology, not to mention an increasingly assertive Republican Congress. His rhetoric about the end of big government, his campaign to reform welfare, and his efforts to balance the budget led to less emphasis on social spending.

Clinton was followed by GW, who was coping with the start of a recession about two months into his term and terrorist attacks six months after that. Social spending as a share of the budget increased under GW, in large part out of necessity—two recessions sandwiching short-lived recovery meant increased unemployment, stagnating wages, and increasing poverty. The need for social spending was clearly up on GW's watch.

However, this measure is more about priorities than it is about amount. The massive military buildup that followed 9/11 meant that substantial increases in social spending would still be modest relative to the overall budget. Moreover, GW seemed to have few qualms about taking the budget deep into deficit. As Dick Cheney, GW's vice president, famously said, "Deficits don't matter."

Ranking behind GW was the JFK/LBJ administration, which in turn was followed by two administrations that cut the share of the budget going to social benefits: Carter and Reagan. These two men presided over a twelve-year span following the Vietnam War, when military spending declined. Carter started the subsequent military buildup and Reagan dramatically upped the ante. Spending on social issues moved to the rear pews—and looked even worse, when measured against the whole budget.

On average there was no change in social spending as a share of the budget under Democratic administrations, but a big increase under Republicans. How very awkward for both parties! That awkwardness only increases if you recall that, as we saw in Chapter 2, Republican administrations on average increase spending as a percentage of GDP by more than Democrats do. Put another way, if there's a party that really, truly favors social spending, despite its own rhetoric, it's the Republican Party.

Okay, that's not entirely true. The graphs are not—repeat, *not*—showing that the Republicans are the bleeding hearts, and the Democrats are the tough-love types. What's going on may have more to do with the political and human context than budget ideology.

For one thing, a Republican seeking election needs to collect some Democratic votes and lean in some ways just a little left of where he might like to be. Politically, it's a good idea to assuage the Democrats with social spending. In contrast, Democrats have to appeal to some conservative voters if they want to be elected—just look at how Clinton leaned right of his natural constituency, pushing issues previously identified with Republicans like free trade and a balanced budget.

But perhaps there is also a compelling economic reason behind this. The administrations that produced the fastest growth had the least need for social benefits; we need a lot less unemployment compensation when good-paying jobs are plentiful. It may be more than coincidence that the four administrations that produced the biggest annualized increases in social spending as a percentage of the budget were also the four administrations that produced the slowest economic growth.

That's not to say that some presidents aren't more generous than others—and generosity is evident even when things are going well (the way that flint-heartedness is evident especially when things are awful).

As we will see in the next section, poverty decreased much faster under JFK/LBJ than under Reagan, and it decreased faster under Nixon/Ford than under Bush Sr. And yet Reagan cut spending on benefits while JFK/LBJ increased them, and Nixon/Ford increased them by more than Bush Sr.

This difference might be one of the natural penchants of the person in the Oval Office and the politics of the time. Bush Sr. and Reagan were not exactly well-known for their compassion toward those who were hurting. (Bush Sr., of course, came from a famously well-off family, while Reagan's attitude was ironic: His father was aided by the New Deal.) Perhaps more important were the prevailing political winds. Both Reagan and Bush Sr. held office during an era of rhetorical backlash against the poor and backpedaling on government's role in social welfare.

LBJ, on the other hand, came of political age as a New Dealer and took over from an ambitious, martyred president in an era of political activism. He launched a number of programs to help those at the bottom. Nixon, though, he deliberately fueled resentment against some of those same people, he was hemmed in by a Democratic Congress and a still-largely New Deal electorate and, despite often playing to the resentments of the "Silent Majority," he continued many of LBJ's programs.

# Poverty

In the last section, we looked at spending on social benefits. Ultimately, social spending should make people better off and a lot of that spending is geared specifically toward helping the poorest among us. But some programs might do very little good. Worse, some may actually encourage a prolonged dependence. Spending intended to help the poor can be very ineffective in the hands of an incompetent or corrupt administration. Conversely, a president who designs and executes social programs well could improve the lives of many needy citizens.

In this section we'll look at how much was actually accomplished with social spending by measuring the change in the poverty rate over the span of each administration. Information on the percentage of people living in poverty going back to 1959 is available from the Census Bureau. It is shown graphically in Figure 7-5, by administration.[4]

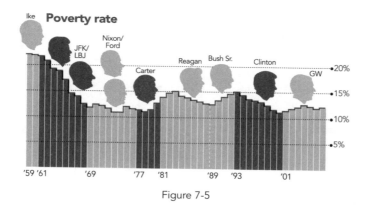

Figure 7-5

Figure 7-5 shows that in the late 1950s, almost 22.5 percent of Americans lived in poverty. During the JFK/LBJ administration, that figure dropped by almost ten percentage points as the rapidly growing economy and the war on poverty strengthened the economic backbone of many families and individuals.

But Johnson's war on poverty was only a small part of his larger, multifaceted Great Society program. The Great Society was a catchall series of initiatives designed to reduce discrimination, improve living and working conditions in urban areas, and increase the availability of educational opportunities and medical care. Well-known programs that formed a part of the war on poverty and are still around today include the Job Corps, Head Start (which provides educational opportunities to poor children), Medicaid, and Medicare.

Poverty stayed fairly steady for the next ten years or so. It began to rise at the tail end of the Carter administration as a result of rampant stagflation (a damaging mix of slow economic growth and high inflation). Poverty continued to rise in the early part of the Reagan administration, though it began to fall once inflation was brought under control and the economy started growing again. In his final State of the Union Address, Reagan said:

> My friends, some years ago, the Federal Government declared war on poverty, and poverty won.[5]

That might have been a poor description of the JFK/LBJ era, but in Reagan's two terms, the fight was pretty much a draw; the poverty rate in 1988, his last year in office, was the same as it was in 1980, the year before he took office.

Poverty rose steadily during the administration of Bush Sr., and then fell steadily while Bill Clinton was president, largely thanks to a growing economy. The percentage of the population that was employed increased and so did real wages. Unfortunately, the trend reversed itself once again with poverty increasing under GW Bush.

The annualized changes, by administration, are shown in Figure 7-6.

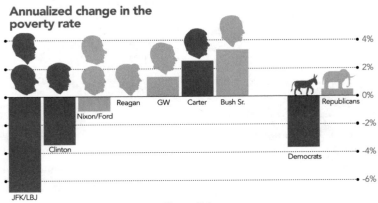

Figure 7-6

We did not include Ike in Figure 7-6 because, with only two years of data, it was not possible to evaluate him fairly. We might guess that poverty decreased during his term; the economy grew, albeit slowly, and so did incomes (both real median incomes and real net disposable incomes increased) and real net worth. Moreover, income disparities were modest by today's standards, so the poor probably received their share of the new income created while Ike was in office. Furthermore, neither Ike nor his Democratic Congress tried to dismantle the New Deal safety net. But that's conjecture on our part. We just don't have the data so we cannot include him.

Of the remaining administrations, poverty fell during only three of them—those of JFK/LBJ, Clinton, and Nixon/Ford. Under Reagan, the poverty rate rose at first, paralleling unemployment, then fell back to where it had started.

Among the administrations with rising poverty rates, the smallest increase was registered by GW, followed by Carter. Bush Sr. brought up the rear. Of these three administrations, Carter is the odd man out. As we saw earlier, despite stagflation and an awful recession toward the end of his term, economic growth under Carter was reasonably strong. However, the real median wage decreased during his administration, and those close to the bottom of the economic pyramid are often more vulnerable to economic turbulence, not to mention policies like Carter's wage controls, discussed in Chapter 4.

Poverty also increased during both Bush presidencies, but as we've seen in previous chapters, their administrations were marked by tepid economic growth, reductions in the percentage of Americans employed, and a scraping-the-bottom-of-the-barrel performance on real net disposable income. To those problems, poverty was a natural concomitant. Nevertheless, of the two Bush presidents, Bush Sr. was the less effective one when it came to addressing poverty. Not only did he preside over the biggest increases in poverty in our sample, but he did so despite coming in second at increasing funding for social issues.

On average, Democrats addressed poverty more effectively; during Democratic administrations, the poverty rate decreased. Conversely, while Republicans were in office, the poverty rate increased. This contrasts with social spending, which, as we've previously noted, increased by more under Republicans than under Democrats. Those greater increases in social spending under Republicans were not effective in lifting people out of poverty, raising some pointed questions: How was the money spent? Were the programs more wasteful? Were they targeted at the wrong people? Or were the effects swamped by larger economic forces?

# Income Inequality

Democrats worry about equity. They feel there is too wide a gap between the earnings of those who make the most money and those who make the least, especially given that family ties and luck—rather than hard work and skill—are often deciding factors in where we end up in life.

A measure of income inequality is produced by the Census Bureau, using the Gini ratio (often called the Gini coefficient). Named after Corrado Gini, an Italian statistician, the Gini ratio ranges between 0 and 100%; the closer the economy is to zero, the more evenly income is distributed throughout the economy. On the other hand, as income inequality increases, the Gini coefficient approaches 1.

Figure 7-7 shows how the Gini ratio, calculated using the income of families, changed from 1952 to 2007, the last year for which data is available.[6]

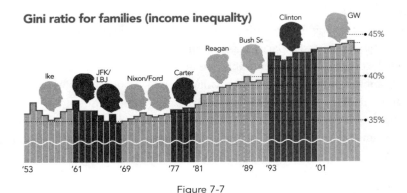

Figure 7-7

Income inequality had its ups and downs during the Eisenhower administration. It jumped during the first year of the JFK/LBJ administration but then decreased, particularly once the war on poverty kicked into gear. After LBJ left office, however, inequality was mostly on the rise. Essentially, growth in high incomes outpaced whatever increases there were among those with low incomes.

Several factors influenced this trend. One was the increase in the number and status of women in the workforce. Until recently, women were rarely hired for high-paying positions, so as women entered the job market, they disproportionately took low-paying jobs. That drove up competition for those jobs and pushed down the wages those jobs could command. Another reason for the increasing inequality was the gradual shift in the economy away from manufacturing toward "knowledge-based" work—including the ever-more lucrative slots on Wall Street. This raised the wages of those at the top, while simultaneously reducing the opportunities (and hence the earning power) of people without college degrees.

The big jump in 1993 was caused by a statistical aberration; the Census Bureau made a major change in the way that it calculates the Gini coefficient:

Direct comparisons with years earlier than 1993 are not recommended because of substantial methodological changes in the 1994 ASEC. In that year, the Census Bureau introduced computer-assisted interviewing, increased income reporting limits, and implemented 1990 decennial census-based population controls.[7]

Because of these methodological changes, Clinton's annualized results are calculated using data from 1993 to 2000 rather than from 1992 to 2000, as we do with other series. However, the annualized changes across administrations should still be comparable, as shown in Figure 7-8.

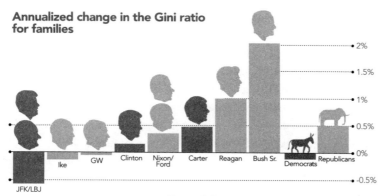

Figure 7-8

The biggest decreases in income inequality were achieved during the JFK/LBJ administration. While the whole economy was growing, the war on poverty helped those at the bottom of the social scale narrow the gap with the middle class and the wealthy. Ike had the second-best performance.

Ranking behind Ike was GW, under whom inequality actually increased almost every year until dropping quite a bit from 2006 to 2007, the last year for which data is available. That one big decrease in inequality might have been due to the first effects of the economic meltdown. Home construction was a source of income for many people during GW's administration, but housing starts began declining at the beginning of 2006. This affected many of those with higher incomes, from mortgage brokers to traders to owners of construction companies.[8]

Among the remaining administrations, inequality increased. Defenders of Clinton's reputation as a growth-happy liberal must contend with that—though the change in the Gini ratio during his administration represents the slowest pace among the inequality-increasing crew. His administration was followed by that of Nixon/Ford and Carter. Bringing up the rear were Reagan and Bush Sr. Clearly, not everyone was going places during the go-go '80s.

Despite Clinton and Carter, inequality declined on average under Democratic presidents because the performance of JFK/LBJ was so strong. Inequality rose under Republican administrations. The Republican focus on tax cuts and deregulation has been used to "frame" the party during elections as pro-growth and populist, sometimes quite effectively. But the data shows that these strategies do not help the needy nearly as much as their proponents contend.

## Tax Progressivity

Democrats believe each of us should pay a fair share of taxes—heck, most people will say that. But what is a "fair share"? Some say the answer typically refers to the ability to pay, and clearly the rich can afford to pay more. Conservatives argue that the focus on ability to pay is counterproductive. People who can afford to pay more, they say, are wealth creators and taxing them more is akin to killing the goose or, rather, the geese that lay the golden eggs.

But Democrats have a comeback to that, focusing not on ability but on benefits. When it comes to who benefits, we often think of handouts and assume that low-income people benefit disproportionately from government programs. After all, those at the bottom of the social scale receive goodies like welfare, food stamps, and government cheese.

However, giveaways to the poor are only a small part of what the government does with the money it collects. Taxes also pay for patent and copyright protection, farm subsidies, scientific research, transportation initiatives, law enforcement at home, and diplomatic efforts as well as military defense for American interests overseas. Depend on air traffic control as you flit from one government-subsidized airport to another? Work in a profession—like medicine—where salaries are higher because entry is limited by law? Make money from the Internet?

Give thanks to somebody's tax dollars.

Democrats feel that those who make the most money are the ones who benefit the most. It's an argument that has lately gotten some high-profile ammunition.

Goldman Sachs might not have survived to continue tapping the government welfare spigot if all it got from the 2008 Emergency Economic Stabilization Act was government cheese, even if its employees had gotten all of it. And speaking of cheese, even the very conservative Heritage Foundation noted that "most farm subsidies are distributed to large farms, agribusinesses, politicians, and celebrity 'hobby farmers.' "[9] In other words, many of the giveaways to the poor are by-products of programs intended to benefit wealthy people.

Even the most basic government functions disproportionately benefit those with higher incomes. For example, everyone agrees that one purpose of the government is to safeguard people and their property. Part of this is keeping foreigners at bay with the biggest, baddest military around. But part of it is a legal system that makes our market economy possible. And while offering a foothold to upstarts, that system of laws and regulations may disproportionately benefit people who are already winners.

Consider, for instance, two individuals working for the same company, Bear Stearns, in 2008 as the company implodes. One individual is a nameless janitor; the other, Jim Cayne, is running the company. Now, we don't know how many homes Jim Cayne has, much less how much money he has in his bank account. But our anonymous janitor probably lives in a rented hovel in East Harlem and is lucky to stay one paycheck ahead of his creditors.

Now consider how the government benefits each of these individuals. What defends Jim Cayne's homes—and all his other assets—is the government. It's not fear of the wrath of Mr. Cayne, much less worries about being fired that keeps some low-paid bank clerk from surreptitiously moving money from Mr. Cayne's account into his own and then disappearing to Switzerland. Nor is it the fear of some private security service that prevents people from moving into one of Mr. Cayne's homes when he's not there. Rather, it's concern about what the government will do that prevents people from trying to take assets that the government says belong to Mr. Cayne. Even the attorneys he employs, however fierce they may be, would be useless if the government decided to withhold its protection.

Now consider the janitor. He doesn't have much property to protect and given the neighborhood where we figure he lives, what he has is more likely to be defended by his baseball bat than by the legal system established and maintained by the government. Yes, he might get the police to come if he has trouble, but most of us recognize that the response from the police to a call from our janitor's neighborhood would be different than it would be to a call from Mr. Cayne's neighborhood. Yes, our janitor can use the legal system, but good luck finding a good lawyer he can afford. How about trouble with the IRS? Think he can retain a top-notch accountant?

This is not just bleeding-heart rhetoric. This is reality. Common sense too: People with resources have a better chance of marshaling the forces of the government to defend their interests than people who have nothing.

There are three reasons why our hypothetical janitor has many fewer assets than Mr. Cayne. One is that Mr. Cayne started out with more assets and more opportunities than the janitor.

A second reason is that, as noted investment guru Warren Buffett has pointed out, the system is set up to reward certain skills and not others, and which skills are rewarded is, to some degree, arbitrary. There is no nonarbitrary reason why the job of leading an investment bank that loses billions of dollars by gambling that home prices would rise forever should pay any more than the job of cleaning toilets and mopping floors, but it does. That the company's shareholders at the time thought that Cayne was more valuable than Bear's janitors is also purely arbitrary; after all, with the benefit of hindsight few of them would still agree that Cayne's compensation package was justified, no matter how rare the ability to lose billions happens to be. The Invisible Hand of capitalism—true capitalism, anyway—does not reward skills for their rarity but rather for their usefulness. Which makes sense since the ability to stuff seven walnuts up one's nose is more rare than any skills that Mr. Cayne might have, but it also less likely to cause damage to a company or the wider economy.

And since we're on the subject of capitalism, a third reason our hypothetical janitor has fewer assets than Mr. Cayne was noted by Adam Smith in the bible of capitalism, *The Wealth of Nations,* published in 1776:[10]

> The necessaries of life occasion the great expense of the poor. They find it difficult to get food, and the greater part of their little revenue is spent in getting it. The luxuries and vanities of life occasion the principal expense of the rich . . .

Put another way, the typical janitor spends much, or most, of his income keeping body and soul together. For folks like Mr. Cayne, however, life's necessities are a fraction of a percent of their income, which allows them to spend the bulk of their assets on luxuries and accumulating more assets, which the government then protects for them. Adam Smith went on to write:

> It is not very unreasonable that the rich should contribute to the public expense, not only in proportion to their revenue, but something more than in that proportion.[11]

In other words, taxes should be progressive—a person with greater income or wealth should pay a higher rate than a person with less income or wealth. So as we noted, there are at least three reasons why Mr. Cayne makes more money than a janitor, and at least two of those reasons justify having Mr. Cayne pay a higher tax rate than the janitor. A lot higher. Which brings us back to the capper: He can afford to pay more. Someone has to pay to maintain the government, which keeps this complex economy going. Relying on a bunch of janitors to pay for it would have resulted in Mr. Cayne ending up no better than, well, a janitor after the implosion of his firm, as there would have been nobody around to offer the inducements necessary for JP Morgan to purchase the remains of Bear Stearns, or to keep the more unbalanced among the angry shareholders from visiting their wrath upon Bear Stearns executives.

To see how Democrats should feel about different administrations when it comes to tax progressivity, we can look at the percentage of total taxes paid by the top 1 percent of income earners. This data is available from the Congressional Budget Office (CBO) for the period from 1979 to 2006.[12] However, before we present our graphs, we should point out that one of the sources of data used by the CBO in compiling this information is the IRS' Statistics of Income. The Statistics of Income uses data from tax forms—data that Americans declared on their income taxes.

This data has several inherent problems. One is that many Americans cheat on their taxes. As we saw in Chapter 6, in 2001, tax evasion reduced government revenues by at least 15 percent.

Furthermore, the ability to cheat tends to increase as one's income and wealth increases. Sure, if you're a waiter, a house painter, or a street performer, you may be paid in cash and you might just be aware that the government would have trouble verifying precisely how much money you made. But if you're a middle-class or blue-collar employee—like our janitor—your income is recorded and you probably get a W-2 form, which would make failing to report income difficult. On the other hand, if you're the boss, the opportunity to underreport is greater. As the IRS notes:

> . . . one percent of all wage, salary, and tip income is misreported, contributing an estimated $10 billion to the tax gap. In contrast, nonfarm sole proprietor income, which is reported on a Schedule C and is subject to little third-party reporting or withholding, has a net misreporting percentage of 57 percent, contributing about $68 billion to the tax gap.[13]

The higher one's income, the easier it is to make that income look smaller than it actually is. Furthermore, those at the top of the pecking order have a wide variety of ways to reduce their taxable income *legally,* from deferring that income through a multitude of tools to writing it off against losses. They can also use insurance schemes or holdings of tax-free municipal bonds. It would take a lot of tax-cheatin' street jugglers to equal the amount of money saved by one clever accountant for a rich client.

All of which is to say: Analyses using the IRS' Statistics of Income data should be taken with a grain of salt, particularly since they are likely to strongly understate the "true" income of the wealthy.

So with that caveat, Figure 7-9 graphically illustrates all this data.

### Effective tax rate of the lowest 20% of income earners relative to the effective tax rate of the top 1% of income earners

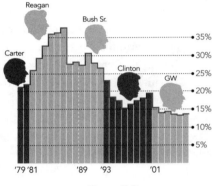

Figure 7-9

Figure 7-10 shows a summary of annualized changes over the span of each administration, beginning with Reagan.

### Annualized growth in the effective rate paid by low-income earners to the effective tax rate paid by high-income earners

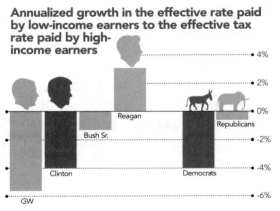

Figure 7-10

Of the four presidents for whom there is four or more years of data, only Reagan actually shifted more of the tax burden toward the lower-income folks. Because, as we saw earlier in the chapter, income inequality increased during his term in office; high-income earners did particularly well under Reagan.

Assuming the data reported to the IRS is within spitting distance of being accurate—we know it isn't but it's all we've got—the best performance on tax progressivity from a Democrat's perspective was turned in by (wait for it...) George W. Bush, followed by Clinton and Bush Sr. This isn't exactly what Democrats expect to read, but it's what the available data says.

# The Environment

Democrats generally favor protecting the environment. They like clean water and clean air, not just for us human beings but also for our fellow creatures like fuzzy rabbits, majestic eagles, and even malevolent marsh monsters.

Measuring the degree to which the environment was protected is hard to do. But we can look at spending on natural resources and the environment as a share of the budget as a measure of an administration's commitment to those issues. Figure 7-11 shows spending on natural resources and the environment, both in real per capita terms, and as a percentage of GDP.[14]

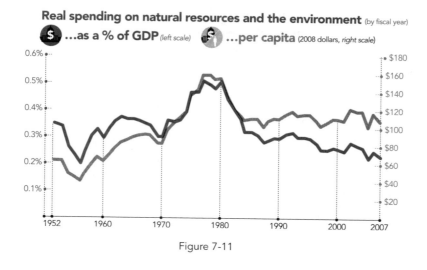

Figure 7-11

Figure 7-11 indicates that the high point of natural resource and environmental spending—in real per capita terms and as a percentage of GDP—came during the Carter administration,[15] and both fell in the early 1980s. Real spending on natural resources and the environment has stayed fairly constant since then, hovering between about $100 per person and $120 person since 1984. Spending on the environment as a percentage of GDP has been slowly drifting down since 1984; in 2007, it was less than a quarter of 1 percent of total GDP.

Figure 7-12 illustrates spending on natural resources and the environment as a share of the budget, by administration since 1953.

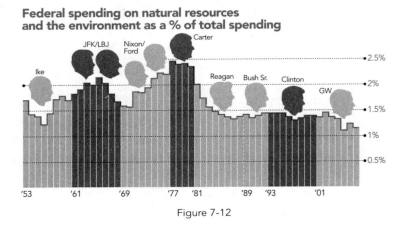

Figure 7-12

Spending on natural resources and the environment has never been a big priority, hovering most years between 1 and 2 percent of the budget. That spending declined slightly under Ike, albeit not very smoothly. It increased in the first half of the JFK/LBJ administration, and then dipped as money was diverted to the war on poverty. The Nixon/Ford administration, on the other hand, made the environment a priority. Nixon mentioned the environment in his First Inaugural Address, and he established the Environmental Protection Agency in 1970. Funding as a share of the budget jumped under Carter, and then suffered a huge decline under Reagan. Since then, it has stayed fairly constant, fluctuating between 1.1 percent and 1.5 percent of the budget.

Figure 7-13 shows the annualized change in spending on natural resources and the environment as a share of the budget over the span of each administration.

The biggest spending increases on natural resources and the environment as a share of the budget came under Nixon/Ford. Carter came in second, with spending on the environment peaking on his watch. Bush Sr. followed, spending part of the peace dividend on the environment. The remaining presidents all reduced environmental spending as a share of the

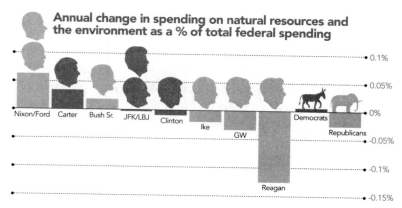

**Annual change in spending on natural resources and the environment as a % of total federal spending**

Figure 7-13

budget—mostly by increasing the budget elsewhere. The smallest reductions came under JFK/LBJ, followed by Clinton and Ike.

GW, second from last, shared a distinction with Carter; they were the only two presidents to have Idahoans as secretary of the interior. However, while environmentalists were generally quite pleased with Cecil Andrus, who served under Carter, they weren't quite as happy about Dirk Kempthorne under GW. Kempthorne's primary distinction seems to have been not placing any creatures or plant life on the endangered species list. He certainly had the opportunity to do so with at least one particularly charismatic species: polar bears. During GW's administration it became apparent that the ice floes from which polar bears hunted for seals were disappearing at an alarming rate. However, declaring polar bears endangered would have had consequences that the Bush administration felt were unfortunate, from requiring that their habitat be protected against mining and oil drilling to offering a tacit admission that global warming was actually occurring.

However, the individual with the most, um, unique approach toward the position of secretary of the interior was the first person to hold that position during the Reagan administration: James G. Watt (who was, by the way, from Wyoming, not Idaho). Watt certainly personified Reagan's slash-and-burn attitude toward the environment: His administration produced the biggest reductions in spending on natural resources and the environment as a share of the budget, averaging about 0.12 percent per year.

Watt took it as his primary mission to block efforts at resource conservation, once proposing that by the end of the twentieth century all federally owned wilderness be opened up to drilling and mining. He was eventually forced to resign after remarking that his staff included "a black, a

149

DEMOCRATIC ISSUES

woman, two Jews, and a cripple." From there, he appears to have turned to less wholesome activities. Watt's career would eventually wrap up on a relative high note: In 1996 he managed to avoid jail time despite being indicted on twenty-five counts of perjury, unlawful concealment, and obstruction of justice, all relating to a housing scandal during the Reagan administration. He plea-bargained his way down to a sentence of five years' probation, a $5,000 fine, and five hundred hours of community service.

## Democratic Issues: Conclusion

In the previous five sections, we looked at five typically Democratic issues: spending on social programs, the percentage of people in poverty, income inequality, tax equity, and spending on natural resources and the environment. We used these five measures to construct an Overall Score on Democratic Issues. The Overall Score has been designed so that it would equal 100 percent for a president who did best on each of the five measures and 0 percent for a president who did worst for each of the five measures.

Figure 7-14 shows each administration's score on Democratic issues.

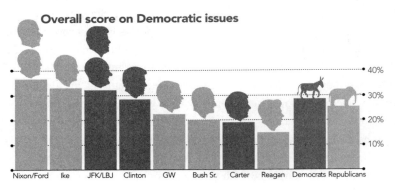

**Overall score on Democratic issues**

Figure 7-14

Nixon/Ford topped the list on Democratic issues. Yes, Nixon/Ford. They warmed Democratic hearts—or would have, had the Democrats been looking at just the data rather than issues like illegal bombing campaigns, dirty tricks, and Watergate—a top finish in natural resources and the environment, a second place on social spending, a third place on poverty, and a fifth place on income inequality.

Ike, another Republican, came next, with the top showing on social spending, and coming in second on reducing income inequality. JFK/LBJ came next, mostly as a result of reducing poverty and income inequality. Fourth was Clinton, and he was followed by both Bush presidents. Seventh was Carter, producing a not-very-Democratic outcome. Reagan came in last, showing the least concern over typical Democratic issues of all the administrations.

Perspective is a funny thing. It's interesting that Republicans, particularly pre-Reagan Republicans, did so well on Democratic issues. These days, many Republicans would be puzzled, if not peeved, to find their party showing concern over issues like poverty or the environment.

## CHAPTER 8

# Health Care

The basic resource of a nation is its people.
Its strength can be no greater than the
health and vitality of its population. Preventable
sickness, disability, and physical or
mental incapacity are matters of both
individual and national concern.

JOHN F. KENNEDY
Special Message to the Congress on National Health Needs, February 27, 1962[1]

N o matter how you slice it, the United States spends more on health care than any other country. In fact, in 2005, at prevailing exchange rates, 45 percent of all expenditures on health care anywhere in the world took place in the United States. On a Purchasing Power Parity (PPP) basis (i.e., adjusting for differences in the cost of living across countries), that figure dropped to 24 percent of the world's spending,[2] but it was still pretty impressive. And still more spending than anyone else.

And that's not just because we're big relative to other wealthy countries or rich relative to other big countries. Even on a per capita basis, we're *still* spending more than everyone else. For instance, among members of the Organization of Economic Cooperation and Development (OECD)—a group of democracies that includes the world's wealthy industrialized countries[3]—we spend almost 50 percent per person more than second-place Norway on a PPP basis.[4]

That might be acceptable if we were getting our money's worth. But we're not. Despite paying more, Americans as a group tend to do worse than people in most wealthy countries. For example, life expectancy (both at birth and at more advanced ages) in the United States is below that of most developed countries, and infant mortality rates—the ratio of children who die at less than a year of age—are higher.[5]

It should be noted that one of the things other countries, at least other industrialized countries, are doing differently is providing some version of "socialized" medicine. Sometimes it's the delivery system that is socialized—as in England, where the doctors work for the state. Other times, as in Canada, the government is just the insurer. In the patchwork U.S. system, the government (state and local combined) paid about 46 percent of the health care tab in 2007; the remainder was paid for by patients and—when they had coverage—their insurance companies.[6]

So it is fair to say that Americans pay more and—in the aggregate—get less. The technical term for this is "getting shafted." And since getting shafted is not a good thing, it's definitely in our best interest to have a president concerned enough about the issue to make things better. In this chapter, we'll look at which presidents made things better and which made things worse with respect to health care.

# Health Care Costs

Regardless of whether health care expenses are paid for directly by those who need it or indirectly through insurance or the government, rapidly rising costs are a problem. The faster health care costs rise, the less health care we can collectively afford. And make no mistake: Health care costs in the United States have been climbing. Rapidly.

To get a handle on the size of the problem, we obtained data on health care costs from the Department of Health and Human Services.

In the last few decades, the rise has been dramatic. In 1960, health care spending in the United States was $148 per person, but by 2007 that figure had reached over $7,400, an increase of 8.7 percent a year. That is, health care costs per capita increased at more than twice the rate of inflation from 1960 to 2007. Real health care spending per capita (2008 dollars) increased from about $1,077 per person to $7,700 per person, an increase of about 4.3 percent a year—which comes out to more than 600 percent!

The change in real health care costs per capita are shown in Figure 8-1.[7]

Notice that the increase in spending is pretty constant; it occurred in every administration. And the increase is steady. Real health care costs per capita have never declined since figures began to be gathered in 1960, and have increased by more than 1 percent a year in all but two years: 1979 and 1980. The Carter presidency, within which those two years fell, was characterized by

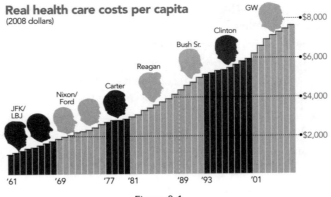

**Real health care costs per capita**
(2008 dollars)

GW

$8,000

Clinton

$6,000

Bush Sr.

Reagan

$4,000

Carter

Nixon/
Ford

JFK/
LBJ

$2,000

'61    '69    '77  '81    '89  '93    '01

Figure 8-1

relatively slow increases in real health care costs per capita. That isn't to say health care costs weren't rising rapidly during the Carter administration, but rather that other costs were also increasing at a fast clip.

Relatively slow increases in real health care costs were also a characteristic of another Democratic administration, that of Bill Clinton, as Figure 8-2 shows.

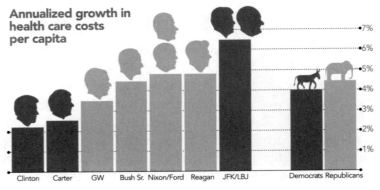

**Annualized growth in health care costs per capita**

7%
6%
5%
4%
3%
2%
1%

Clinton  Carter  GW  Bush Sr.  Nixon/Ford  Reagan  JFK/LBJ    Democrats Republicans

Figure 8-2

Figure 8-2 shows that Democratic administrations bookended the performance on real health care costs per capita; Clinton and Carter produced the slowest increases; JFK/LBJ the fastest. Part of the reason for the rapid increase during the JFK/LBJ years was the Great Society, which created both Medicare and Medicaid, among other things. But health care was a key concern for JFK/LBJ from the beginning; they pushed for grants to hospitals and nursing homes, more money for health research, and increased immunization. Costs were not as much of an issue to them as was increasing access, availability, and quality for all Americans. So costs went up.

Still, this is not a fair way to look at health care costs; after all, while real health care costs per capita increased quickly under JFK/LBJ, as we noted, real GDP per capita and real incomes also increased rapidly during that administration. Conversely, real health care costs per capita rose more slowly during the GW administration, but then so did real GDP per capita and real incomes. Therefore, to understand the true impact on our collective pocketbooks of rising health care costs, we should look at health care costs as a percentage of GDP.[8] That will give us a sense of how much of a burden paying for health care is on the economy (see Figure 8-3).

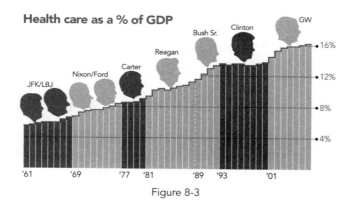

Figure 8-3

Figure 8-3 is similar to Figure 8-1; however, it is much flatter during administrations that produced rapid economic growth and steeper during administrations that grew more slowly. One other thing to note: There was a virtual plateau during the Clinton administration, but costs began rising again immediately after Clinton left office.

All of which tells us that real health care costs have been rising at a steady pace. When the economy booms, the increases have seemed more manageable, but they are still there. As Figure 8-4 shows, none of the administrations from 1960 to 2008 managed to reduce health care's share of the nation's pocketbook.

The slowest growth by far occurred during the Clinton administration; this was a function of relatively slow dollar increases in the cost of health care and a rapidly growing GDP. One factor that contributed to the relatively slow growth in health care costs as a share of the economy was Hillary-care, an initiative, led by Hillary Clinton, to enact a universal health care system based

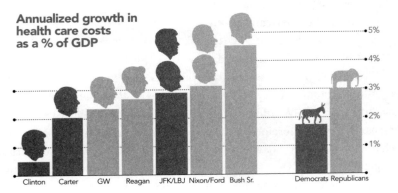

Figure 8-4

on mandating employer-provided health insurance. Even though it would have allowed the big-money players—especially insurance companies—to retain their favored position at the trough, the plan took so much fire from the industry that it went down in flames.

Another factor that might have contributed to the plateau in costs during the Clinton administration was the Reinventing Government initiative, the process led by Vice President Al Gore to find cheaper, more effective ways to do what government was already doing. The process of reinventing government gets a lot of credit for, among other things, turning around the Veterans Administration hospital system (the "VA system"). By the end of Clinton's term, the VA system, which less than a decade earlier was considered a basket case, was widely recognized as one of the most effective and efficiently run medical systems in the country.

While Hillary-care was a debacle and the VA system initiatives were successful, together they served as a reminder to the health care industry that the president was watching, and he was willing to expend political capital to try to keep costs down. The health care industry got the message, but perhaps they also understood that the threat applied only while Clinton was in office; as soon as Clinton was safely out the door, health care costs as a percentage of GDP started rising rapidly again.

Carter was the second most effective president at containing health care costs. In his first year in office, Carter recognized that rapidly increasing health care costs were a problem and proposed several measures to deal with them. These included a national health insurance plan and price controls in the form of the Hospital Cost Containment Act of 1977. The health care industry responded by organizing a "voluntary effort" at cost containment, which, predictably, evaporated once the threat was neutralized by Carter's voter-facilitated departure from the White House after one term.

Third and fourth were GW and Reagan, with JFK/LBJ coming in fifth and Nixon/Ford coming in sixth. Bush Sr. came in last. Overall, Democrats did a better job of keeping health care costs in check than their Republican counterparts, despite JFK/LBJ's massive expansion of the entire system.

Interestingly enough, many Republicans blame rapidly rising health care costs on Democratic policies, lawsuits, or demographic issues, like changes in population. As Figure 8-4 seems to show, Democratic policies aren't the biggest problem when it comes to rising health care costs. Similarly, lawsuits aren't the problem either: The Congressional Budget Office found that "Malpractice costs amounted to an estimated $24 billion in 2002, but that figure represents less than 2 percent of overall health care spending."[9] Furthermore, the fact that health care costs rose more slowly under Democratic administrations, which have a reputation of being more "lawyer-friendly" than Republican administrations, tends to indicate that lawsuits aren't the issue.

Demographics also shouldn't be significantly different under Democrats than under Republicans. How could long-term trends in the population be different under Clinton, the top performer when it comes to keeping health care under control, than the two Bushes, whose administrations flanked his, and who did significantly worse?

Which leads us to the following conclusion: What doesn't work at containing health care costs is the health care market as it existed in the United States from 1960 to 2008. The presidents that were most successful at keeping health care costs down were Clinton and Carter, the two who presented the most credible threat to the various players in the industry.

# Infant Mortality

Costs are only part of the equation. It is also important to know whether the health care system is, well, making us all healthier. That is surprisingly hard to measure. We can look at whether more people are getting diagnosed for or treated for cancer or asthma, for example. But treatments may or may not be effective. And diagnoses may be wrong.

So any measure of the health care state of the nation has to take into account mortality. It may be a bit simplistic, but if people are living longer, that is generally a sign that people are getting more and better access to doctors and hospitals, epidemics are being kept under control, and fewer people are hopping into a swimming pool within thirty minutes of eating. The problem with trying to make a snapshot evaluation of the health care system based on mortality rates is that people often die of diseases they contracted years or even decades earlier. Deaths in one administration could easily be attributable to things that happened decades earlier.

But that's not as true of infants. In general if the rates of child mortality go up, it's because of conditions the infants face or their mothers faced while they were pregnant. And because care for infants and expectant mothers rarely exists in isolation—a medical system that fails babies and pregnant women probably fails everyone else—looking at infant mortality is a good way to measure how well the medical system is doing overall. There is also a moral component to infant mortality: It has been said that you can judge a society by how it cares for its weakest members. Who is more vulnerable and more at risk than infants?

Data on infant mortality—that is, children under one year of age, excluding fetal deaths—is collected from the Centers for Disease Control (CDC).[10] In Figure 8-5 we have overlaid that with the average infant mortality rate of OECD member countries.[11]

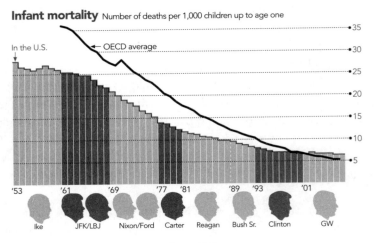

Figure 8-5

The infant mortality rate has dropped; in 1915, 99.9 out of every thousand children born failed to make it to their first birthday. By 1952, that figure had fallen to 28.4, and it would continue to drop, more or less continuously, reaching 6.6 per thousand in 2007.

The annualized change in infant mortality over the span of each administration is shown in Figure 8-6.

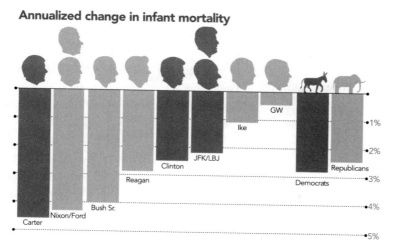

**Annualized change in infant mortality**

Figure 8-6

The biggest reduction in the infant mortality rate came during the Carter administration, followed by Nixon/Ford and Bush Sr. Middle positions are occupied by Reagan, Clinton, and JFK/LBJ. Ike came in seventh and GW came in last. The infant mortality rate fell more while Democrates were in office than when Republicans were in office, but the difference was slight.

We can learn a lot from the different approaches of two Republican administrations: Nixon/Ford and GW Bush. Of all the presidents since 1952, Nixon was arguably the most concerned about population issues, mentioning them frequently in communiqués to Congress early in his administration. Nixon felt that one way to deal with "our distressingly high infant mortality rate, the unacceptable level of malnutrition, and the disappointing performance of some children in our schools"—not to mention "poor physical and emotional health for all members of the family"—was to ensure that "no American woman should be denied access to family planning assistance because of her economic condition."[12] Nixon's focus on family planning paid off. Arguably, some of the benefits carried over into the Carter administration, helping to explain his first-place finish.

At the other end of the spectrum was GW. One reason worth noting for his poor showing is the age of the mother; it is generally accepted that the optimal age for most women to give birth is between twenty and thirty-five years old. Teenagers are unlikely to have the maturity and resources to take proper care of a child. On the other hand, as women (and their partners!) get older, the likelihood of miscarriages and low birth weights increases. Unfortunately, under GW, trends were not favorable at either end of the scale.

For instance, the adolescent birth rate, which had long been in decline, slowed, and then, by 2006, registered its first increase since 1991.[13] In the aggregate, abstinence-only education apparently has not worked all that well.

At the other end of the age distribution, births to women in their late thirties jumped dramatically during GW's administration, increasing at their fastest rate in decades.[14] Many professional women hold off on having children until they are financially secure, and financial security came a little bit later, if at all, while GW was in office.

It is also worth noting that America does not have a monopoly on health care. You can get health care in other countries too, and that health care is usually cheaper and often better than what you can get here. Furthermore, some factors that improve health care, such as new developments and technology, are available everywhere, not just in the United States.

For example, it has been noted that the traditional neonatal intensive care units are less effective than "womb rooms"—relatively dark, quiet rooms intended to replicate the womb as closely as possible. Building womb rooms is essentially a low-tech tool in the fight against infant mortality; the only real roadblocks to its use are the money needed to build such rooms and the willingness to do it. This is true of many new medical tools and techniques.

As a result, the proper way to measure improvements in infant mortality is to compare the change in infant mortality in the United States to that in other countries. Despite our self-image, and despite the posturing of pandering politicians, facts are stubborn things, as John Adams said. While the reduction in infant mortality in the United States is wonderful, representing a huge number of lives saved, it isn't very impressive when compared to the gains observed abroad. In fact, we can do much better. In 1960, the United States had the thirteenth-lowest infant mortality rate in the world; by 2005, the last year for which most OECD countries reported data, it had fallen to twenty-fifth. Clearly, other countries are improving much faster than we are.

# Health Insurance

One problem the American health care system has typically had is one of access: Not everyone can get the care they need. There are a number of reasons for this, but cost is always at the top of the list. Insurance is a way to help people afford health care.

In much of the developed world, the government pays for health insurance, or is the insurer, thus seeing to it that everyone has access to health care. In the United States, people can buy their own insurance, but that is often costly. It is more common for people to get health insurance through their employer or their union (or that of a family member). This arrangement dates back to World War II, when the government froze wages, so employers provided benefits like health insurance in order to lure or reward workers.

But over the past few decades, unions have gotten weaker, and health care has gotten more expensive; as a result, many employers have trimmed the health insurance they offer their employees. Additionally, millions of people work for themselves or for small companies and cannot afford insurance. Nearly 50 million Americans are without health insurance.

Some of those people are young and healthy and can get by without insurance but, as we noted, in other industrialized countries they generally don't have to take that risk. Regardless, young people usually do get older, and older people get sick more often than their younger counterparts.

Besides the impact that lack of health insurance can have on the individual, beyond any question of morality, there are obvious costs to the nation in having vast numbers of uninsured people. Among them: the waste in hospital resources from treating uninsured people who use the emergency room for what should be routine visits to a doctor, the loss of productivity among workers who are sicker than they would be with better coverage, and the workers who die from inadequate treatment.

Additionally there is a psychological cost. The vast number of uninsured serves as a reminder to the rest of us that we could, one day, be uninsured too. It is not the sort of thing to inspire a potential entrepreneur to leave her job.

So how have our presidents done in this category? We used data from the Census Bureau to graph the percentage of Americans with health insurance and how it has evolved (see Figure 8-7). We were not able to find data going back earlier than 1987, which means that we can only fairly evaluate three presidents—Bush Sr., Bill Clinton, and GW.[15]

The percentage of Americans with health insurance declined just about every year, but it jumped quite a bit at the tail end of the Clinton administration. (And no—this is not due to the change from one Census series to another—the break is there regardless of which series is used in Figure 8-7.) The reason for this jump under Bill Clinton, which reversed earlier declines in the percentage of Americans with health insurance, was the State Children's Health Insurance Program, commonly known as SCHIP. The federal government provides matching funds to states that pony up money to pay for health insurance for families with children; by early 1999, forty-seven states were participating in the program.[16]

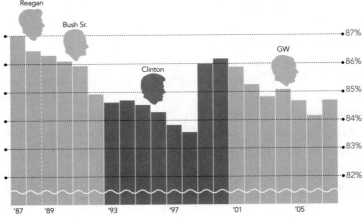

**% of Americans with health insurance**

Figure 8-7

The program has increased the percentage of Americans with health insurance and it has also reduced health care costs; children in the program are less likely to visit the emergency room or require a hospital stay.[17]

The annualized changes in the percentage of Americans with health insurance over the span of the three administrations beginning with Bush Sr. are shown in Figure 8-8.

As Figure 8-8 shows, the percentage of Americans with health insurance increased under Bill Clinton and decreased when men named George

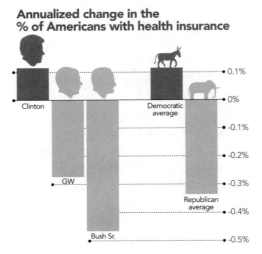

**Annualized change in the % of Americans with health insurance**

Figure 8-8

Bush lived in the White House. And there were reasons other than SCHIP for the difference.

One reason is the employment situation. As we saw in Chapter 4, the percentage of Americans who were employed increased under Bill Clinton and fell under the two Bushes. At the same time, incomes and wages rose much more swiftly during the Clinton administration than while either Bush was in office. Thus competition for good employees was more intense while Clinton was president than during the administrations preceding and following him. Many employers competed by offering benefits like health insurance. Given that health care costs rose relatively slowly when Clinton was president, health insurance was a particularly attractive benefit to offer employees. Furthermore, because jobs were more plentiful, incomes were rising quickly, and health care costs were relatively stable, health insurance became more affordable even to people who weren't offered that benefit at work.

By contrast, under the Bush presidencies, we witnessed stagnant real incomes and job losses. Many Americans did without extras; for a lot of people that included health insurance. Ironically, but perhaps not surprisingly, the percentage of Americans with government-provided health insurance increased under both GW and Bush Sr., as more Americans came to qualify for programs like Medicaid. Under Clinton, on the other hand, the percentage of Americans with government-provided health insurance declined even as the total percentage of Americans with health insurance climbed. The free-market solution didn't work as well while the two Republicans were in office.

# Health Care: Conclusion

In the last three sections, we looked at three aspects of health care: the cost of health care, the infant mortality rate, and the probability that people had health insurance.

Because each of these factors captures a different facet of the health care issue, we combined them into an index that measures how well each president did on these issues overall. The index was built in such a way that a president who was ranked first on all health care issues would have a score of 100 percent and a president who was ranked last on all these issues would earn a score of 0 percent.

The overall score on health care is shown graphically in Figure 8-9. Note that Ike was not included, as there was only enough data to include him on a single series.

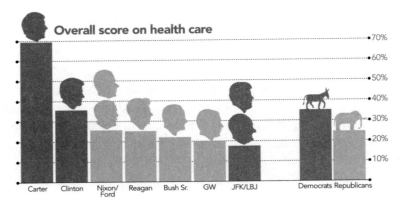

Figure 8-9

Of the remaining administrations, Carter made far and away the best showing. He presided during the largest annualized decline in infant mortality, and yet he did the second-best job at keeping health care costs under control. Carter was followed by Clinton, whose best scores came at keeping down health care costs and increasing the percentage of Americans with health insurance. Nixon/Ford came in third, largely by virtue of finishing second on reducing infant mortality. Reagan, Bush Sr., and GW came next, and JFK/LBJ turned up in last place.

On average, Democrats scored better on health care than Republicans. The best-performing Republican administration—that of Nixon/Ford—achieved its ranking in large part by acting like Democrats on health care issues. Nixon promoted a plan that would require employers to provide health coverage to all their employees. The plan hewed so closely to the Democrats' playbook that similar proposals were advanced by the three main contenders for the 2008 Democratic Party's presidential nomination—Barack Obama, Hillary Clinton, and John Edwards.

The American health care system is more costly and produces poorer results than the health care systems of most industrialized countries. Democrats may have shied away from fully challenging the insurance industry, but they have tended to push for approaches that are more like those of other countries having better, cheaper systems. As a result, Democrats have obtained better results for the American public. Whether because of ideology or their desire to appeal to corporate constituencies, Republicans have not.

## CHAPTER 9

# Crime

The entire nation is united in concern over
crime. The entire nation shares in the
resolution to deal effectively with crime.
But national concern is not enough.
National resolution is not enough.
We must match our will with wisdom.

LYNDON B. JOHNSON
Special Message to the Congress on Crime and Law Enforcement, March 9, 1966[1]

Ask Americans what they want the government to do for them and responses are likely to include the following: Provide jobs, build highways, keep taxes low, and give out free bagels on Sunday mornings. But the starting point for Americans—and what people around the world want from their governments—is to be kept safe and secure.

For many people being kept safe and secure is so important that they're willing to let the government off its leash in exchange for a bit more perceived protection against perceived threats. Presidents and aspiring presidents take note of that tendency and often take advantage of it, whipping up public fervor to advance their own ends. As a result, the government itself can, on occasion, be the biggest threat to the people's safety. But just because the government sometimes goes too far does not change the fact that one of the most basic functions of government is to keep people safe and secure.

The president doesn't decide spending and policy for the town police, the county sheriff's department, or the district attorney. But he does have a pretty muscular enforcement arm. He can set budgets and make policy for the Justice Department, which includes drug enforcement, the FBI, and an assortment of other law enforcement organizations and federal attorneys. He appoints judges.

He has agencies like the Securities and Exchange Commission overseeing white-collar activities. He can also help state and local law enforcement agencies by funneling money and resources toward them. And of course, he can set a tone, perhaps going so far as to declare a war on drugs or a war on terror.

But all that is theory. In this chapter, we look at what actually happened on the crime front from Ike to GW.

# Public Order and Safety

Superman promised to fight for "Truth, Justice, and the American Way." And we like Superman. But setting aside the issue of where he was born, would the Man of Steel have made a good president? It's hard to say . . . we aren't exactly sure what the American Way is, but it does sound like something we support and it certainly makes for a great campaign slogan. And if he really is big on Truth, well, that gives him a leg up on many presidents we've had. But what about Justice? Just about all the candidates running for president, if asked, will say they are for justice. But are they really? And do they put their money—that is, *our* money—where their mouth is?

The federal legal system, admittedly a very different animal than justice, is part of what the federal government calls "public order and safety." Other components of public order and safety include the police services (federal police agencies such as the FBI or the U.S. Marshals, funded directly by the federal government, and grants to state and local police agencies), fire services, and prisons.[2] That amounts to nearly $153 per person in 2008 dollars. Sounds a bit shabby considering how much noise politicians make about fighting crime or keeping us safe. Despite all the jabbering and chest pounding, public order and safety clearly isn't a top priority to the federal government: Only about 1.5 percent of the federal budget went toward public order and safety in 2007.

Figure 9-1 shows how spending on public order and safety as a percentage of the federal budget evolved from 1959, the first year for which we have data.

Though it doesn't constitute a big part of the budget, the issue of public order and safety has slowly been growing as a priority. Nevertheless, it has never gone much higher than 1.5 percent of the federal budget. No wonder Superman has a job; he works for free.

Annualized changes in the percentage of the budget going toward public order and safety by administration (not counting Ike, as there is not enough data for his administration) are summarized in Figure 9-2.

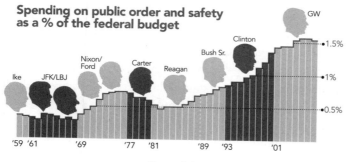

Figure 9-1

Figure 9-2 shows that five administrations increased the share of the budget going to public order and safety, and two reduced it. Interestingly enough, the five administrations that put an increased emphasis on public order and safety—those of Nixon/Ford, Clinton, Bush Sr., GW, and Reagan—were all known for at least one celebrated breach of the law: Watergate for Nixon, Clinton's lying under oath about the Lewinsky affair, the Iran-Contra affair for Reagan and Bush Sr., and issues regarding the allegedly illegal holding and treatment of detainees in the war on terror for GW.

Richard Nixon, a man who at one point found it necessary to tell the American public that he was not a crook, was a strong proponent of "doing something" about crime. He put a lot of political capital into a somewhat vague "crime program." This didn't result in much legislation but it did funnel a lot of money to state and local crime prevention initiatives. Even if Nixon didn't have any real solutions to the problem, he had good reason to throw money at it; crime soared from the mid-1960s to the mid-1970s. The murder rate,

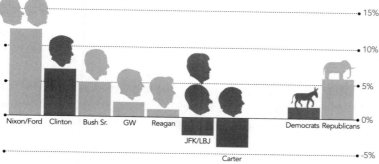

Figure 9-2

for example, more than doubled between 1963 and 1973. As a result, over the span of the Nixon/Ford administration, on average, the share of the budget combating crime and administering justice rose by more than 12.1 percent a year, or by a total of 2.5 times! However, the increase wasn't evenly distributed throughout the term; under Gerald Ford the share of the budget going to public order and safety stayed pretty constant. Perhaps he felt much of the crime problem had been contained when his predecessor resigned.

The Clinton administration came in second, but the rate of increase in spending on public order and safety as a share of the budget rose by only about half as much as it did under Nixon/Ford. When he ran for office, Clinton portrayed himself as a new kind of Democrat, one who was tough on crime. And it was a good time to be tough on crime; in the early 1990s, the myth of the "superpredator" began to circulate. This cohort of extremely ruthless young sociopaths was about to unleash an unprecedented crime wave on the unwitting American public, driven by its members' voracious addiction to drugs and Air Jordan athletic shoes. The term *superpredator* was coined by John Dilulio, one of a small group of mostly conservative academics who promoted the theory. Dilulio, incidentally, would eventually became head of the White House Office of Faith-Based and Community Initiatives under President George W. Bush.

As we will see later in this chapter, this supposed wave of superpredators never materialized. Nevertheless, Clinton fought that phantom crime wave with money and political capital. Among the steps taken to prove his crime-fighting bona fides was passage of a new crime bill, which led to the hiring of up to 100,000 new police officers, and tougher sentencing requirements for certain crimes and career criminals.

Bush Sr. and Reagan, who came in third and fifth, respectively, were in the Oval office when the so-called "crack epidemic" was sweeping the streets of America. A glut of cocaine on the American market led to a lot of competition among drug dealers, which in turn ushered in the development of crack. Crack has several advantages over powder cocaine from the perspective of dealers and suppliers: It is cheap, easy to produce, more addictive, and can be sold in "dime bags."

JFK/LBJ and Carter both decreased the share of the budget that went toward public order and safety. It's fair to say that fighting crime wasn't a big priority under any of these administrations. As we will see later in the chapter, this was not a very smart move, and its effect should have been easily predictable. On average, Democrats increased spending on public order and safety by quite a bit less than Republicans did.

# Murder

In the previous few pages, we looked at federal spending on public order and safety. But as we have seen in earlier chapters, spending money on an issue doesn't always lead to the desired results. So it is natural to wonder: Did putting more of a priority on crime reduce crime rates? In this chapter we look at arguably the worst crime of all—murder. Figure 9-3 shows the homicide rate per 100,000 people, using data provided by the FBI's Bureau of Justice Statistics.[3]

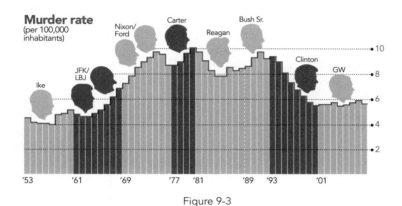

Figure 9-3

The murder rate stayed mostly constant until the mid-1960s, when it began a meteoric rise, more than doubling between 1963 and 1973. It dipped for a few years, then rose again, peaking at 10.2 murders per 100,000 people in 1980. The Clinton years were almost a mirror image of the rapid rise of the 1960s, posting year-after-year declines in the murder rate. Those declines ceased immediately upon Clinton's leaving office.

The annualized percentage change in the murder rate is shown in Figure 9-4.

The biggest declines in the murder rate by far occurred under Clinton; during his administration, the murder rate declined by 6.4 percent a year, more than two-and-a-half times as quickly as the 2.3 percent a year declines under Reagan, the second-place finisher. All other administrations presided over increases in the murder rate, with the largest coming under Carter and JFK/LBJ, who, as we have seen, also produced the biggest cuts in spending on public order and safety as a share of the budget.

Looking back at the increase in the murder rate from 1963 to 1973, you might think there should be some simple, powerful explanation for this. Perhaps there was some sort of collapse of moral order. But if so, what would

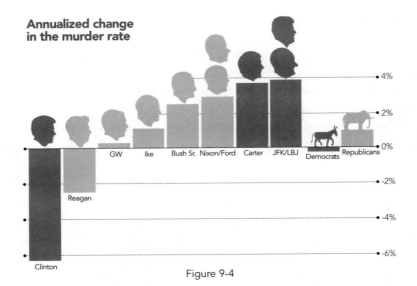

**Annualized change in the murder rate**

GW · Ike · Bush Sr. · Nixon/Ford · Carter · JFK/LBJ · Democrats · Republicans

Reagan

Clinton

4%
2%
0%
-2%
-4%
-6%

Figure 9-4

have caused it? The shocking assassination of John Kennedy? The upheavals of the civil rights movement? Was it spillover violence from the Vietnam War, or maybe fear of nuclear war with the Soviet Union? Or what about Vatican II?

Conversely, what about the 1990s decline? Was there suddenly a sea-to-sea return of moral backbone? Did a booming economy suddenly turn potential killers into more productive citizens? Perhaps the record pace of drug-related incarceration in the 1980s had locked up millions of potential triggermen. Or, as the authors of *Freakonomics*[4] argue provocatively—was it the predictable result of millions of abortions in the preceding two decades that inadvertently eliminated so many potential killers?

One explanation that comes up a lot is "more policing." The idea is that having more police on the street reduces crime. And there is some truth to that: The correlation between the number of federal police officers and the murder rate is –0.76. The correlation between the number of all police officers (at the federal, state, and local levels) and the murder rate is higher still: –0.84, which indicates a fairly strong negative relationship between the number of officers and murders.[5] The correlation is even stronger between the number of officers in one year and the murder rate several years out, which indicates that the benefits of a greater police presence can increase with time. Cops walking the beat might dissuade potential criminals from engaging in petty crimes, making it less likely they will graduate to more serious crimes later on.

The president has a great deal of control over federal police staffing. However, he can exert considerable influence over the size of state and local police forces as well. For instance, early in his tenure, Clinton pushed for and signed into law the Violent Crime Control and Law Enforcement Act of 1994. The act provided more than $30 billion for crime control programs (including social programs geared toward crime control), more than one-third of it going to state and local law enforcement. One stated goal of the law was the addition of 100,000 police officers throughout the country.

Of course, merely beefing up police ranks is not enough; it is important to put those forces to work where they are needed. For instance, the economic meltdown of 2007 and 2008 caused tremendous hardship to many, many people across the United States and around the world, and not a few deaths. It arguably caused more disruption to the American way of life than 9/11. And yet the economic disaster was caused in large part by mortgage fraud. The FBI, which normally monitors such things, was aware of large-scale mortgage fraud going on as far back as 2002, but the agents with the expertise to deal with that issue had been diverted to counterterrorism.[6]

In the next few pages, we will consider two other explanations for the murder rate.

# Murder and Gun Control[7]

A common misconception about murder involves guns. Many gun advocates are fond of pointing out: guns don't kill people; people kill people. However, what these same advocates gloss over is that the people who kill people generally use guns to do it; according to the FBI, guns were used in over two-thirds of all murders committed in 2007.[8]

So maybe the availability of guns and gun control laws help account for the murder rate. For example, the Brady Bill, which became law in 1994, put a five-day waiting period on the purchase of handguns. Is that the cause of the decline in the murder rate under Clinton? Did it make any difference?

Guns were involved in **2/3** of all murders

It's actually very hard to answer that question because data on the availability and the sales of guns is simply not available (partly because the pro-gun lobby convinced legislators to limit it). But we can look at the stock price of companies whose income depends primarily on gun sales to the public. If the murder rate is going up, we might expect their stock price to go up too; after all, people who are fearful might buy guns to protect themselves.

But what if a rise in the stock price of gun manufacturers tends to be followed by an increase in the murder rate and a fall in the stock price tends to be followed by a decrease in the murder rate? In that case we can either conclude that gun buyers are clairvoyant, able to divine ahead of time what the FBI and police forces across the country cannot, or that increased gun sales do in fact contribute to the murder rate.

Perhaps the best example of a company that relies mostly on gun sales to the public is Sturm, Ruger and Company ("Ruger"). We hasten to add that we're not picking on Ruger. Among the guns owned by one of the two authors of this book is a revolver made by that company. The author is pleased with that handgun.

According to Reuters:

> The Company's design and manufacturing operations are located in the United States and substantially all product content is domestic. The Company offers products in four industry product categories: rifles, shotguns, pistols and revolvers. Its firearms are sold through a select number of independent wholesale distributors, principally to the commercial sporting market. The Company manufactures and sells investment castings made from steel alloys for both outside customers and internal use in the firearms segment. Approximately 96% of the Company's total sales for the year ended December 31, 2008, were from the firearms segment, and approximately 4% were from investment castings.[9]

The company began trading on the New York Stock Exchange on March 26, 1990, and data on its stock price is available since that date from numerous sources. Figure 9-5 shows the annualized percentage change in the ratio of the company's share price to the S&P 500 ratio, where both Ruger's share price and the S&P 500 are adjusted for stock splits and dividends.[10] For comparison, Figure 9-5 also shows the murder rate.

The Ruger-to-S&P 500 ratio tends to bounce around a lot, which makes it hard to determine how closely the ratio corresponds to the murder rate. However, Figure 9-5 does seem to indicate that both series had a tendency to decrease during the 1990s, and from about 2003 on, both series stayed relatively flat. For the period for which we have data on Ruger's share price, the correlation between the two series is about 34 percent. During two of those years—2001 and 2008—the country languished mostly in recession, and during times of economic stress, violence tends to rise. Removing those two

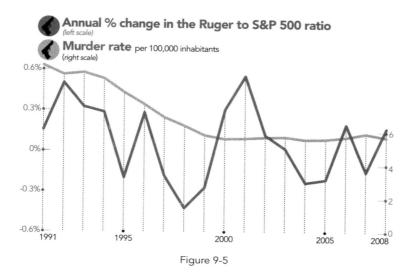

**Annual % change in the Ruger to S&P 500 ratio** *(left scale)*

**Murder rate** per 100,000 inhabitants *(right scale)*

Figure 9-5

years from the calculations because they might represent unusually violent periods raises the correlation above 50 percent.

But does the share price lead to the murder rate, or does the murder rate lead to the share price? Well, it turns out that the correlation between the murder rate in one year and the ratio of Ruger's share price to the S&P 500 in the next year is only 26 percent—less than the correlation between the two series in the same year. In fact, looking at even longer correlations, it doesn't seem like an increasing murder rate helps spur gun sales.

On the other hand, the correlation between the ratio of Ruger's share price to the S&P 500 in one year and the murder rate in subsequent years is 46 percent, an increase over the correlation of the ratio of Ruger's share price to the S&P 500 and the murder rate in the same year. Removing the Ruger share price to S&P 500 for 2001 raises the correlation above 60 percent. (Because our data ends in 2008, the ratio in 2008 cannot be compared to a subsequent murder rate.)

Causation we can't give you. These numbers are not conclusive. But for the period for which we have data, at least, it is clear that the murder rate tends to rise following years in which Ruger's share price does well, and it tends to fall following years in which Ruger's share price does poorly. Ruger's share price, on the other hand, is much less influenced by the murder rate than the other way around. Since the factor most likely to cause an increase in the share price is a profit increase, and since Ruger's profits presumably increase as sales go up, for the period in question increases in the murder rate tended to follow increases in gun sales. Conversely, declines in the murder rate tended to follow decreasing gun sales.

If gun control is one of the things that can help affect the murder rate, does it also help explain the murder rate by administration we presented earlier? Clinton, the president under whom the murder rate had its biggest decline, was a proponent of gun control, pushing for and signing two major pieces of gun control legislation: the Brady Handgun Violence Prevention Act (which mandated background checks for anyone seeking to purchase a gun) and the Federal Assault Weapons Ban. On the other hand, Reagan, under whom the murder rate had its second-largest decline, was an opponent of gun control. Other than Clinton, the only president to sign a major piece of gun control legislation was Lyndon Johnson, and that bill, preventing convicted felons and insane people from legally buying guns, came only in his last year in office and thus is unlikely to have had a major effect on crime during his term.

Which means that while gun control may be an important variable and is certainly worthy of further study, when it comes to the performance of the presidential administrations on murder, there are other factors that matter more. So what are they? Well, we have a little theory that we present in the next few pages.

## The Murder Rate and Demographics

In the last two sections, we looked at the murder rate and spending on public order and safety. Presumably the two should be related: We should expect that more spending on deterring and punishing crime would reduce the rate of crimes, including murders. To some extent that's what we see in some of the graphs in this chapter. The two presidents under whom the murder rate dropped (Clinton and Reagan) both increased spending on public order and safety as a share of the budget and the two administrations under which the murder rate increased the most (JFK/LBJ and Carter) reduced the share of the budget dedicated to law and order.

But spending money isn't always a guarantee of success; Nixon/Ford increased spending on public order and safety as a share of the budget by more than any other administration, and yet the third-biggest increase in the murder rate occurred from 1969 to 1976.

Similarly, while the murder rate did increase under GW, it was still the third-best performance in the sample. And yet GW's administration was also the third-stingiest when it came to funding the justice system.

Both the Nixon/Ford and GW administrations might have benefited (or suffered consequences) from actions of their predecessors; the relatively small increase in the murder rate under GW may have had something to do with policies that made Clinton successful at reducing the murder rate, whereas the poor showing by Nixon/Ford may have been related to the spectacular rise in the murder rate under JFK/LBJ. After all, as we showed earlier, law enforcement funding in one year can affect murder rates years later.

But then why did the murder rate spike under Bush Sr.? After all, he followed Reagan, under whom murder rates declined and spending on public order and safety increased. Bush Sr. also increased spending on public order and safety as a share of the budget by more than any other administration except that of Nixon/Ford and Clinton. So, clearly, something else matters.

All of which brings us back to the notion of the "superpredator" mentioned earlier in the chapter. It turns out that one thing the promulgators of the superpredator myth got right was this: Males eighteen to twenty-four tend to commit a disproportionate percentage of violent crimes. In 2005, for example, of murders committed in the United States whose perpetrators were identified, 40 percent were committed by people eighteen to twenty-four.[11] "[M]ales were almost 10 times more likely than females to commit murder"[12] according to the Department of Justice. This means that as males eighteen to twenty-four become a larger proportion of the population, it makes sense for a president to spend more to combat crime, and failing to do so might result in an uptick in the crime rate. Let's check if that's true.

Figure 9-6 shows what the number of males eighteen to twenty-four as a percentage of the population looks like.

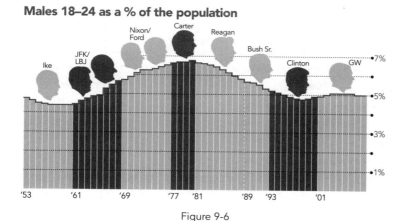

**Males 18–24 as a % of the population**

Figure 9-6

The first thing we notice is that the crop of superpredators that was expected during the Clinton administration never materialized. There was a slight uptick in that cohort toward the end of the Clinton administration, but on average about the same percentage of Americans qualified as males in the eighteen- to twenty-four-year-old demographic when Clinton left office as when he took office. (This should have been obvious ahead of time both to the peddlers of the superpredator theory and to those who bought into it.)

Thus Clinton's big increase in spending on fighting crime came at a time when the threat was not rising; it was at a multidecade low for that matter. Reagan's spending increase came at a time when the criminal cohort was a bit bigger, but shrinking rapidly. So it's no wonder that murder rates dropped so precipitously while Clinton and Reagan were in office.

The percentage of males eighteen to twenty-four, coupled with changes in spending on public order and safety, go a long way toward explaining changes in the murder rate during most of the other administrations as well. For example, among administrations under which the murder rate increased, the smallest increases came under Ike and GW. Even though these two presidents left spending on public order and safety as a share of the budget relatively unchanged, the murder rate didn't spiral out of control. That seems to be in part because the murderous cohort was relatively small in both administrations. The percentage of the population made up of males aged eighteen to twenty-four rose more rapidly under Nixon/Ford than under any other administration; hence, the large increase in spending wasn't enough to keep the murder rate from escalating rapidly. Jimmy Carter, on the other hand, decreased the share of federal spending going to public order and safety at a time when the percentage of the population made up of males eighteen to twenty-four was hitting its peak; as a result, his administration turned in the second-worst performance on the murder rate. The worst increase in the murder rate came under the JFK/LBJ administration. Like Jimmy Carter, their priorities were elsewhere, as evidenced by how they put together their budget. Unfortunately, this was a time when the percentage of the population made up of males eighteen to twenty-four was increasing rapidly, from 4.5 percent in 1960 to 5.7 percent in 1968. It was also a time of great strife in American cities with riots over the civil rights movement and the Vietnam War. Many people were disillusioned and angry. And armed.

The only administration whose performance seemingly cannot be easily explained by the combination of spending and demographics is that of Bush Sr. While he was president, the percentage of males in the "dangerous demographic" decreased from 5.6 percent in 1989 to 5.2 percent in 1990, well off the 6.7 percent peak during the Carter years. Furthermore, Bush Sr. increased the share of the budget going to justice issues more quickly than any other administration except those of Nixon/Ford and Clinton. And yet the murder rate increased. One possible explanation for this anomaly is that Bush Sr.'s focus on combating illegal narcotics, the so-called "war on drugs," diverted efforts from other forms of crime. Furthermore, the crack epidemic being fought by the war on drugs itself escalated the violence. Ironic though it might be, the tough attempts at policing cocaine and crack cut supply, making their sale that much more profitable. Higher stakes meant harsher tactics in the streets.

There's one more thing: Like JFK/LBJ, Nixon, and GW Bush, three other administrations under which the murder rate increased, Bush Sr. presided over a war. Sure, it was a different kind of war—sterile and clean on CNN, and one that most Americans felt good about, but wars have consequences, and sometimes those consequences come home. Among the consequences of war that can lead to increases in the murder rate are post-traumatic stress disorder (PTSD) and the notion (even among civilians viewing events from afar) that violence is a suitable way to solve problems.

# Public Corruption

Everybody who pays enough attention to politics to be a member of a political party knows who the most corrupt president was. Just ask one of these astute political observers and he'll name some guy from the other party. But we suspect the answer you get is not the whole story. It's pretty obvious that both parties have had their share of scandals. Some of the scandals aren't difficult to name: Watergate, Iran-Contra, Monica Lewinsky. But how can they be rated? Watergate led to the resignation of Richard Nixon. And the Monica Lewinsky, er, affair led to the impeachment of Bill Clinton. But was the Lewinsky scandal really worse—more corrupt and more damaging—than selling high-tech missiles to the Iranians in violation of the National Security Act? It depends who you ask.

If we can't rate how scandalous scandals are, maybe we can talk about people the president chooses to appoint to his cabinet. Shouldn't an honest person surround himself with honest people, the kind who won't get arrested with their hands in the cookie jar? Nixon, who seems to be among our most corrupt presidents, named numerous people of questionable character to serve in his administration. His first vice president, Spiro Agnew, was forced to resign when it became known that he had sought and accepted bribes before and after becoming vice president. John Connally, Nixon's secretary of the treasury from 1971 to 1972, was eventually tried (though acquitted) on a number of charges, including bribery, perjury, and conspiracy to obstruct justice. John Mitchell,

U.S. attorney general from 1969 to 1972, served nineteen months in jail for conspiracy, obstruction of justice, and perjury, resulting from the Watergate scandal. His successor, Richard Kleindienst, pleaded guilty to providing false testimony to a Senate panel and received a thirty-day suspended sentence. (Yes, that's right—two of the men Nixon selected to head the nation's law enforcement apparatus got into trouble for breaking major laws they should have been enforcing.) Maurice Stans, secretary of commerce from 1969 to 1972, pleaded guilty to five misdemeanor violations of campaign law and was fined $5,000. Caspar Weinberger, the first budget director and later secretary of health, education, and welfare during the Nixon administration, proved to be one of the more patient individuals in the Nixon cabinet. He held off until the Reagan administration to commit the acts that brought him a felony indictment on two counts of perjury and one count of obstruction of justice. . . or perhaps he simply wasn't snagged for anything until then.

For those keeping count at home, that's six cabinet-level members of the Nixon administration in serious trouble with the law, not counting Nixon himself. There's a reason Nixon's reelection campaign committee was called CREEP (the Committee to Reelect the President). As for Caspar Weinberger, well, proving that patience is a virtue, he was one of several Reagan administration conspirators pardoned by Bush Sr. one fine Christmas Eve.

And it's not just the quantity of crime in Washington that is noteworthy. Some of the plots these folks engage in are—let's call it like it is—cartoonish. Consider, for instance, the Iran-Contra affair, a convoluted scheme by which American weapons were sold to Iran in exchange for Iran's exerting influence on Hezbollah, Iran's terrorist buddies in Lebanon, to release American hostages. (Hezbollah, not incidentally, is thought to be the group responsible for the 1983 U.S. barracks bombings in Lebanon, in which 220 U.S. Marines and 79 international peacekeepers were killed.) To bring the complication of the scheme to the level worthy of a comic-strip villain, much of the loot resulting from the sale of American weaponry to an extremely hostile country would go toward funding the Contras, a rebel group in Nicaragua, thus providing the Contras with a much-needed source of funding that did not involve drug trafficking. A number of administration officials were convicted for their role in the affair. This included the secretary of defense (that would be our friend Weinberger, previously featured in Nixon's White House), as well as two successive national security advisors (Robert McFarlane and John Poindexter). The president, Reagan, insisted that he knew nothing about it, though he said he took full responsibility (whatever that meant) for the affair. The vice president, Bush Sr., claimed to have been "out of the loop."

However, the independent counsel who examined the whole mess, Lawrence Walsh, begged to differ and noted pointedly that Bush Sr. had withheld his notes on various meetings from the investigators.

Regular Washington watchers are rarely surprised when one or another corruption scandal, big or small, emerges. There is the natural lure of money and power. But perhaps another reason corruption seems rampant is that there doesn't seem to be much of a price to be paid for corrupt acts. It wasn't until the Reagan administration that a sitting cabinet member was indicted while in office (Secretary of Labor Raymond Donovan, who was charged with crimes unrelated to his official duties; he was eventually acquitted). Many of those who are caught are pardoned, and just about all of them seem to end up with cushy jobs someplace else later on. Heck, as we learned when GW appointed Elliot Abrams to the National Security Council, even people who have *already* pleaded guilty to crimes seem to be welcome at the highest echelons of government in Washington.

But can we turn this into data? Can we graph it and chart it? For that we need numbers and figures, and surprisingly, we have not been able to find an official list of scandals by administration. But we did find something else that is interesting, if very incomplete. It is too incomplete for us to draw definitive conclusions from it, but it is also too interesting to ignore. So let us tell you an unpleasant story.

In 1976, the Department of Justice created the Public Integrity Section (PIS) in its Criminal Division. (Despite being a Nixon appointee, Gerald Ford was considered an honest guy, and given the circumstances, he had good reason to be concerned about the appearance of impropriety.) The Public Integrity Section was charged with prosecuting corrupt federal, state, and local public officials, including federal judges. Beginning in 1982, the PIS has issued annual reports to Congress, and those reports provide information on the number of public officials charged, convicted, and awaiting trial each year, going back to the year 1980. Let's look at each of these measures: arrests and convictions.

But before we do, we should note that this sort of data isn't necessarily a good measure of the level of corruption in a given administration. For instance, more arrests and convictions could be a symptom of corruption, but it could also signal the arrival of a competent and honest administration that is cleaning house. It might be a sign that even politically connected targets aren't scampering away untouched. Examples of that include the administrations of, well, come to think of it we really can't come up with any examples. Alternatively, it might be a situation where prosecutors are given the green light or encouraged to engage in political vendettas. But one thing is certain: Even a relatively honest administration will appoint its share of crooks and many public officials are elected or appointed at the state and local level, so it's hard to imagine that any recent administration has suffered, if that's the right word, from a dearth of public officials to arrest.

Figure 9-7 shows the number of public officials arrested and charged with crimes, going back to 1980, the first year for which the PIS provides data.[13]

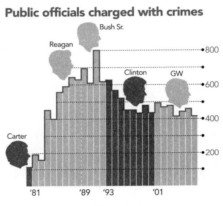

Figure 9-7

The biggest increase in the number of public officials charged with corruption occurred under Reagan. This may be partly due to the fact that the Public Integrity Section was a relatively new entity, created in 1976. It may also be due to a lot of low-hanging fruit; many federal agencies, including HUD, had well-earned reputations for corruption by the early 1980s, and cleaning up the mess required arrests.

Arrests peaked in 1991, and by the end of Bush Sr.'s term the arrest rate had begun to decrease. It decreased further under Clinton, and then had a slight uptick early in the GW administration.

But were those arrests warranted, or were they politically motivated? Were they handled well, or poorly? This the data doesn't reveal. But there is other data that does point to an answer; namely the conviction rate. The conviction rate is the number of people convicted as a percentage of those charged in any given year. If an administration is careful about arresting the right people, and it puts enough resources into prosecution, the conviction rate will (hopefully) be high. Figure 9-8 shows what that looks like.[14]

But of course, arrests and convictions aren't enough to tell us conclusively that one administration is more corrupt—or more aggressive in the prosecution

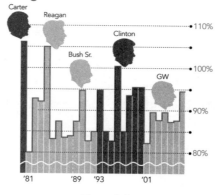

**Conviction rate of public officials charged with crimes**

Carter
Reagan
Bush Sr.
Clinton
GW

110%
100%
90%
80%

'81    '89   '93    '01

Figure 9-8

of public corruption—than another. Prosecutors know that if their bosses want high conviction rates, they can be more selective in what they take to court or offer more plea deals. They also know how to pile up arrest numbers if that is what matters most.

The conviction rate might have fallen under Reagan because he produced the most arrests. Or maybe it was because he arrested the wrong people. Similarly, Clinton may have had the best conviction rate because he reduced the number of people being arrested and therefore could put more resources into prosecution.

This data can't tell us whose was the most corrupt or the most honest administration. But it does provide some indication of which administrations pursued criminals most zealously and which did the best job of convicting them.

# Crime: Conclusion

In this chapter we looked at crime in America. We looked at spending on public order and safety, the murder rate, and the arrest and conviction of public officials. We have conclusive figures for only the first two issues—spending on justice and the murder rate. From those figures, we have constructed an Overall Crime Score that measures each president's performance on crime. The Overall Score on Crime is constructed so that a president who did best at both crime measures would have a score of 100 percent, and a president who was at the bottom for both measures would have a score of 0 percent.

The scores on crime are shown in Figure 9-9.

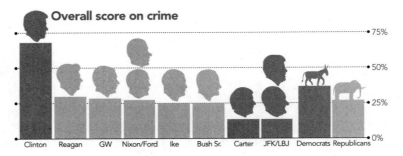

Figure 9-9

Easily the best performance was turned in by Clinton—he increased spending on crime-fighting as a share of the budget by more than any president except Nixon/Ford, and he oversaw the biggest decrease in the murder rate. The second through fifth spots were all held by Republican administrations, and all were tightly bunched.[15] JFK/LBJ and Carter brought up the rear. They got there by spending very little on public order and safety and, at least partly in consequence, saw the worst increases in the murder rate occur on their watch.

## CHAPTER 10

# The Public Mood

Americans live on the sunrise side of [the]
mountain. The night is passing.
And we are ready for the day to come.

GEORGE W. BUSH
Address Accepting the Presidential Nomination at the
Republican National Convention in Philadelphia, August 3, 2000[1]

To some analysts, the mood of the country matters more than just about anything else, since it affects everything else. Economic growth, productivity, prosperity, the length of skirts, the width of ties, the length of beards, hair, good times, bad times, war—they're all about the underlying rhythm of human psychology. That rhythm, that mood, may be hard to measure, but it's a big driver of the economic indicators that get most of the attention.

After all, people who are fearful have different spending habits than people who are confident. People who are optimistic start businesses or new ventures, while those who are barricaded in the pantry, quivering behind the canned corn, do not.

But it's not a one-way street, and it's not always the mood that shadows reality. Sometimes it goes the other way around. If your neighbors lose their jobs, you may fear that you are going to be next and curtail your economic activity as a result. And when enough people do that, it just makes the mood (and the economy) worse.

Worries and hopes can both be exaggerated. People can be slow to see the termites in the walls or too quick to believe the snake-oil guy's version of tomorrow. But sometimes the economy changes—for better or worse—quicker than the experts believe it will. That's because consumers—that would be you and us—know better than any economist whether we're having trouble making the mortgage, keeping the kids in decent clothes, or paying Grandma's upkeep. And so our mood affects the economy.

Although the executive branch has no budget for public feelings, no Office of Mood Management, the president still affects the mood. Some presidents do not inspire, do not make us feel prosperous, do not make us feel good. But some instill a vision, a feeling of prosperity, combined with hope that the future will be more prosperous. And these attitudes help bolster—if not create—the reality that follows. They also sometimes place a lens over reality so that we see it a certain way—a bit rosier, a bit bleaker, perhaps, than the facts might warrant. And we act accordingly, more confidently or cautiously. In this chapter, we'll see how each of the administrations from Ike to GW has done at improving the public mood.

## Consumer Confidence

You've had a long day at work and you want to do what you do best: Prop your feet on the ottoman, turn on the TV, and eat some pork rinds. You get the process started—you're resting comfortably on the couch, there's a rerun of *Seinfeld* you've seen six times before. And then the phone rings: "Damn telemarketers!"

Because you decide to ignore the call, you'll never learn that tonight's phone call isn't from someone trying to sell you a beachfront time-share in Fargo or get you to contribute to the Benevolent Order of Fraternal Grifters. Nope. This time it's from some folks trying to conduct a survey to determine the public mood. And maybe it's just as well that you let it go to voice mail; after you've been interrupted your mood is bound to be pretty foul.

One survey whose results are frequently reported on the news is the Consumer Confidence Survey, conducted by the University of Michigan. Every month they call and call until they manage to corral about five hundred adults into answering five questions. Those questions deal with people's perception of their own economic situation, the broader economy, and where it's all headed over the next twelve months to five years. Even though the survey only includes the opinions of people who have nothing better to do than answer questions from a complete stranger on the phone during dinnertime, the survey is widely respected and is even used as a leading indicator by the BEA.

The survey is conducted monthly,[2] and is normalized so that values of 100 equal the level of consumer confidence at the beginning of 1966. Figure 10-1 shows how consumer confidence has evolved since it was first measured at the end of 1952.[3]

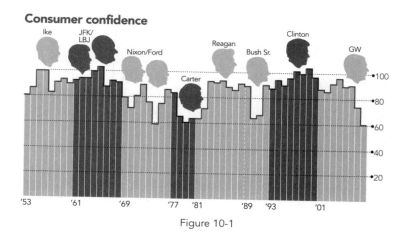

Figure 10-1

Notice that consumer confidence bounced around quite a bit, but the low points came in the 1970s, 1990, and 2008, which were periods when the country's economic situation was rather shaky.

The high points came during the LBJ and Clinton administrations, periods in which the economy was growing rapidly and the lot of the average person was improving.

Figure 10-2 shows a summary of how consumer confidence changed over each administration.

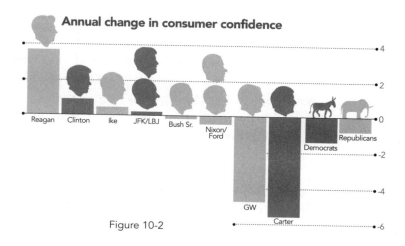

Figure 10-2

Reagan was the big winner at improving the public mood, though you wouldn't know it if you looked only at his first year and change in office. However, after the Fed finally brought inflation under control, a combination of factors—some we can credit to Reagan—sparked growth that helped fuel optimism. The Great Communicator was able to make the public believe in America again after a dismal decade. Reagan was followed distantly by Clinton, another great communicator. Ike came next, then the Camelot of JFK/LBJ. Under the rest of the presidents, consumer confidence actually declined, with the biggest drops occurring under Carter and GW.

GW's administration ended poorly, with a financial crisis and a deteriorating situation in Afghanistan. Under Carter, the big drops came early in his presidency; consumer confidence had risen dramatically in the last two years of the Nixon/Ford administration, apparently in response to the departure of Nixon. However, there is no denying that the public was also happy to see Jimmy Carter's departure from the White House, though that feeling of malaise would stick around a bit longer.

# Suicide

Committing suicide is the ultimate act of despair. A person who commits suicide thinks life itself is not worth living and doesn't see much hope for improvement.

But while committing suicide is a personal issue, it is strongly correlated with a person's economic well-being. Economic setbacks for people who had previously been well off, as well as unemployment and low status, increase the likelihood of a person committing suicide.[4] Wherever you might start on the happiness scale, a run of dismal financial luck can only be bad for your state of mind. And since this is true of all of us, suicide can be a pretty good measure of the state of the economy.[5]

But suicide is affected by more than just personal factors and the state of the economy—it depends in part on the availability of services intended to help people who are at risk of committing suicide or are otherwise in despair.[6] Suicide may be more likely among those who seek help but cannot find it, and sometimes finding help might be a function of the government's making such help available. That in turn depends in no small part on where the president chooses to put his priorities.

Figure 10-3 shows the change in the suicide rate from 1953 to 2006.[7]

While the suicide rate was fairly stable during the early part of the Eisenhower administration, it began to rise in the late 1950s, and eventually peaked at 13.7 deaths per 100,000 people in 1977. After that, it began to fall,

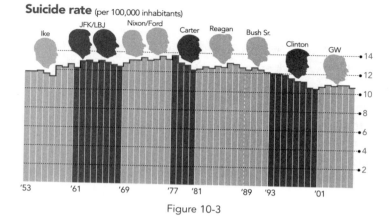

Figure 10-3

bottoming out at 10.4 deaths per 100,000 in the year 2000. After 2000, suicide rates first rose, then fell back to 10.6 in 2006.

Figure 10-4 shows a summary of the annualized changes in the suicide rate.

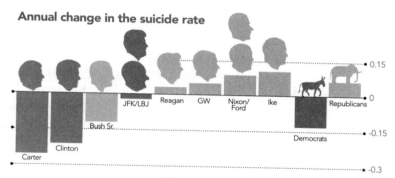

Figure 10-4

Suicide decreased under four administrations—those of Jimmy Carter, Bill Clinton, George Bush Sr., and JFK/LBJ. The strong reduction during the Carter administration may owe something to the First Lady, Rosalynn Carter, who was a strong proponent of mental health research and treatment. As a result, early in his administration, Jimmy Carter created the President's Commission on Mental Health, and the administration put a lot of resources into serving the needs of those with mental health problems.

Mental health was also a priority under Bill Clinton, who pushed for and signed the Mental Health Parity Act (MHPA). The MHPA ensured that insurance policy holders had the same yearly and lifetime limits on access to mental health

as they did on access to other forms of health care. An additional factor that may have reduced suicides in the Clinton administration was the state of the economy; unemployment fell and real incomes rose during the Clinton administration.

Bush Sr. also put a strong emphasis on mental health issues, going so far as to proclaim the 1990s the Decade of the Brain in October of 1992. Furthermore, the collapse of the USSR, as well as Gulf War I, a conflict in which the country was successful and the moral ambiguities were at a minimum, helped many Americans feel righteous about their place in the world, even if the economy wasn't exactly going anywhere. The fourth administration under which suicide rates declined—that of JFK/LBJ—was, like Clinton's, an era of a booming economy and a strong emphasis on social services.

Under the remaining administrations, suicide rates rose. Reagan famously reversed Carter's policies on mental health; the Omnibus Budget Reconciliation Act of 1981 killed many provisions of Carter's Mental Health Systems Act and at the same time shifted responsibility for mental health and substance abuse services to ill-prepared state and local communities. GW came in just about tied with Reagan, but the data is missing for his last two years. Given the dismal state of the economy in 2008, GW might end up looking worse when all is said and done. Ike, who came in second to last, also wasn't known for putting much emphasis on mental health issues or suicide prevention.

The Nixon/Ford administration came in last. Nixon, it should be noted, did have one famous interaction with the mental health care field; the break-ins at the Watergate Hotel were preceded by a similar break-in at the office of the Beverly Hills psychiatrist who treated Daniel Ellsberg. Ellsberg had made Nixon's "enemies list" by leaking the Pentagon Papers to the *New York Times*.

## The Stock Market

Pssst. Want a hot stock tip? Well, so do we, buddy. So do we. Why? Because Americans love to gamble. One popular way to gamble is on the stock market. Buying stock is betting that the shares of the company you bought—run by people you will never meet in an industry you know nothing about engaging in accounting tricks you don't understand—are going to rise in value. If you want to bet on a bunch of companies, you can buy shares of a mutual fund. Perhaps the broadest of the widely reported indices is the Standard and Poor's 500 (i.e., the S&P 500). If the S&P 500 is rising, it's a sign that people are betting that things are going to go well for a broad range of American business. If it's falling, people are betting against that broad range of American businesses.

Yahoo's finance page provides data on the S&P 500, adjusted for dividends and splits. Figure 10-5 shows how the stock market has performed (with dividends reinvested) since 1952.

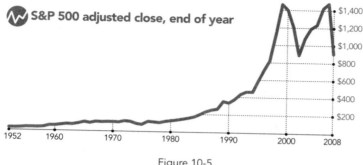

Figure 10-5

It certainly appears that investing in the stock market is a good idea over the long run; the annualized rate of return for the S&P 500 is about 6.5 percent. The market slowly trended up until about 1982, at which point it picked up its pace, accelerating again in 1995. The market peaked in the year 2000, and had a big decline until 2003, when it started rising again. However, there was a second big decline in 2008.

But what about inflation? How does that 6.5 percent a year stack up after the effects of inflation have been taken into account? Figure 10-6 shows the real adjusted close of the S&P 500, taking into account the effects of inflation, by administration.

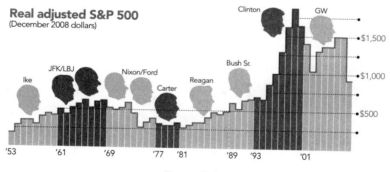

Figure 10-6

The ride is a bit bumpier with inflation thrown in, and the annualized growth rate drops almost in half, to 2.7 percent a year. The market first hits a peak in 1965, and then drops for a long time. If you had invested $1,000 at the end of 1965, in real terms, you would have been underwater until 1991. In other words, it would have taken you a quarter of a century to make up your losses! We suspect that's not something any investment advisors ever told you, is it? Kinda like they never told you that what happened to your retirement money in 2008 was possible, right?

But in the early 1980s, the market began rising again. Not surprisingly, the rising stock market inspired Americans to keep their money at home, and foreigners (we'll be discussing them again later in this chapter) to invest in the United States. In 1983, the United States went from being a net creditor to a net debtor. In other words, before 1983 the value of foreign assets (stocks, bonds, land, etc.) that Americans owned exceeded the value of American assets owned by foreigners.[8] Beginning in 1983 foreigners had a greater claim on Americans than the other way around.

And no wonder everyone wanted to invest in American stocks: Once the market started to rise, it continued for quite a while, slowly at first but later accelerating. And speaking of accelerating, if there's one thing in our chart that stands out like a Las Vegas showgirl in full regalia in a roomful of accountants, it's the huge increase under Bill Clinton. Part of that run is due to the tech and telecom bubble when everyone wanted to play the stock market. Naturally, it was followed by a big collapse. These cycles of boom and bust have repeated themselves throughout the stock market's history; a similar situation followed the run-up in prices that peaked in 1965. And within these cycles, there are other cycles. During the Reagan administration, the market rose at (what then appeared to be) an impressive clip, but after the Black Monday collapse in 1987, it took a couple of years to recover fully.

Figure 10-7 shows a summary of the annualized gains and losses, by president, in the inflation-adjusted S&P 500.

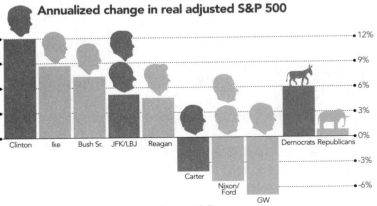

Figure 10-7

From Figure 10-7, it is evident that the fastest growth in real S&P 500 occurred under Clinton, followed by Ike, Bush Sr., JFK/LBJ, and Reagan. Declines were registered under Jimmy Carter, Nixon/Ford, and GW Bush, with GW posting the biggest drop of all.

Interestingly enough, contrary to popular belief, the performance of the stock market does not appear to be highly correlated with the strength of the economy. For instance, the top spot was taken by Bill Clinton, a strong performer when it came to the economy, but he was followed by Ike and Bush Sr., neither of whom goes on anyone's short list of economic superstars. Similarly, being "pro-business" doesn't appear to make the stock market surge; the two presidents most often described that way—Reagan and GW—presided over so-so (4.9 percent a year) and abysmal (–6.9 percent a year) real returns on the S&P 500, respectively. In fact, real returns on the stock market grew almost six times faster under Democrats than under Republican administrations.

So what causes the stock market to go on a tear? We have no idea. But as we learned in 2008, neither do most investment bankers and fund managers.

# The Value of the Dollar

Not everyone is an American. In fact, studies show that more than 95 percent of the world's population is made up of foreigners. While foreigners come in many varieties, they can generally be recognized by a few traits most of them have in common. For instance, most foreigners live outside the United States, don't speak proper American English, and use funny-looking currency.

And just as you can use dollars to buy stuff, if you choose, you can use dollars to buy some of that exotic foreign currency that foreigners use. And the foreigners can use some of their foreign currency to buy dollars, if they choose. Why would a foreigner want American currency? Well, maybe she wants to buy stuff that's made in the United States. Most things Americans buy and sell, including their labor, is priced in dollars. So if a Swiss woman wants to visit the United States, purchase a few hundred tons of American corn, or buy a home in Vermont, she'll find it useful to have dollars. Similarly, an American planning to visit Switzerland, import some Swiss chocolate, or buy a farm in Switzerland will want to buy some of the funky paper Swiss people use.

But what is the price of a dollar? And what is the price of a Swiss franc? That depends on the supply and demand of the dollar and the Swiss franc, but, for the most part, if people start wanting francs a lot more and dollars a lot less, the price of a dollar (in francs) will fall and the price of a franc (in dollars) will rise. As we already noted, one reason people want more (or fewer) dollars or francs or euros or any other currency is because they expect to be able to use that currency. The dollar rises in value if the United States is producing more stuff people want to buy or becoming (in many people's opinion) a better place to invest money. Don't forget that supply-demand principle either: If the U.S. government prints a whole bunch of dollars, the dollar is likely to decline in value.

All in all, the value of the dollar indicates how people all over the world, including in the United States, collectively, feel about the current and future prospects of the United States. Now is a rising dollar a good thing or a bad thing? The answer to that is: It depends. If the dollar increases in value, it makes American goods and services more expensive relative to foreign goods and services, so an increase in the value in the dollar can actually cost jobs. On the other hand, a strong dollar makes it cheaper to buy stuff made by foreigners, which is good for American consumers. While a rising dollar is not unambiguously a good thing, it does indicate increased faith in the United States. Thus, in this section we will be treating a rising dollar as an improvement in the public mood, and a devaluation of the dollar as a sign of a deteriorating public mood.

But what if the dollar rises in value relative to the British pound sterling, but loses value against the Brazilian real? Overall is the dollar rising or falling in value? One way to answer this question to see how the dollar is doing relative to many currencies. The Federal Reserve does this by keeping track of the value of the dollar relative to a basket of major foreign currencies. This value is called the Trade Weighted Index of Major Currencies.

This index hasn't been around forever. Until 1973 the United States and most other developed countries were operating on the Bretton Woods system. That arrangement came about in the closing days of World War II, when delegates from all the Allied countries got together to decide how the world economy should run in the postwar era. What they cooked up was a gold standard. The U.S. dollar was "priced" at $35 for one ounce of gold and the rest of the currencies could be exchanged for fixed quantities of dollars.

The system eventually fell apart during the Nixon administration when inflation became a problem. This means that there was a lot of money floating around and over time each dollar would buy less stuff. Well, less stuff like cans of peas, pickles, and Picassos. But not less gold—the amount of gold you could buy per dollar stayed the same because of the Bretton Woods system. So more and more dollars were exchanged for gold, partly because the amount of dollars increased so much, and partly because the dollars bought less and less of everything else. Eventually, Nixon had an unhappy epiphany—if inflation weren't brought under control, sooner or later the government would run out of gold and the entire Bretton Woods system would fall apart. Not one to wait around for the inevitable, Nixon unilaterally withdrew the United States from the gold standard. Other countries soon followed suit, and by 1973 the major currencies were allowed to float freely (more or less) against each other.

Figure 10-8 shows the value of the dollar, as measured by the Trade Weighted Exchange Index of Major Currencies—the basket of currencies we described earlier—since 1973, using data for December, the last month of the year.[9]

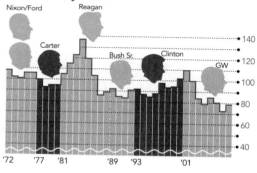

Figure 10-8

In the first couple years after the end of the gold standard, the value of the dollar declined a bit, stabilizing by the end of the Nixon/Ford administration. The high point came in the 1980s when, as Reagan put it, it was morning in America. The country was on the ascendance; Americans and foreigners alike believed that.

And then in September 1985 there was the Plaza Accord, and it was afternoon, if not early evening, in America. The Plaza Accord was an agreement between the United States, France, West Germany, Great Britain, and Japan, all of which were worried about the massive trade and budget deficits the United States was running. The consensus was that those deficits had to be contained or the U.S. economy would be in trouble, and if the U.S. economy got in trouble, sooner or later its major trading partners would be in trouble too.

Among the steps agreed to by all parties to the Plaza Accord was reducing the value of the dollar. The intervention of these governments had an immediate impact on the value of the dollar. The Reagan administration's budget deficits did shrink somewhat in 1987 and 1988, as we saw in Chapter 2, but how much of that was due to the dollar losing value is hard to say.

After the Plaza Accord, the dollar puttered along for about ten years, and then, following several years of solid growth and continuously falling budget deficits, it began to rise in value. This despite the constant warnings found on the op-ed pages of the *Wall Street Journal* that Clinton's tax hikes were going to harm the economy. The value of the dollar (as measured by the Trade Weighted Exchange Index of Major Currencies) continued to rise through the early part of the GW administration, reaching as high as 113 in January of 2002, before dropping.

A summary of the growth rate by president is shown in Figure 10-9.

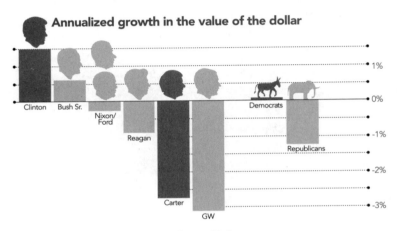

Figure 10-9

Of the five administrations, the biggest increase in the value of the dollar occurred under Clinton—good for American consumers, bad for exporters whose products were becoming more costly overseas. There was also a small rise under Bush Sr., but the dollar declined in value under the other three presidents. The biggest decline, by far, was under GW, under whom both the economy and perceived prospects for the future declined markedly.

# The Public Mood: Conclusion

In the preceding sections of this chapter, we looked at four different measures of the public mood: consumer confidence, the suicide rate, the stock market, and the value of the dollar. Each of these measures captures different aspects of people's faith in the American system.

To evaluate how well a president did overall, we developed a measure of public mood from the rankings each president had on all four measures. The measure was designed so that a president who scored first in each of the aspects of the public mood would have a score of 100 percent, and a president who came in last place in all of these measures would have a score of 0 percent.

Figure 10-10 shows the public mood value for each of the presidents, and a final ranking.

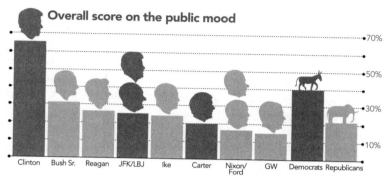

Figure 10-10

Figure 10-10 shows that Clinton scored best; in fact, his score is more than twice as high as that of his nearest competitor. This is not surprising; Clinton scored first when it came to increasing the value of both the stock market and the U.S. dollar, and second when it came to consumer confidence and reducing the number of suicides. The Clinton administration oversaw a booming economy, plentiful jobs, and peace. There was also a technological explosion that returned the United States to preeminence after a decade in which it appeared that the nation was falling behind Japan.

Bush Sr. came in second place, a result of a second-place finish in the value of the dollar and strong showings when it came to the stock market and reducing the suicide rate. His administration oversaw a period in which there were no threats on the horizon; the Soviet Union had collapsed, and U.S. muscle was only flexed against far weaker opponents (e.g., the first Gulf War and the invasion of Panama). However, the economy wasn't all that great, and by the end of his presidency, the nation was only slowly emerging from a recession.

Reagan closely followed his successor in the rankings in terms of the public mood. The man who told us it was "morning in America" did, in fact, convince many people that he was right, producing a first-place finish in improving consumer confidence. But despite Reagan's upbeat rhetoric, not everyone fared so well during his administration; Reagan's performance on other measures of the public mood was only middling.

The JFK/LBJ administration followed on Reagan's heels, also producing middling scores on consumer confidence, suicide rates, and the S&P 500. (Because the Bretton Woods system was in effect at the time, they did not receive a score for the value of the dollar.) That administration was characterized by a booming economy on the one hand and a deteriorating Vietnam War on the other. The civil rights movement, perhaps not ironically, led to further frictions in society.

Ike—also too early to be graded on the value of the dollar—had more ups and downs, scoring well on the stock market and consumer confidence, but overseeing the worst increase in suicide rates observed in the sample. His was a period of hopefulness but uncertainty—even fear—as *Sputnik* was launched, Soviet allies made inroads in various countries, and the premier of the Soviet Union threatened to bury us.

Sixth place belongs to Carter. The malaise presidency had one bright spot—the biggest reduction in suicide rates. But that was the only bright spot, as the mood rings people wore at the time would have attested. The economy grew rapidly but people's incomes didn't keep up, forcing them into polyester and platform shoes lest they have nothing whatsoever to wear.

Nixon/Ford ranked next. What with inflation, the oil embargo, and a president who apparently was a crook, it was hard for people to maintain a positive mood.

Which leads us to the last and the least of the presidents when it comes to the public mood: GW. Dubya produced mediocre performances across the board—last place in stock market growth, second to last in consumer confidence, a tie for fifth on suicides, and a sixth-place finish on the exchange rate. No wonder he did so poorly—the best predictor of the Bush years came from, of all things, the satirical news magazine *The Onion,* which stated just before GW took office that "Our long nightmare of peace and prosperity is over."[10] Sadly it was. From 2001 to 2008, America got a mediocre economy and an exploding debt, and by the end of GW's term many Americans were worried we might be heading into a second Great Depression. On the international front, there was the rise of China, increasing ill will toward Americans in other countries, two wars, and no sign of Osama bin Laden after the destruction of the World Trade Center. The president who came to office promising to be a "uniter, not a divider" did, in fact, unite much of the country and even the world, at least in their negative opinion of him.

## CHAPTER 11

# Family Values

> But America was a good country. America stood for
> spiritual and moral values that far transcended the
> strength and the wealth of the nations of the Old World.

RICHARD NIXON
Remarks at the National Prayer Breakfast, February 2, 1971[1]

It seems kind of odd that we'd be talking about how each president performs on family values. But many of our presidents do like to tell us what our family values should be, all the while failing to live up to their own lofty words. They tell us marriage is sacred, but at least three of them had affairs and one was divorced. (One of the adulterers was going around telling churchgoers about the need for more discipline and self-restraint, right around the time he was cheating on his wife.) They tell us to instill virtues in our children, but presidential offspring have included a surprising number of drunkards. And then there's Tricky Dick!

So who are these people in the White House to lecture the rest of us on family values? Yet we have come to expect the president to help lead the national conversation and even to promote those values we supposedly share. Then again, most of us don't want the government, the president—or anyone else—dictating our behavior. After more than 230 years of the American republic, tension still surrounds the proper role of government in our lives. Some of the questions batted around in the Federalist Papers 1787–88 are still getting a bit of a workout. Just what restraints should government impose on us when it comes to human behavior? How much should government intrude in citizens' private lives, and how much should it enforce social rights?

Even without having the government directly dictating family values to us, the president can still take steps to move us in the direction that most

Americans, regardless of their place on the political spectrum, want us to go: fewer abortions, more stable marriages, and more children raised in two-parent families.

When it comes to influence, the president has many tools at his disposal. First, he has the bully pulpit. When the president talks, he moves the meter on debate (although, as Jimmy Carter found, not always in the direction he wants the meter to go). Suddenly, the *New York Times* has an investigative series on the subject, CNN is doing specials, *Time* and *Newsweek* run cover stories, and Congress is holding hearings.

The agencies that the president controls can also be used to promote family values through education, health care policies, housing programs, and even tax regulations. Make no mistake: If the president thinks he's making a positive difference or if he thinks he can spin it in a way that benefits his administration, he and his people are going to place a premium on a family-values agenda.

Perhaps, if we can find the right data and look at it hard and well enough, we can figure out just who should get credit for promoting family values, how much credit they should get, and just how they compare to the rest of the Oval Office crowd. That's what we try to do in this chapter.

# Abortion

Contentious as the issue is, pretty much no one is actually in favor of abortion. All sides seem to be in agreement that reducing the number of abortions is a good thing. The argument seems to be about *how* to reduce the number

of abortions. One side says it is simple—abortion is wrong, it's murder, and it should be illegal in all (or, depending on who you ask, at least in most) cases. The other side says—either out of the principle of choice or perhaps sheer pragmatism—that the focus should be on access to birth control and sex education, especially for young adults, and that simply making abortion illegal won't prevent unwanted pregnancies and won't cut down on the abortion rate.

But what do the numbers say? Which side seems to have the better handle on reducing the number of abortions? For that, we turn to the data. The Centers for Disease Control (CDC) has figures for the number of abortions going back to 1970. (Remember that *Roe v. Wade*, decided in 1973, didn't make abortion legal in the United States; rather, the Supreme Court ruled in *Roe v. Wade* that individual states could not make abortion illegal.)

Unfortunately, the data isn't going to make it easy for us. From 1998 to 2003, the data is missing for a number of states; therefore the bottom line is probably somewhat inaccurate—that is, understated—for those years.

Still, to paraphrase Donald Rumsfeld, you go to your analysis with the data you have, not the data you might want. According to the data we have, as illustrated in Figure 11-1, the number of abortions moved up and then down after 1970.[2]

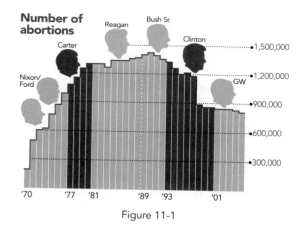

Figure 11-1

As Figure 11-1 shows, the number of abortions increased rapidly throughout the 1970s, leveled off in the 1980s, and then peaked in 1990, when more than 1.4 million abortions were reported to the CDC. It has declined ever since. In 2005, about 820,000 abortions were reported to the CDC.

Because of the missing data from 1998 to 2003, we won't calculate the annualized rate of change for abortions over the span of each administration. Still, Figure 11-1 does seem to indicate that the fastest declines in the number of abortions occurred under Clinton, even if we leave out the data from 1998 to 2003.

In a sense, the numbers overstate how common abortion has been. After *Roe v. Wade*, the number of abortions steadily increased, peaked, and then declined. During that time, the number of women who might under some circumstances have an abortion in any given year—the number of women of reproductive age (which the CDC considers to be those between the ages of fifteen and forty-four years old)—has grown by 45 percent.[3] In 1970, there were 42.6 million women of reproductive age. That figure grew to 52.8 million in 1980, 58.6 million in 1990, and 62 million in 2005.

Notice that the growth rate in the population of women who could potentially have an abortion has been increasing more slowly since 1990. In fact, from 1990 to 2005 that population grew by less than 6 percent, while at the same time, the number of abortions dropped by about 40 percent. Put another way, if women of reproductive age weren't having fewer abortions than they had in 1990, there would have been more than 1.5 million abortions in 2005, a figure 85 percent higher than the 820,000 that actually occurred in that year. So one important way to reduce the number of abortions overall is to reduce the likelihood that a woman in the fifteen- to forty-four-year-old demographic will get one.

Figure 11-2 shows the rate of abortions per thousand women between the ages of fifteen and forty-four.

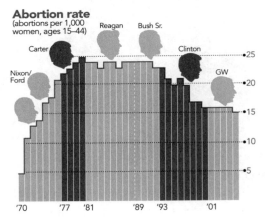

Figure 11-2

For states missing data on the number of abortions in a given year, the number of women of reproductive age was also not included for that year. Assuming that the states for which data is available do not vary significantly from the norm, the abortion rate is probably reasonably accurate even in the years for which data is missing. (That was obviously not the case when we were discussing the total number of abortions.)

Abortions per thousand women of reproductive age rose throughout the 1970s and peaked in 1980 at twenty-five. The rate meandered very slightly downward through 1991, when it began to decline more rapidly, eventually leveling off at about sixteen abortions per thousand women of reproductive age in the year 2000.

The annualized decrease in the number of abortions per administration is shown in Figure 11-3.

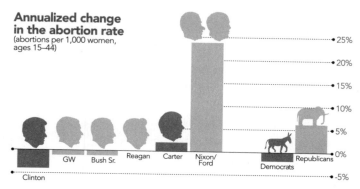

Figure 11-3

Figure 11-3 shows that the likelihood that a woman of reproductive age would get an abortion decreased more markedly during the Clinton administration than at any other time. But why? Is the decline due to more women deciding not to have abortions when they got pregnant or simply to women not getting pregnant when they did not want to have children? To answer that, let's look at things yet another way: comparing abortions to their most obvious alternative, namely giving birth rather than terminating the pregnancy. Figure 11-4, therefore, shows abortions per thousand live births.[4]

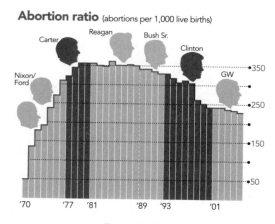

Figure 11-4

The ratio of abortions to live births follows a pattern (more or less) similar to the number of abortions over time—but the parallel is not exact. The ratio increased throughout the 1970s, peaked in 1984 (when there were 364 abortions per thousand live births), and has declined ever since. Now this doesn't tell us how many women are using birth control in the decades since it became widely acceptable. But when the ratio drops, it does tell us about the *choices* made by pregnant women: They are—proportionally—choosing to bring pregnancies to term more often, and have abortions less often.

The changes in the ratio are dramatic only under Nixon/Ford. That makes sense, since abortion was suddenly legal and available at that time. In economic terms, there was pent-up demand. That may help explain the less stunning but still significant increase under Carter.

Figure 11-5 presents a summary.

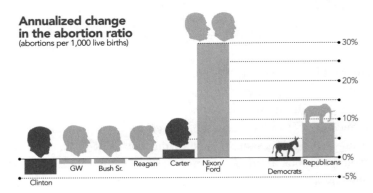

**Annualized change in the abortion ratio**
(abortions per 1,000 live births)

Figure 11-5

So what is the story all these figures are telling us? Nixon/Ford and Carter were presidents right after abortions became legal in most of the country, and the number of abortions would have risen no matter who was president at that time. There were also some powerful social factors pushing in the same direction. The movement for women's rights gave ideological and political support to choice. Meanwhile, a huge cohort of women were reaching adulthood and entering the workplace in record numbers. Some of these same factors may have affected results in the beginning of the Reagan administration as well.

So maybe, just maybe, if we're going to assign a score to each administration (and if you've read this far, you know we're going to do just that!), it wouldn't be fair to grade Nixon/Ford, Carter, and Reagan. Leaving out those administrations moves us a full fifteen years after *Roe v. Wade* was decided, more than enough time for a lot of its immediate effects to fade and for the proportion of abortions to decline.

It also leaves us three presidents whose performance we can judge more fairly: Bush Sr., Clinton, and GW. Of the three, the best results came under Bill Clinton, regardless of the measure we use. Under Clinton, the abortion rate dropped the fastest, the rate at which women chose to bring pregnancies to term increased the fastest, and the percentage of women opting to have abortions also dropped at the most rapid clip. Thus, Clinton ranks first. The two Bush presidents produced very similar results, so we can say they're tied for second.

Furthermore, for each of the abortion measures, there was a marked difference between the numbers turned in under Clinton and those turned in by the two Bushes. Given that Clinton outperformed both his predecessor and his successor, it is very tough to attribute his success to social trends or demographics, either of which would have benefited Bush Sr. or GW as well. So why did Clinton produce better results than the two Bushes? There's probably no single answer, but one thing is obvious: Clinton's approach to abortion infuriated social conservatives. Gary Bauer, one of the leaders of the social conservative movement, wrote in 1994:

> The words "safe, legal, and rare" were still warm on Bill Clinton's lips when, less than 24 hours after taking office, he signed an executive order making abortions easier to obtain. Later he tried to establish public funding of abortion through repeal of the Hyde amendment; promoted abortion overseas through the United Nations Family Planning Association; mandated the provision of abortion on military bases; included abortion in his health-care plan; and brought RU-486, the French abortion pill, to the United States. [5]

And what Bauer wrote is not the only indication that Clinton made it easier to get abortions. For instance, Clinton ordered the Department of Justice to be particularly zealous at prosecuting violence against women's clinics, which are often major providers of abortions.

Which raises the obvious question: If Clinton made it easier to get an abortion, why did the number of abortions, the abortion rate, and the abortion ratio all come down so much while he was in office? We think the answer lies in his policies toward sex and reproductive issues, which were markedly different than the other presidents in the sample, at least after 1980. They were also different from the approach preferred by Republicans in Congress, who became the majority party in 1995.

Clinton's focus on sex education, easily obtained contraceptives, and initiatives to combat the spread of STDs (especially AIDS and syphilis) may have contributed to the big drop in the abortion rate. But there was something else, something that Clinton contributed to the zeitgeist. Issues pertaining to sex somehow just weren't as private during the Clinton administration as before. (Hey, long before that blue dress was part of the national conversation, this was a guy who people felt comfortable asking about his choice of underwear on national television—and he was willing to answer. It is hard to imagine anyone asking one of the Bushes that same question.) Discussion often sheds light, especially when we're dealing with taboo issues. Perhaps even a small increase in knowledge about sex, combined with greater availability of birth-control options, can make the difference between whether a teenager—or a twenty-four-year-old for that matter—finds herself pregnant and unable to support a child.

Fortunately, regardless of how well or how poorly the presidents have dealt with the issue, since the 1980s, the number of abortions—as well as the abortion rate—has been dropping. Perhaps for that reason the issue has become a priority for proportionally fewer voters and a decisive factor in only a handful of elections. That is partly because, at least for now, most of the country considers the issue settled. The frequency of abortion, the demographics and politics driving its availability, the public fatigue with the argument—all have shifted over time. But even with all that, and with all our differences over how to approach the issue, one thing remains true: Most people would prefer that there be fewer abortions. So the data reinforces the muting of the debate.

## Marriage and Divorce

At the end of World War II, the return of a large percentage of the American public to our country's shores led to a spike in the marriage rate: A greater percentage of Americans got married in 1946 (16.4 out of every 1,000 Americans alive that year walked down the aisle) than in any other year, at least going back to 1867, the first year for which we've been able to track down data.[6] The divorce rate also spiked in 1946, hitting a then-unprecedented high of 4.3 divorces per 1,000 Americans, more than twice what it had been before the United States entered World War II. The divorce rate would not get that high again until 1973.

What this tells us is that Americans like to get married, or used to anyway. Many of us do so at the first decent opportunity, even when no shotguns are involved. But not all of us find we like to stay married, so many of us get divorced at the first opportunity too. But the fact of the matter is that Americans are not getting married as much as they used to, and while the divorce rate has also been dropping, it has been dropping much more slowly than the marriage rate. The result is that the "net marriage rate," the difference between the rate of Americans getting married and the rate of Americans getting divorced, is lower than it has been at any point since 1867. Furthermore, while we don't have the data to know for certain, given social mores before 1867, it is likely that the country's net marriage rate is now at an all-time low.

We hasten to mention that we take no position on gay marriage in this book; our emphasis is on issues for which we could find readily available reliable data that has been tracked for many years, and this hasn't been the case for gay marriage.

Figure 11-6 shows the net marriage rate since 1952.

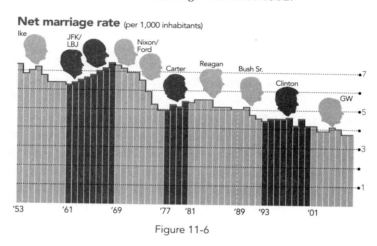

Figure 11-6

From 1952 to 2007, the net marriage rate decreased by half, from 7.4 per thousand to 3.7 per thousand. Along the way, the marriage rate fell from 9.9 per thousand to 7.3 per thousand, and the divorce rate increased from 2.5 to 3.6 per thousand. Figure 11-7 presents a summary of the annualized change in the net marriage rate by administration.

The only two administrations that saw increases in the net marriage rate were those of Jimmy Carter and JFK/LBJ. During both of those administrations, the divorce rate increased, but the rate at which people got married increased even faster.

Marriage and divorce were clearly important issues to Jimmy Carter. The man who admitted to committing adultery in his heart many times (but not, mind you, in the flesh!) was concerned enough to convene a Conference on Families at the White House to find ways to decrease the marriage rate

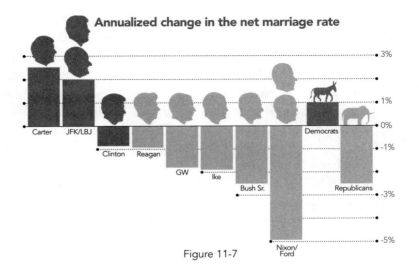

**Annualized change in the net marriage rate**

3%

1%

0%

-1%

-3%

-5%

Carter JFK/LBJ Clinton Reagan GW Ike Bush Sr. Democrats Republicans Nixon/Ford

Figure 11-7

and reduce the number of children born out of wedlock.[7] If it did little else, the conference helped sharpen the debate over the role of families in society, and in particular the role of each member of the family. This was the era of the ERA (the Equal Rights Amendment); the battle raged over whether a woman's place was in the home or the workplace. Similar conferences were held throughout the country, and for many, the issue is still not resolved. Carter was also concerned that the welfare system was antifamily, and he worked to make it more family-friendly.

The increase in the net marriage rate under JFK/LBJ probably has more indirect origins—namely, the improving economic condition of most Americans, and in particular, of the poor. This made it possible for more Americans to contemplate marriage and to stay married rather than skipping town at the first sign of economic trouble.[8] We note that things can go the other way. Sometimes, when the economy is awful it encourages people to get married in order to pool their resources; as to divorce, who could afford it?

The third-best performance—albeit one in which the net marriage rate declined—came under the third Democratic administration we examined, that of Bill Clinton. As with JFK/LBJ, a big part of the reason for the improvement in the net marriage rate was probably the improved economic condition of the poor and the middle class; fewer money woes led to stronger marriages. Clinton was closely followed by Reagan.

At this point, it is worth asking: Is there anything differentiating the top administrations from the others in the sample that might explain their net marriage rates? One possibility is that the top four administrations were also the top four when it came to economic growth. Another thing to keep in mind is that the top three were all Democrats, and the two parties have very, very different views on keeping families together. Republicans tend to use the term *family values* to refer to abstinence, opposition to same-sex marriage, and, often, living according to biblical injunctions and precepts. Republicans tend to think that if families need aid, it should be provided by churches and private citizens. Democrats rarely use the term *family values*, but they do tend to feel there's a role for the government in ensuring that families have some minimum level of income and access to food and health care.

But can we say that the Democratic policies are "better" for the net marriage rate than Republican policies, based on the fact that the three top spots are held by Democrats? Maybe, but we need something more. One possible corroborating factoid came during the Clinton administration. Let's consider, first, the period from 1992 to 1997. During that time, the net marriage rate increased a smidge, from 4.5 per thousand to 4.6 per thousand. Given how dismal the marriage picture had been over the previous decades, not losing ground looks like a major success.

But then the net marriage rate retreated. Interestingly enough, the divorce rate also decreased during that time, which means that the drop in the net marriage rate came entirely from a decrease in marriages and not from an unfavorable change in the divorce rate.

So what happened to marriages beginning in 1997? Did a lot of people just get cold feet? Did men learn to string their fiancées along better than they had before? It shouldn't have been economic disincentives: Potential spouses should have had at least marginally better prospects since economic growth was stunningly, even unnaturally, strong. Maybe we have to look at welfare reform, which arrived in the snappily labeled Personal Responsibility and Work Opportunity Reconciliation Act of 1996. Though the new law began as an initiative of the Republican Congress, it was virtually hijacked by the Great Triangulator, Bill Clinton, and then made into a centerpiece of his administration. However, it retained a very Republican-ish approach toward welfare. The act limited the amount of time a person could receive welfare and forced many recipients to work in exchange for the aid they did receive.

The Personal Responsibility and Work Opportunity Reconciliation Act of 1996 was followed by other tools designed to reform welfare (we will look at one of these in a few pages), many of them intended to encourage unmarried parents to tie the knot or keep families together. Clearly, this very Republican approach to strengthening families did not work. In fact, if it didn't actually cause the decrease in the marriage rate that began in 1997, it certainly came about at a coincidental time. We don't know why this would cause a decrease in the marriage rate, but it may be that by encouraging people to get jobs as quickly as possible, it reduced their ability to obtain training and education, which would have resulted in greater future income. Alternatively, the new law might have reduced the incentives for fathers to come forward and confirm paternity of their children.

For the second time in a few pages, we want to remind readers that we do not take a position on gay marriage in this book. Nevertheless, we note that these days, in socially conservative circles the term *defense of marriage* has come to mean opposition to gay marriage with a sprinkle of abstinence-only policies thrown in for good measure. The ironic thing about those who tout their defense of marriage credentials is that, were they to rank the administrations on the effectiveness of their policies at promoting marriage, most of them would probably rank the three administrations that actually performed best as dead last.

## Unmarried Mothers

Raising children is a tough job. It's expensive, time-consuming, and often requires cleaning up malodorous body fluids. Put another way, it's a tough job for two people to do together, and quite a bit harder for a single person to do herself or (less frequently) himself.

As a result, most Americans, if asked, would express a desire to see more children entering the world in a family with two parents. Not that most Americans get asked or are likely to have their way on the issue any time soon: In 2006, over 1.6 million children in the United States were born to unmarried mothers, which represents about 38.5 percent of all births in the country. And as Figure 11-8 shows, that percentage has been growing.[9]

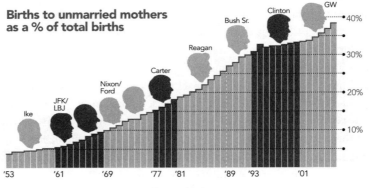

Figure 11-8

The percentage of children born to unmarried mothers increased almost tenfold, from 3.9 percent in 1952 to 38.5 percent in 2006. Furthermore, that percentage increased every single year, except for a short stint between 1994 and 1997. From 1997 to 2000, it would begin rising again, albeit at a relatively slow pace. A few years into the new millennium, however, the rate of increase in the percentage of children born to unmarried mothers was climbing relentlessly again. All of this seems to indicate that the Clinton administration was doing something different to cause these big changes in the rate of unwed motherhood.

As noted during the discussion on abortion, the Clinton administration spent considerable time, money, effort, and political capital changing the way that sex education was taught in the nation. The goal was multifaceted: By trying to ensure that if people did have sex they used contraceptives, the country could see a reduction in the rate of unwanted pregnancies, abortions, births out of wedlock, and STDs. And as we've seen, the Clinton administration certainly did preside over reductions in abortions and the rate of unmarried motherhood.[10]

So perhaps that explains why births out of wedlock actually stopped rising for a few years. But did anything happen in 1997 to bring this happy trend to a halt? Well, the funny thing is, one thing that did happen, or began, in 1997 was TANF, which stands for Temporary Assistance for Needy Families. TANF was introduced in the Personal Responsibility and Work Opportunity Reconciliation Act mentioned earlier and replaced Aid to Families with Dependent Children, the main source of welfare for, well, families with dependent children. What makes TANF particularly interesting in any discussion about changes in the rate of children born out of wedlock is that TANF was specifically designed by the Republican majority in Congress to reduce that rate.

The TANF approach to reducing the number of children born to single mothers had three main prongs. The first was to require single parents to work at least thirty hours a week in order to receive aid, making welfare a less attractive proposition than it had been before, according to the members of the Republican Revolution. And since most single parents who were raising children were mothers, the second prong dealt with the father: Child support enforcement was increased. Finally, funds were allocated to abstinence-only education. Members of the Republican Revolution explained that TANF would eliminate incentives to having children out of wedlock and strengthen families. The rest, as they say, is history. With the arrival of TANF, the only period in which the rate of children born to single mothers remained constant came to an end.

Figure 11-9 shows the annualized rate of increase in the percentage of children born to unmarried mothers.

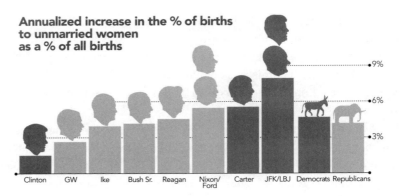

**Annualized increase in the % of births to unmarried women as a % of all births**

Clinton · GW · Ike · Bush Sr. · Reagan · Nixon/Ford · Carter · JFK/LBJ · Democrats · Republicans

Figure 11-9

As Figure 11-9 shows, the best performance was turned in by Bill Clinton, who, as we noted earlier, managed to hold the line steady for almost half of his administration. Clinton is followed by GW Bush. This could partly be due to happenstance or perhaps to following Bill Clinton. After all, the longer GW was in office, the more the rate of unwed motherhood appears to have picked up, and the data does not include his final two years.

For the most part, other than Clinton, we didn't find much evidence that any of the presidents put a lot of effort or political capital into dealing with unwed motherhood except Jimmy Carter—think of the aforementioned Conference on Families. However, Carter's efforts appear to have been unsuccessful, and he came in second from last in this measure. And since none of the presidents was particularly successful at reducing the percentage of children born out of wedlock, perhaps we should focus on failures—is there any particular reason, for instance, why the JFK/LBJ administration would come in dead last?

One reason for the dismal performance by JFK/LBJ may have to do with the very nature of the 1960s. It was the era of upheaval, a cultural and demographic earthquake when nearly everything was questioned. By mid-decade, the country was suffering through a prolonged infestation of flower children and hippies. Peace and love—especially love—was in the air. That kind of love can lead to children by anonymous fathers—or fathers sent to the rice paddies of Vietnam. Additionally, around this time, many people stopped considering out-of-wedlock births to be shameful; that is, the stigma of unwed motherhood was fading. As a result, more women who were unmarried but pregnant brought their pregnancy to term.

Despite the chance to balance free love against easily available contraception, during the JFK/LBJ administration the rate of unwed motherhood increased faster than during other administrations. This was at least in part because of events beyond their control. Does

that absolve JFK/LBJ from culpability? In a word, no. After all, if a tsunami is coming, the authorities should be trying everything to get people off the beach—and not engaging in business as usual. With societal mores changing, the need for action was even more urgent. Doing nothing—at least nothing useful—was worse from 1960 to 1968 than during other periods precisely because it led to worse results. We acknowledge that each administration faced different circumstances, but we have to hold each one responsible for managing its own era.

# Family Values: Conclusion

In the last three sections, we looked at family values–type issues: abortion, the net marriage rate, and unwed motherhood. The Overall Score on Family Values Issues we constructed would rank a president first on all the family values issues by giving him a score of 100 percent, and a president who ranked last on all these issues would earn a score of 0 percent.

Figure 11-10 shows how the presidents are ranked.

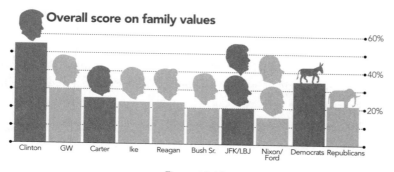

Figure 11-10

Clinton came out on top, far outdistancing all the others. His administration came in first on two family values–type issues—reducing the rate of abortions and reducing the rate of births out of wedlock—and he turned in a third-place finish on the net marriage rate.

One noteworthy point about Clinton is that his administration differed significantly—on message and approach regarding family values—from that of his predecessors and his successor. But messages and education—on issues like abortion and marriage and unwed motherhood—may stay in people's minds for a while and thus have an influence for a while. How long? Well, it turns out, not long. When we look at measures like the net marriage rate or births out of wedlock, we see that the trend under Bush Sr. continued for a year or two under Clinton, and the trend in Clinton's last few years continued for a year or two under GW, but that's about it.

Which leads us to GW, the self-proclaimed compassionate conservative, who came in second on family values. As we noted, on a few of these issues GW continued Clinton's very favorable trends for a few years, but only for a few years. Whether GW would have done as well following a president with less effective policies, we do not know. However, at the time of this writing, data for GW's entire term wasn't available; it will be interesting to see whether he looks as good once all the data is in.

GW was followed by Jimmy Carter, largely on the strength of his first-place finish on improving the marriage rate. As we noted earlier, Carter went so far as to hold a conference on strengthening families, but he had only mixed success; the number of births out of wedlock and the abortion rate increased rapidly during his administration.

The next four administrations all produced similar results. Which leaves the Nixon/Ford administration. Even discarding their results for abortions, they came in last on the net marriage rate and sixth on births out of wedlock. Clearly, that administration was not one during which the families of America were strengthened.

It is clear that neither party has a monopoly on family values. However, the Democrats on average do better than the Republicans. This is ironic considering how many Republicans run for office campaigning on family values. But given how many folks who talk the talk don't walk the walk, perhaps that should come as no surprise.

CHAPTER 12

# Investing in the Future

Throughout our history, the building and improvement
of transportation links have been vital to the
exploration and settlement of our country and to the
development of its commerce. We can all be
grateful that these processes have never ceased
and that the spirit of enterprise that motivated early
American pioneers still thrives today.

RONALD REAGAN
*Proclamation 5636—National Defense Transportation Day
and National Transportation Week, 198, April 23, 1987*[1]

Call it Daddy's Dilemma. We don't mean to be sexist, it's just that the guy
in the Oval Office has so far always been a guy. The point is this: Like
a parent holding the family purse strings, the president has to make choices
about how to spend money. Those choices sometimes boil down to making us
feel good now or making us feel good later.

Let's talk about feeling good now. For Daddy Feelgood, that could mean
using Friday's paycheck on a trip to the mall. He could buy the kids gourmet
pizza and ice cream, sponsor an evening of indulgence at the theater, and cap
it off with some high-end French pastries.

Daddy springs for the Missus to enjoy a buying spree at Abercrombie
and Fitch—and she returns the favor, picking up a new top-of-the-line fishing
rod, the one with the built-in GPS unit. On the way home, Daddy pulls into one
of those big box stores so little Suzie can buy herself a couple of DVDs. What
the heck, thinks Daddy, and he pulls out his wallet: one flat-panel, widescreen
plasma television to go, please.

You may be thinking that this was already covered in the chapters on fiscal responsibility and debt. And you're right, but there's another side to it. See, when Daddy is spending on fun stuff, there are some other things Daddy is not doing. He's not putting money away for the kids' education. He's not making home improvements. He's not buying a piece of property that he thinks might grow in value.

But come on. Those things are like, so *tomorrow*. What do they do for Daddy and his family today?

Odds are the people from Gallup or Harris are not going to call the various family members and ask how they feel about ol' Dad. But if they did call, we're thinking his approval rating would be through the roof, especially when everyone is down at the ice cream shop gorging on something decadent.

But years from now, there might be no money to pay for the kids' schooling, nothing but laughs from potential buyers when Daddy tries to sell the run-down house, and—despite years of healthy paychecks—nothing on the asset side of the family's ledger. So how would the family feel about Daddy and his financial choices then?

Of course, we could go the opposite way and make this a story about Daddy Scrooge—the guy who invests and socks money away and constantly prepares for a solid future. But doing things for the here and now? Not so much. This Daddy takes care of his family's future, but the family's present tense isn't just unhappy—it's shabby and unhealthy. Worse, by saving money now, Daddy has probably set up some higher costs down the line (like paying for a therapist).

The parallel is obvious. The president must constantly choose between taking care of the country's current needs and desires and making investments that will provide for its future health.

If he follows the first path, he'll be more likely to have the support of voters. If he follows the second, he'll get kudos from the historians. Is the verdict of history enough of an incentive for presidents to do the right thing? Well, it might be based on two things we know about people who run for president. One is that everyone who runs for president claims to be very patriotic, and patriotic people want the country to succeed. The other trait common to every person who has ever run for president is a healthy ego. Nobody with that kind of personality wants to be remembered as the worst president ever.

So the presidency, like parenthood, is a balancing act: Every president wants the nation to be better off in the future (we think so, anyway), even if taking care of business right now is generally the priority. But striking the right balance is not easy. Some presidents have been more courageous, more farsighted or luckier, and they were able to take the longer view. We've already seen that some presidents paid down the debt, but others did not. That's just one way some presidents have shown how they feel about the future. But a president's concern for the future can manifest itself many ways.

Take Eisenhower's massive plan for a national highway system, one of the grandest examples of an investment that has paid dividends for decades. But from Eisenhower's perspective, the money might have bought more political bang if spent another way. Yes, the program did provide thousands of jobs and pump money into the economy, but the lion's share of the benefits came long after Ike had retired.

It's a matter of degree, a sliding scale where the more farsighted of our leaders push a little harder to invest in the American future. Let's see how the presidents did on this measure.

# Education

We believe that children are our future. Teach them well and let them lead the way. . . Wait a second—why are we channeling Whitney Houston? We aren't going to be able to hit those high notes. But Whitney does make a good point—education matters. And not just for children; training adults in new skills can help them find jobs and move the economy forward.

This notion that education is vital and that the state has a role to play in it dates back a long way. After leaving office, our third president, Thomas Jefferson, wrote in a letter to our second president, John Adams:

> A bill for the more general diffusion of learning . . . proposed to divide every county into wards of five or six miles square; . . . to establish in each ward a free school for reading, writing and common arithmetic; to provide for the annual selection of the best subjects from these schools, who might receive at the public expense a higher degree of education at a district school; and from these district schools to select a certain number of the most promising subjects, to be completed at an University where all the useful sciences should be taught. Worth and genius would thus have been sought out from every condition of life, and completely prepared by education for defeating the competition of wealth and birth for public trusts. [2]

Jefferson and Adams were often at odds about, well, nearly everything. Jefferson was a firm believer in states' rights with many checks and balances.

Adams, on the other hand, was a proponent of a strong federal government. He had signed into law the Alien and Sedition Act, which bore more than a passing resemblance to the USA Patriot Act of 2001. Yet the two agreed on the government's role in ensuring that everyone had an education, as we can see by one of Adams's "Thoughts on Government":

> Laws for the liberal education of youth, especially of the lower class of people, are so extremely wise and useful, that, to a humane and generous mind, no expense for this purpose would be thought extravagant. [3]

Unfortunately, measuring the quality of education is difficult. How can you tell if people are actually learning more or if what they're learning is useful? Testing helps. But consider the No Child Left Behind law. It requires plenty of testing. However, there is a fair amount of debate about whether teachers "teach to the test" and whether kids develop the skills needed to answer questions on which teachers don't expect their students to be tested. Similarly, measuring graduation rates or the percentage of children of a certain age in school is problematic because there's no guarantee that the children are actually learning anything.

We can't measure how well each administration does with education—we're not saying it is impossible, merely that we don't see how to do it with publicly available data. But we can measure an administration's financial commitment to education; all else being equal, the more an administration values education, the more it will be willing to spend per student.

Figure 12-1 shows total federal spending per pupil in public elementary and secondary schools since 1952, adjusted for inflation.[4]

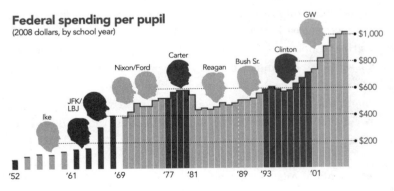

Figure 12-1

In the school year ending in 1952, the federal government spent $69.13 per student (in 2008 dollars) enrolled in public elementary, junior high, and high school. Spending rose slowly but steadily until the mid-1960s, when it began increasing more rapidly as part of the Great Society and the war on poverty. By 1980 real spending on education and training had reached $589 per person—a level that it would not reach again until 1993. However, beginning in the mid-1990s education spending appears to have increasingly been a priority, and it increased rapidly through the end of our sample period.

Broken down by administration, Figure 12-2 shows the annualized change in real spending per pupil.

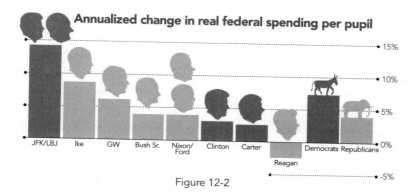

Figure 12-2

The biggest annualized increases in spending per student by a long shot occurred in the JFK/LBJ years, with the biggest spending increases occurring in the last four years when Johnson was president. Johnson, whose first job was that of schoolteacher, was aggressive about using the national government and the federal purse to fight the war on poverty as well as to advance his Great Society and civil rights programs. Among other efforts, he shepherded into law the 1965 Higher Education Act—a proposal meant to strengthen the country's education system.

The second-fastest increases in education spending per student occurred under Ike. Like LBJ, Eisenhower was from Texas (though he was raised in Kansas). He made education and training a part of what he called "dynamic conservatism." One tangible component of dynamic conservatism was the creation of the Department of Health, Education, and Welfare at the cabinet level.

Education also figured heavily in Eisenhower's actions to comply with the Supreme Court's landmark 1954 ruling in *Brown v. Board of Education*, which declared segregation in the public school system unconstitutional.

The ruling was contested for years, sometimes in events that forced the administration to respond. Most notably, an angry mob of white people tried to prevent nine black students from enrolling in Little Rock Senior High School on September 23, 1957. Eisenhower—who was often disparaged by liberals for his cautious conservatism—sent troops from the 101st Airborne Division and federalized the entire Arkansas National Guard in order to ensure that the students received the education that the Supreme Court had ruled was their right.

Coming in third on education spending on public elementary and secondary schools is GW. The man who famously observed, "Rarely is the question asked, is our children learning?" was himself the product of a very, very expensive education,[5] and he married a one-time schoolteacher. GW made the No Child Left Behind legislation a signature element of his administration's education policy.

Interestingly enough, Bush's first secretary of education, Rod Paige, was selected for having presided as superintendent over the so-called "Houston miracle"—a dramatic reduction in the dropout rate in Houston high schools. It would later turn out that the dropout rate had, well, dropped so low in large part because the school system Paige had overseen was simply dropping the dropouts from its books. Controversy followed Paige to the Department of Education. During his tenure there he began paying several syndicated columnists to write glowingly about No Child Left Behind (all the while failing to disclose those payments).

GW was followed (in close succession to each other) by his father, Nixon/Ford, Clinton, and Carter.[6] President Carter is noteworthy on this list not just for the mediocrity of his ranking, but also because he finished so low despite pushing for and signing into law a measure establishing the Department of Education.

And that department was a thorn in the side of the president who finished in last place on education: Reagan. Reagan believed the federal government had no place in education and that government spending on education was just a way for government bureaucrats to tell people what they could and could not do. One of his early goals as president was to abolish the Department of Education, which he referred to as Carter's "new bureaucratic boondoggle."

Reagan failed in this goal, partly because of his first education secretary, Terrel Bell. Although appointed by Reagan to dismantle the new department, Bell wasn't your typical Reagan appointee. For one thing, he drove a U-Haul to Washington when he got the job. And while Bell admired Reagan deeply, he described the president's cabinet meetings wryly like this: "I didn't like jelly beans and my chair didn't fit."[7] Despite Bell's avowed dislike of jelly beans, he was apparently fond of blue ribbons. He established the Blue Ribbon Schools Program to honor high-performing schools and convinced Reagan that it would be a good idea to appoint a blue-ribbon panel to look into the state of American education.

The end result was a report titled "A Nation at Risk." In many ways the report mimicked Reagan's own utterances on education, being long on opinion and devoid of anything resembling actual facts or data. But the opinion it did present was very different from Reagan's, namely that "The Federal Government has the primary responsibility to identify the national interest in education." Making matters worse from the perspective of many Reagan loyalists, the report made absolutely no mention of prayer in school.[8]

Reagan wasn't happy. He formally accepted the report, but in the subsequent press conference he gave a speech completely ignoring its findings.[9] Despite that, the report's conclusions caught on with the American public. Bell resigned from his post a year after the release of "A Nation at Risk," but by then Reagan was no longer talking about dismantling the Department of Education. Instead, he was telling the nation "The Federal Government is doing its part."[10] And years later, Reagan would be quoting from "A Nation at Risk" as if he had approved of its conclusions all along.[11]

# Research & Development

Federally funded research has brought us all sorts of things many of us use every day, from the Internet to thermonuclear warheads. That funding has led to improvements in the nutritional yield of farmland, reductions in the incidence of many diseases, better and faster transportation, souped-up surveillance technology, and more efficient weapons of war.

But the federal government's role in research and development (henceforth R&D) extends further than opening its wallet. It can create conditions that make the private sector more (or perhaps less) likely to put its own dollars into R&D. This can be done directly, through tax incentives on the one hand or laws prohibiting certain types of research on the other. It can also be done by creating a climate—in times and places where research is valued and encouraged, bright people brimming with intellectual curiosity find themselves able to make a living developing new things. But in times and places where a premium is placed on mythology rather than science, bright people brimming with intellectual curiosity will find other outlets, such as creating opaque–financial instruments that bear a certain resemblance to time bombs.

As with much else that goes on in the country, the president has a lot of influence over the amount of R&D that takes place. As we've noted throughout the book, he shapes the federal budget and influences the laws. But he also sets the tone, partly through his appointments to key positions, such as secretary of energy and director of NASA, and partly through the very words he uses. A president who sees "controversies" in geology, biology, or cosmology, where none are recognized by reputable geologists, biologists, or cosmologists, sets the country on a different course than one who keeps his cherished but ignorant beliefs to himself.

Figure 12-3 shows total spending on R&D from 1953 to 2007, the last year for which data is available, as a percentage of GDP.[12]

Perhaps the most interesting feature of Figure 12-3 is the increase in spending on R&D as a percentage of GDP during the 1950s. The big increase was largely due to competition between the United States and the USSR to develop technology that could be militarized. While the United States perceived itself as technologically superior in the 1940s and 1950s, the Soviet Union announced in 1954 that it would be launching an artificial satellite. Eisenhower "me-tooed," telling the world that the United States had the same intentions in the following year. However, the Soviets succeeded first with the launch of *Sputnik* in 1957. The already alarmed American public panicked, and the result was a new agency, the National Aeronautics and Space Administration—NASA (shepherded through Congress by then–Senate majority leader Lyndon Johnson)—and the National Defense Education Act of 1958, both of which were used to funnel research money into the sort of scientific research deemed necessary to beat the Soviet Union.

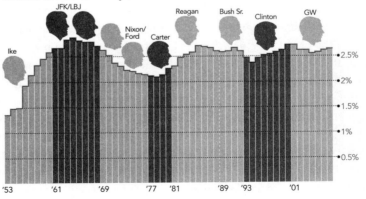

**Research and development as a % of GDP**

Figure 12-3

The annualized change in spending on R&D as a percentage of GDP by administration is summarized in Figure 12-4.[13]

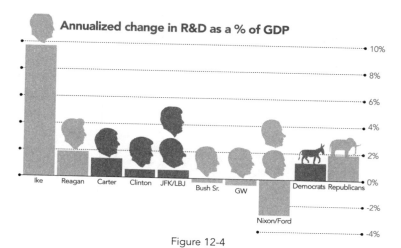

**Annualized change in R&D as a % of GDP**

Figure 12-4

By far the biggest increase in R&D spending as a percentage of GDP took place under Eisenhower. As noted earlier, this was in large part because of the space race and competition with the USSR. There were other factors at play as well. The national fascination with science had started before Eisenhower took office; the National Science Foundation—the government's premier agency for funding R&D and education in the nonmedical sciences— had been formed in 1950. Even Hollywood was doing its part, combining fear of annihilation with an awe of technology in films like *The Day the Earth Stood Still* and *Forbidden Planet*.

Reagan came in second, with a big chunk of the spending going toward the Strategic Defense Initiative. Colloquially referred to as "Star Wars," this was Reagan's plan to defend the country against nuclear attack by shooting down incoming ballistic missiles. While the goal never came remotely close to being accomplished, a number of Reagan supporters insisted—albeit based on limited evidence—that Star Wars was in large part responsible for bringing down the USSR.

Following Reagan came the three Democratic administrations. After years of science having been starved for spending under the Nixon/Ford administration, Carter resurrected a number of previously halted high-profile, high-tech projects, including the Hubble telescope and the MX missile. He also funded the start of a number of completely radical technologies, including the Advanced Technology Bomber (which became the B-2, also known as the "stealth bomber").

Clinton followed Carter. Fifth place was occupied by JFK/LBJ.[14] The relatively mediocre showing by JFK/LBJ is surprising; putting a man on the moon was not cheap, after all. But spending on R&D during the JFK/LBJ administration peaked in 1964 as other priorities, including the war on poverty and the war in Vietnam, took priority.

Ranking behind the Democrats were the two Bush presidents, both of whom reduced spending on R&D as a percentage of GDP. However, the biggest reduction came under Nixon/Ford. The administration that started the National Oceanic and Atmospheric Administration (NOAA) and the Environmental Protection Agency (EPA) cut R&D spending each and every year. Sometimes forming new agencies is much cheaper than funding the sort of work those agencies are intended to carry out.

## Infrastructure

One way to invest in the future is to build infrastructure. Roads, ports, and bridges make modern commerce possible; dams and levees prevent damaging floods; and power plants and transmission lines help illuminate our lives. Heck, even a short fence will keep the alligators out. All these things cost money. Lots of it. But we all like toilets that flush, roads without potholes, bridges that let us get across the river, and knowing that the water coming out of our taps isn't going to kill us.

In this section, we look at spending on the sorts of infrastructure that just about everyone uses every day. Nonmilitary infrastructure, or what the Office of Management Budget refers to as nondefense physical capital, is the sort of infrastructure spending that has the most impact on the average American. This money includes direct expenditures by the federal government as well as grants to states and local governments. We will measure infrastructure spending by the priority each administration gives it; that is, according to its share of the budget.

Figure 12-5 shows infrastructure spending as a share of the budget going back to 1940, the first year for which data is available.[15]

In 1940, with the economy still recovering from the Great Depression, the New Deal at full throttle, and military spending at pre–Pearl Harbor levels, more than a quarter of the federal budget went toward nondefense physical capital. A lot of us attended schools built many decades earlier during the New Deal, then hung out in the afternoons at New Deal–built libraries. Many of those buildings are still in use, just as there are still neighborhoods with sidewalks, staircases, and bridges bearing the Works Progress Administration

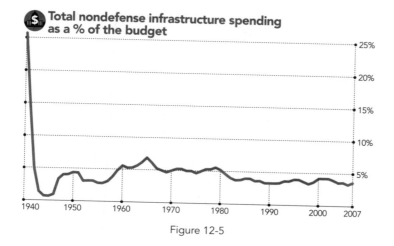

Figure 12-5

logo. But after the attack on Pearl Harbor, spending was diverted toward the war effort and infrastructure spending fell to a fifth of 1 percent of the budget. After the war, as military spending ebbed, nondefense infrastructure spending rose slightly as a percentage of the budget, but only slightly. The postwar high-water mark came in 1965 with spending on nondefense infrastructure reaching 6.8 percent of the budget.

Figure 12-6 shows infrastructure investment from 1953 on, by administration.

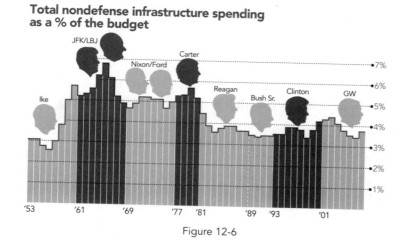

Figure 12-6

The annualized changes in civilian infrastructure investment by administration are summarized in Figure 12-7.

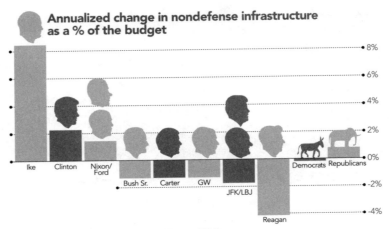

**Annualized change in nondefense infrastructure as a % of the budget**

Figure 12-7

The biggest annualized increases in nondefense physical infrastructure investment, by quite a bit, occurred under Ike. Perhaps the signature investments occurred as part of the construction of the interstate highway system, authorized by the Federal-Aid Highway Act of 1956. Eisenhower's zeal was due in part to his experience in World War II, when he saw firsthand the usefulness of the German autobahn network.

The Clinton administration came next, followed by Nixon/Ford. The remaining administrations all reduced spending on nondefense infrastructure as a share of the budget, with the biggest reduction occurring under Ronald Reagan.

Emblematic of his relationship with nondefense infrastructure spending, Reagan vetoed the Surface Transportation and Uniform Relocation Assistance Act of 1987 (STURAA), considered by many to be the last authorization bill of the interstate era. This was the first and last veto of a highway bill in the twentieth century, but it was overridden[16] so the money was spent anyway. Given Reagan's views on nondefense infrastructure spending, perhaps it is ironic that the largest and (at the time it was built) the most expensive building in Washington, D.C., used for nondefense purposes bears his name (i.e., the Ronald Reagan Building and International Trade Center). On the other hand, as we saw earlier in the book, despite all his rhetoric, Reagan wasn't averse to increasing the size and scope of the federal government or spending vast sums of taxpayers' money, so maybe the building is a fitting monument after all.

While infrastructure is an easy part of the budget to shortchange, we do so at our peril. Or rather, presidents do it at *our* peril—though the danger is often invisible at the time. Just as individuals must spend time and money maintaining their homes to avoid trouble later on, infrastructure that isn't maintained will fall apart. When bridges collapse and drivers plunge into the river, when levees break and cities are submerged underwater, that's when we pay the price for our government skimping on infrastructure.

# Energy Independence

To many Americans, the Middle East and North Africa (MENA) are complex and almost incomprehensible places. We don't understand the languages, the religions, the feuds, or sometimes even the food of the people who live there. And yet there have been many crises in those regions that have involved the United States, beginning in the earliest days of the Republic ("to the shores of Tripoli," anyone?). In recent decades such involvements have ranged from Ike's intervention in the 1956 Suez crisis to GW's invasion of Iraq in 2003, with a sprinkling of crises in between, including the 1973 oil embargo, the 1979 Iranian hostage crisis, the –1983 Beirut barracks bombings, and the first Gulf War in 1991.

What makes MENA important to most Americans is oil, one of our main sources of energy. In 2008, Americans consumed 19.4 million barrels of oil a day, of which we imported 11 million.[17] While our next-door neighbor, Canada, is the biggest exporter of oil to the United States, the second largest, from which we obtained about 1.5 million barrels a day, is Saudi Arabia. Put another way, our imports helped fund the education and training for fifteen of the hijackers on 9/11. Other countries in MENA on which we depend for imports include Algeria, Chad, Iraq, and Kuwait. The list of countries from which we obtain substantial amounts of oil also includes somewhat unfriendly countries like Venezuela, and countries whose stability is sometimes in question, like Nigeria, Azerbaijan, and Republic of the Congo. All told, almost half of U.S. oil imports come directly from the aforementioned countries.[18]

While oil makes up almost 40 percent of total U.S. energy consumption,[19] the United States also consumes substantial quantities of

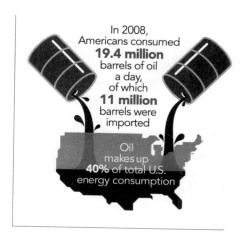

In 2008, Americans consumed **19.4 million** barrels of oil a day, of which **11 million** barrels were imported

Oil makes up **40%** of total U.S. energy consumption

coal, natural gas, and nuclear power. Parts of the country also obtain a lot of energy from hydroelectric dams, and in recent years, we've been getting increasing (but still relatively very small) amounts of renewable nonhydro-electric energy (e.g., solar, wind, and geothermal). However, the tremendous thirst that we Americans have for energy has by far outstripped our domestic production.

In 2007 Americans produced about 71.7 billion BTUs (British Thermal Units) of energy and we consumed about 101.6 billion BTUs.[20] The difference is imported, making us vulnerable to the whims of the suppliers on whom we depend. That lesson was driven home during the 1973 Arab oil embargo. Since then, most presidents have, to some degree, endorsed the idea of energy independence—some much more than others.

Fortunately, there are ways to reach that goal. Unfortunately, paying it lip service is not one of them. To cut our dependence on foreign energy sources, we need to increase production of energy, decrease consumption, or both. These are goals that whoever sits in the Oval Office can help us achieve. For example, parts of the United States have vast potential for generating energy from wind; unfortunately, most of that potential resides in areas like North Dakota, where there are few population centers and much of the wind tends to blow through the night when electricity consumption is lowest. By building out the grid to transport wind-generated power to metropolitan areas or encouraging work on methods of storing that power (e.g., tax incentives for battery development or for the increased use of "pump storage" by power companies),[21] the government can help the country become more energy independent.

The president can also encourage Americans to consume less. Making the electrical grid more efficient, providing incentives for Americans to weatherize their homes and use energy-efficient appliances, and demanding more fuel-efficient vehicles would all go a long way toward reaching the goal of energy independence.

So there's a lot a president can do if he cares to. However, it's pretty hard to see much evidence that most of our recent presidents have cared to. Perhaps the most notable energy-related action taken by a president since 1952 was the creation of the Department of Energy by Jimmy Carter. But, the position of head of the Department of Energy, held through 2008 has largely been by politicians, political hacks, and attorneys. Reagan went so far as to appoint a dentist to the spot (in fairness, the man had been governor of South Carolina, which means that at least he had political experience), but then Reagan's goal was to dismantle the entire department. Few secretaries of energy displayed anything remotely resembling expertise in the field, yet these were the people making policy decisions on such inconsequential trifles as nuclear power regulation.[22]

So maybe it's not surprising that presidents haven't been doing a whole lot to ensure our energy independence. Take a look at Figure 12-8, showing domestic energy production as a percentage of domestic energy consumption.[23]

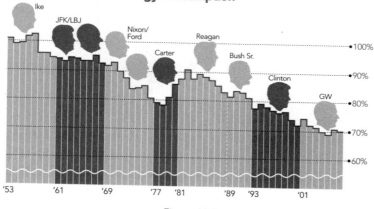

**Domestic energy production as a % of domestic energy consumption**

Figure 12-8

When Ike was inaugurated, the country produced more energy than it consumed—just barely—but that changed by the time he left office. Since then Americans have become more and more (and more) dependent on energy imports.

As we've noted before, the president has many tools at his disposal to promote energy independence, but there are also many factors beyond his control. Some make it harder, but some help. Manufacturing, which tends to be energy-intensive, has become less important to the overall economy. Improvements in technology have made the remaining factories vastly more efficient. From the standpoint of supply, there is the undeniable fact that the pool of oil beneath U.S. soil may be vast, but it is not infinite. Neither does the president control how other nations handle their own oil. Decisions about how much they tap and bring to market are made in their own best interests, not ours.

Still, we judge the presidents on how they cope with what they've got, so let's look at the trends year to year. Figure 12-9 illustrates advance or retreat toward energy independence, summarizing the annualized changes in energy consumption as a percentage of energy production over the span of each administration.

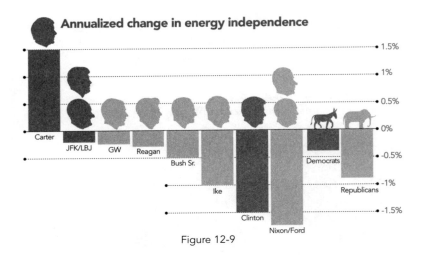

Figure 12-9

The only administration to move the country in the direction of energy independence was Jimmy Carter. Carter took energy issues seriously. Spurred along by an oil crisis and energy prices that almost doubled over four years,[24] he got Congress to create the Department of Energy and expand fuel economy standards. He even referred to the 1979 oil crisis as "the moral equivalent of war." In one of his best-known—and most mocked—speeches he asked Americans to turn down their thermostats, and he led the way symbolically, wearing sweaters, installing a woodstove in the president's quarters of the White House, and having solar panels placed on the White House roof.

Americans have tended to resist being lectured—and in the late 1970s they were especially unenthusiastic about being asked to make sacrifices. Carter's high tone, moral urgency, and symbolic displays would have had a lot less impact without support of a more potent force: higher prices. After all, nothing says carpool like paying a buck and a quarter a gallon to fill up the old Pacer, at least in 1980. (That was about $3.25 a gallon in 2008 dollars.) But Carter should still get credit for responding to the crisis and for pushing changes—like higher-mileage cars—that helped people save more and continue to have an impact today. On the production side of the ledger, Carter pushed for a tax on oil profits that would be used to fund research on synthetic fuels.

The remaining administrations all stood by while the nation became ever more reliant on foreign energy. The least bad job was turned in by JFK/LBJ. A recession had been ongoing when that administration was elected, and was still in progress when they took office. As part of his plan for economic recovery and long-term growth, laid out less than a month after he became president, JFK explained that the easy availability of energy was vital. He favored nuclear power and more efficient usage of existing resources by "regional cooperative pooling of electrical power."[25]

JFK/LBJ were followed in the rankings by George W. Bush. GW didn't do much to encourage conservation. He didn't have to, given the rapid rise in energy prices over which he presided.[26] However, the man who had failed in the oil business before becoming president and whose vice president had been CEO of Halliburton did encourage more production of oil and natural gas. During his tenure, oil and gas producers received new tax breaks, were exempted from compliance with certain portions of the Clean Water Act,[27] received protection against some lawsuits, and were given more access to drill on public lands.[28] The high prices didn't exactly dissuade producers either.

Reagan came in fourth place, despite removing the solar panels from the White House roof. He benefited from many of the programs—or the price-induced conservation—begun during the Carter era. Bush Sr., Ike, and Clinton followed Reagan.

Nixon/Ford had the worst record on energy independence of any administration. The Arab oil embargo, the dramatic spike in the price of energy—which nudged the U.S. economy further into recession—came on their watch. Interestingly enough, so did the peak domestic production of oil, which occurred in 1970. Nixon reacted by relaxing emissions standards, pushing forward the Alaska pipeline, and promoting more nuclear power research. However, most of his initiatives didn't have much effect, at least over the long term.

# Investing in the Future: Conclusion

In this chapter, we looked at ways the president could invest in the future by building nondefense infrastructure, promoting R&D, spending on education, and leading the county toward energy independence. We constructed an Overall Score on Investing in the Future in such a way that the president who came in first on all four measures would have a score of 100 percent, and the one who came in last in all four would have a score of 0 percent. Figure 12-10 summarizes the results.

The best score went to Ike, who came in first in R&D promotion and infrastructure construction, and second on education spending. His only less-than-stellar performance came on energy independence, in which he ranked sixth.

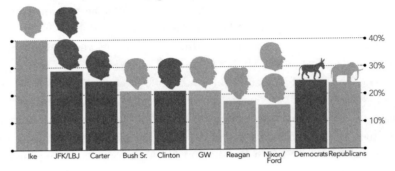

**Overall score on investing in the future**

Figure 12-10

Second and third place went to two Democratic administrations, those of JFK/LBJ and Jimmy Carter. They were followed by the two Bushes and Clinton, who were tied for fourth. The Nixon/Ford administration just managed to edge out Reagan to take last place. In general, Democrats did a smidge better than Republicans by the measures used in this chapter. But it was basically a tie.

However, in this chapter we did neglect one way in which presidents can invest in the future, which we covered earlier in the book: by paying down debt. Sometimes it's important to spend—even run up deficits—but an administration that pays down debt frees up options for its successors, options that may be sorely needed in times of crisis. Had each administration's performance at fiscal responsibility been included here, Reagan, Bush Sr., and GW would all look somewhat worse when measured on their performance at investing in the future.

# Conclusion

★ ★ ★

So there it is. A group portrait in data. A look at the last five decades of presidential performance from a range of directions. More like a series of group portraits, actually—with some of the guys in the foreground looking confident and others in the back looking befuddled. And which presidents were in the foreground seemed to change somewhat from portrait to portrait.

We covered many issues with these data portraits, and we ranked the administrations on how they did on those issues. We tried to cover the important issues—issues like economic growth, jobs, family values, and crime. There were some key issues we did not cover because we simply could not find adequate data to quantify them—issues like gender inequality, race relations, and immigration.

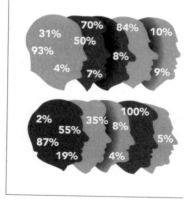

Data was a problem throughout the book—there's a lot of data out there but it doesn't always come prepackaged in a way that answers relevant questions. So we repackaged the data, sometimes adjusting for population or inflation, other times looking at spending on an issue relative to total spending. But we tried to answer the key questions: Did a president pay down the debt? Did he reduce the crime rate? Are we better off now than when he took office?

In this conclusion, we take the logical next step. We rank the administrations based on their performance on all the issues. The overall score leaves out obviously partisan issues that matter mostly to either Democrats or Republicans. Instead, it focuses on things that most Americans care about. We've also wrapped some issues into larger categories; for example, we do not include performance on abortion reduction, but rather "family values," an overarching category that includes reducing the overall number of abortions.

Similarly, we have included fiscal responsibility (but not ranked the presidents on government spending and government revenues, since both are crucial to fiscal responsibility). We also left out the growth in real GDP per capita and the growth in the national debt, but included overall economic growth; that is, growth in the real net GDP per capita. Real net GDP per capita, after all, encompasses both growth in real GDP per capita and growth in the national debt.

Here is the complete list of categories on which we are ranking the administrations:

- Fiscal Responsibility
- Economic Growth
- Jobs
- Income and Wealth
- Health Care
- Crime
- The Public Mood
- Family Values
- Investing in the Future

Our approach is similar to the one we followed elsewhere in the book; the scores were constructed so that a president who was ranked first in each of the issues would have a score of 100 percent, and a president who ranked last would have a score of 0 percent.

So, without further ado, who scored worst? Who scored best? The envelope, please . . . . (See Figure C-1.)

Scoring highest by far was Bill Clinton, with a score of 64.6 percent. He came in first in six of nine issues: fiscal responsibility, jobs, wealth creation, crime reduction, the public mood, and (much to our surprise) promoting family values. He also turned in second-place performances on economic growth and health care. His worst performance was a three-way tie for fourth place on investing in the future.

Reagan came in a distant second with a score of 26.5 percent; his best performance was a second-place finish (after Bill Clinton) on crime. He also posted third-place finishes in economic growth, job creation, and the public mood. He came in fourth on fiscal responsibility, the growth of wealth and income, and family values. However, investing in the future wasn't his thing. In that category, he came in second to last, doing just barely better than the Nixon/Ford administration.

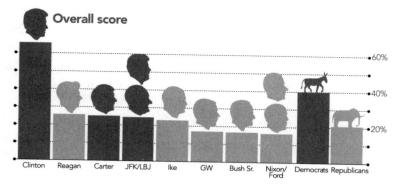

Figure C-1

Reagan's score on the public mood bears noting: The Great Communicator did create—or at least influence—the perception that it was "morning in America," that "America was back," and so on. Consumer confidence rose steadily on his watch. But he also came in fifth place on suicide rates, which may mean his message did not resonate among those in despair.

Contrary to current mythology, Reagan's message did not resonate very much with the investor class of the time either; Reagan came in fifth in terms of real growth in the stock market. Nor did Reagan's message necessarily shape larger economic realities: The value of the dollar actually fell during his administration, despite his upbeat tone. Morning in America was also the age of the Rising Sun. But savvy investors and foreign exchange traders also understood that without strong investments in the future, the future could not be very bright after all.

Reagan was followed closely by Jimmy Carter (25.5 percent) and JFK/LBJ (23.9 percent). Carter had a first-place finish on health care, a second-place finish on fiscal responsibility, three third-place finishes (income and wealth creation, family values, and investing in the future), and a fourth-place finish on jobs. The man whom the public associated with the word *malaise* came in sixth on the public mood and seventh on crime.

The JFK/LBJ administration scored fourth. It came in first on economic growth and had three second-place finishes: jobs, wealth and income, and investing in the future. It also came in fourth on the public mood, but its remaining scores were all subpar: fifth on fiscal responsibility, seventh on health care, and dead last on crime.

Ike came next with a score of 22.2 percent, though it should be noted that he was not ranked on health care issues due to lack of data. In issues for which there was data, Ike's best score came on investing in the future, where he ranked first. That is no surprise for the political architect behind America's freeway system. Keeping with the theme of investing in the future, Ike also came in third in fiscal responsibility, diligently working to pay down debt. He also had a pair of fourth-place finishes (economic growth and family values), but he did below average on crime (fifth place), the public mood (also fifth place), wealth and income (sixth place), and jobs.

The last three administrations were all pretty tightly bunched. The best of the bottom three was GW, with a score of 18 percent. He produced a second-best finish on family values, a third place on crime, and he tied for fourth on investing in the future. GW also came in sixth on jobs and health care and dead last on fiscal responsibility, economic growth, and wealth creation. It bears noting that while GW's best score came on family values, data for several of the issues that go into the family values score were not available for the last few years of GW's administration. For example, as of this writing, data on abortions ran only through 2005, data on births out of wedlock was only available through 2006, and data on net marriages was only available through 2007. It may be more than just a coincidence that GW's best performance was on the issue that is missing the most data, in which case his ranking may yet drop as more information becomes available. But we have to go with what we've got.

So for now GW did better than his father, Bush Sr., who had a score of 17.6 percent. Bush Sr. scored in the top half on only two issues: the public mood (second place) and investing in the future (fourth place). He also came in fifth on health care, and had a pair of sixth-place finishes (crime and family values). On all the economic issues—fiscal responsibility, economic growth, jobs, and income and wealth creation—he came in seventh.

Last place, with a score of 17.5 percent, was the Nixon/Ford administration. Its best scores were a third-place finish on health care, a fourth-place finish on crime, and a trio of fifth-place finishes (economic growth, jobs, and income and wealth). It also came in sixth on fiscal responsibility, seventh on the public mood, and last on investing in the future.

Democrats easily outdistanced Republicans, 40 percent to 21 percent.

So as much as we have tried to stick to the facts and leave our opinions at home, we're stuck with an uncomfortable conclusion: From 1953 to 2008,

Democrats outperformed Republicans on most of the measures covered in this book.

Is it possible that this is all due to chance? Are the Democrats simply luckier than their Republican counterparts—perhaps things just happen to go wrong when Republicans are in office and they just happen to go right when Democrats are in office? Maybe the various cycles we have seen are beyond presidential control and just happened to go wrong more often for Republicans. Let's consider some things that might go wrong:

- It could be control of Congress. But as we saw in Chapter 1, economic growth doesn't seem to be affected much by which party has control of Congress. And as we will see in Appendix 1, control of Congress is a red herring; the president has a lot more control over what goes on in the country than Congress does.

- Maybe the American public elects Democrats when things are good and elects Republicans when things need cleaning up. This explanation also doesn't work—or at least, it requires a little finagling. That is, in 2000 GW didn't win the popular vote. In 1992, Clinton had only a plurality in a three-way race. If Gore was "supposed" to win because things were good, then shouldn't GW have had good numbers? If Clinton wasn't supposed to, then shouldn't his numbers have been bad?

- Alternatively, it could be easier to put up good numbers when following a poor performer and harder when following a great performer. But that doesn't fit the facts either. Reagan's second-place finish looks pretty good, and it followed Carter's third-place finish. Conversely, Bush Sr. did poorly, and he followed second-place Reagan. On a more granular level, on a number of issues GW's best performances came early in his administration, before he reversed many of his predecessor's policies.

- It could be that Republicans actually have better policies than Democrats but there's a lag before those policies produce results. Democrats look better simply because they follow Republican administrations. This reasoning also doesn't quite wash. Bush Sr. followed not only a Republican, but the man who is often held up as the Republican Party's paragon, so he should have had a very strong performance. Similarly, this line of reasoning would require Republicans to attribute part of Reagan's performance to Carter, which few Republicans are willing to do.

So if none of the bad-luck scenarios fit, what else is there? Well, perhaps we are asking the wrong questions, or we are looking at the wrong data. But it is difficult to see how economic growth or the national debt or jobs don't matter. We also don't believe we looked at the wrong data, or the right data the wrong way, though if that happened, perhaps someone smarter than we are can show us how it happened.

But maybe, with a bit more data on social issues or crime or the public mood, or even on topics we haven't examined at all, the rankings on noneconomic issues might look better for Republican presidents. Perhaps Republicans have done a better job reducing gender or income inequality after all. But on economic issues we think we have been pretty thorough, seeking out the best available data covering a broad swath of the economy. We don't see how the discrepancy between Democrats and Republicans can be due to our negligence.

For instance, consider the major economic meltdowns of the last hundred years and change, the events that required massive amounts of (usually government) intervention to mitigate: the Panic of 1907, the Depression of 1920–1921, the Great Depression that began in 1929, the collapse of the Bretton Woods system and the stagflation of the 1970s, the S&L debacle of the 1980s, and the Great Recession that began in 2007. During all but one of these debacles, the president was a Republican. And in all but one of the instances in which the president was a Republican, the start of the problem began well over four years after a Democrat had last occupied the Oval Office.

None of this is to say that Democrats do well on the economy, merely that they don't do as poorly as Republicans. So why the difference? Well, maybe Democrats simply had better policies, as noted below:

- The Democrats' inclination to spend more on the poor and middle class versus the Republicans' focus on big business and the wealthy tends to be better for society because it is more likely to make use of otherwise idle resources. Maybe by paying more attention to the needs of the have-nots, Democrats remedy imbalances in the economy, whereas by focusing on the needs of the haves, Republicans tend to exacerbate those imbalances, as the haves generally get their way anyhow. That raises an intriguing notion: Giving in to business may not actually be good for business. In the long run, the economy thrives on competition in which strong companies survive and the weak ones are driven out of business, not coddled and protected with subsidies and regulatory protections.

- Following up on the previous point, the Republican concept of rights is geared toward "active rights" rather than "passive rights." That means, for example, that one person's right to do what she wants on her property, including emitting dangerous pollutants, may override another person's right not to breathe polluted air. This viewpoint may impose heavy costs on third parties (what economists call "externalities") and, ultimately, society at large.

- Maybe Republicans focus too much on lowering taxes as the solution to all the country's ills. As we noted earlier, every Republican administration cut the real tax burden. Every Democrat raised it. Perhaps taxes have been too low to fund the optimal level of government activity in society, and Democrats are more likely to move the economy toward the optimal point, while Republicans are more likely to move the economy even further away from that point. Or maybe the emphasis on taxes just distracts Republicans from potentially more productive policies.

- Similarly, Republicans tend to view government with suspicion, if not disdain. This may make them less likely to try to use the government to its full potential. Furthermore, the Republican focus on a laissez-faire approach may create, or at least encourage, a culture of cheating—not just on taxes—that is detrimental to society as a whole.

Better policies can also come from preparedness, and in some ways Democrats have simply been better prepared than their Republican rivals for the rigors of the presidency. Elsewhere in this book, we noted that Alan Greenspan mentioned Clinton's willingness to sacrifice political capital for long-term economic good. By contrast, Greenspan felt Reagan "had no patience for discussing economic policy"[1] and that the GW administration failed to think through the consequences of its economic actions.[2]

It bears repeating that Greenspan is a self-described "lifelong libertarian Republican,"[3] so his views would probably have been aligned more closely with those of Reagan and GW than with those of any other presidents in our sample.

Does all this mean that a Democratic candidate for president is automatically a better choice than a Republican? We don't think the data necessarily implies this. Certainly, each presidential candidate should be evaluated based on his or her policies. Candidates for president who promote policies that have failed in the past should be rejected. This is especially so when those candidates insist, despite all evidence to the contrary, that these failed policies succeeded. That is one goal of this book—to set out facts that can be used to judge those claims.

But candidates—even those from the same party—have different policies. And regardless of their views, candidates offer varying levels of judgment and competence. Moreover, the world is always changing. In evolving circumstances, a good president not only needs good policies, a good president must be flexible enough to figure out how best to apply them. That means learning from the past, whether one is a Democrat or a Republican. It also means learning from past presidents, whether they are Democrats or Republicans.

Republican presidents may have a harder time doing this; after all, many of the policies that failed in the past are part of the party's platform and gospel to the Republican faithful. But to be successful, which is to say to serve the American public well, they will have to break with their party's past and develop new policies. Being for tax cuts and economic growth is like wanting to lose weight on an all-you-can-eat ice cream sundae diet. It sounds like it would be great if it worked, but it never produces the desired results. You can pick one or you can pick the other. Just don't lie to us and claim you're going to do both—much less follow GW's lead and claim you will not only do both, but also pay down the debt to boot.

None of this criticism warrants any smugness on the part of Democrats; just because Democrats have done better than Republicans on average doesn't mean Democrats have done well. Earlier in the book, we noted that crime soared under JFK/LBJ and Carter, in part because they failed to react to obvious changes in demographics. That failure to react may have stemmed from a reluctance to state things the public did not want to hear, or worse, from a failure to recognize that a given demographic might be more crime-prone than others. Reality is not always politically correct and to pretend otherwise is to fail the American people.

What we, the American public, need from our leaders is performance, not platitudes, tired theories, or political correctness run amok. Ideas help. But a hard look at the past will help all of us hone our ideas—whatever our politics. We all must test our ideas and recast them in the harsh light of history, and we look away from its glare at our peril. After a long and careful reading, that is the story told by the facts.

# Is It Congress?

If you've read this entire book so far, you've noticed that Democrats outperformed Republicans on many of the issues we've examined. If you're a Republican, this is a problem, and therefore it's a problem for us as authors; those who don't like the message often attack the messenger, even when the messenger is trying to be as data-driven as possible. So we discussed these findings with Republicans we know and invariably, once it sank in that Democratic presidents did generally outperform Republican presidents, we got the same response from all of them: It was Congress. Congress was responsible, not the president. Congress did the good things and the bad. In particular, a Republican Congress did the good things, the things that produced growth and prosperity, and a Democratic Congress did the bad things, the things that slowed down growth and caused misery.

This seems simplistic to us. It assumes that Democrats just happened to be in the White House when a responsible Republican Congress ran the country, and a Republican was in the Oval Office when Congress was controlled by irresponsible Democrats. It also doesn't entirely match our recollection of past events. For example, the American public seemed to fare well on many issues, particularly economic ones, during the JFK/LBJ administration when Democrats controlled both the White House and Congress. But many of the same Congress members were still around, with Democrats controlling both the House and the Senate, during the administration of Nixon/Ford, when the economy was shakier.

Now we could pontificate or we could do what we have done so far in this book, which is to look at the data. So once more into the breach . . .

Congress was controlled by Republicans from 1953 until 1955, and then by Democrats until 1981. In 1981, Republicans took control of the Senate, but the House of Representatives remained in Democratic hands. From 1981 to 1987, control of Congress was mixed. The Democrats took back the Senate in 1987 and controlled Congress until 1995, when the Republican Revolution took over both the House and the Senate.

The Senate began 2001 evenly split. Control of Congress changed hands a few times until 2003, leading us to call the 2001–2003 period a split Congress. From 2003 to 2007 Republicans controlled both Houses, but in 2007 control reverted to the Democrats.

So let's look at how control of Congress affected some of the issues covered in this book. As with presidents, we will look at changes from the last full year before a party took control of Congress to its last full year before being booted out. We've already done a bit of that. Remember this chart from Chapter 1 (relabeled Figure A1-1 here), showing the growth rate in real GDP per capita, by Congress? Growth rates of real GDP per capita are essentially the same, regardless of who is in charge of Congress. But let's consider another issue—paying down debt, as shown in Figure A1-2.

At first glance, Figure A1-2 looks as if it might support some version of the Congress-did-it story. Mixed Congresses run up the debt and both Democratic- and Republican-controlled Congresses pay it down. Democrats outperform Republicans by a smidge, but just as was the case with real GDP per capita, mixed Congresses underperform. If control over Congress is what really matters when it comes to growth in real GDP per capita or debt repayment, then perhaps when the Congress is united, it is more likely to get

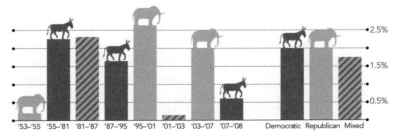

**Annualized growth in real GDP per capita, by control of congress**

Figure A1-1

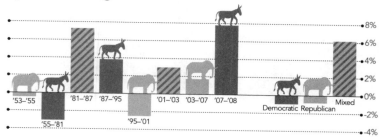

**Annualized change in debt as a % of GDP, by control of congress**

Figure A1-2

done what needs to be done. On the other hand, when Congress is divided, the parties pull in opposite directions and go nowhere.

But Figures A1-1 and A1-2 also show something else. Republican Congresses did best from 1995 to 2001 (which is to say, when measuring the change from 1994 to 2000). That period mostly overlapped the Clinton presidency, and as we saw in Chapter 2, during the Clinton administration the federal government's spending decreased faster before the Republicans took control of Congress than after. Furthermore, while Clinton was in office, federal tax collections as a share of GDP also increased every single year. This is probably not something for which the Republican Congress would want to claim credit. However, those two facts taken together—reduced government spending and increased revenues—were what allowed the debt to be paid down rapidly. And both these factors owed more to Clinton than to the Republican Congress, as we have seen. They also helped create some of the conditions that led to the impressive growth in real GDP per capita in the late 1990s.

Now that certainly seems like anecdotal evidence that control of Congress does not explain what we see in the economy. Still, that evidence is not definitive. So we asked ourselves this: How do we nail the coffin shut? Is there anything else we can look at that might tell us unambiguously whether Congress or the president is in the driver's seat?

And the answer is yes. As we just noted, no Republican Congress would want to take credit for increases in the tax burden that occurred during its watch. So let's harken back to when we looked at the tax burden, by administration (see Figure A1-3).

Given Republican and Democratic views about taxes, Figure A1-3 suggests that presidents are at least peripherally involved in determining the tax bite. After all, taxes are perennially important to Republicans—not only

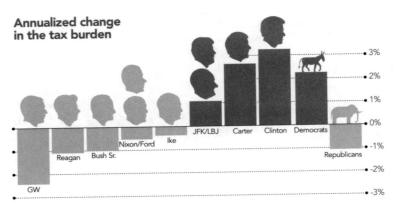

**Annualized change in the tax burden**

Figure A1-3

do they feel that lowering the tax bite increases growth, they tend to feel that decreasing tax rates is in itself a laudable goal.

Which leads us to believe that if Congress were really in the driver's seat, the difference between changes to the tax bite under Republican and Democratic Congresses should be at least as stark as the difference under Republican and Democratic presidents. But what we see is something very different, as shown in Figure A1-4.

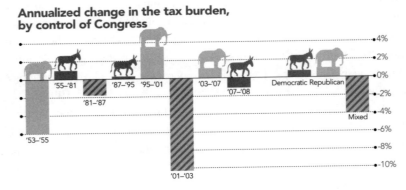

**Annualized change in the tax burden, by control of Congress**

Figure A1-4

As Figure A1-4 shows, on average mixed Congresses delivered reductions in the tax burden. On the other hand, while Democratic Congresses raised the tax burden on average, the *biggest* increases in the tax burden tended to occur while Republicans controlled Congress. Allow us to repeat: When Republicans were in control of Congress, not only did the tax bite go up, it went up by more than when Democrats were in control of Congress. In fact, as Figure A1-4 makes clear, the biggest average annualized increase in the tax burden occurred in the years following the Republican Revolution. (We're betting you never heard Newt Gingrich mention that on TV.)

Our conclusion from this is obvious: The president is more likely to get his way than are congressional leaders. The president sets the agenda, his administration speaks with one voice, and he has veto power. He also controls the executive branch, which not only enforces laws, but also writes rules and regulations. Directly—or through his appointees—the president provides guidance to the government and the rest of us about how laws are to be interpreted. Furthermore, no matter what the president wants to do, he generally has at least some allies in Congress who want to do the same thing. For these reasons we have to assume that the State of the Union is more related to actions of the president than to the desires of Congress.

That is not to say that Congress does not have a lot of power and influence. After all, Congress passes laws. It can refuse to act in ways the president wants, pulling the president's agenda in one direction or another. Congress can even simply flat-out oppose the president at every turn. The Republican Congress did just that from 1995 to the end of Bill Clinton's term, going so far as to impeach him. On the other hand, Congress can give the president everything he wants: GW Bush, for instance, went his entire first term without having to wield the veto pen. But for all its power and influence, Congress simply does not have the control that the president does.

# Explaining Growth in Real GDP per Capita

Elsewhere in the book, we noted that the economy generally grew more quickly under Democratic administrations than under Republican ones, and we suggested some explanations for why that might be the case. In the next few pages, we will revisit and expand on those explanations, and then formalize them into a simple economic model.

In the first few chapters of the book, we pointed out that real GDP per capita is a commonly used measure for the size of the economy among economists. So what explains the growth in that measure? As we saw in the first chapter of this book, one of the things that affects growth is out of the president's control; that is, the real money supply. The real money supply is controlled by the Federal Reserve, which buys more Treasuries when it wants to increase the amount of money in the economy and sells Treasuries to decrease the money supply. When the Fed keeps the economy well-lubricated with an ample money supply, the added money sloshing around makes people *feel* wealthier, which in turn stimulates the economy.

Think of it this way: If the Fed injects a lot of money into the economy, banks and bondholders find themselves flush with money and are more likely to lend it out. That means consumers and companies that could use money have an easier time getting their hands on funds they would like to use (and pay less for those funds too). Companies engage in more projects (which means more hiring) and people buy more stuff (which also means more hiring).

As a result, people are more likely to buy things and start businesses, so the economy will generally grow faster. When the Fed tightens the real money supply, it works the opposite way. Money is a little harder to come by, and people feel a little poorer, buy less, and take fewer risks. Growth has a tendency to slow down.

In Chapter 1, we tracked the real money supply using real M1 per capita. The data is available only from 1959 onward, so Figure A2-1 shows the change in real M1 per capita and the growth in real GDP per capita for each administration beginning with JFK/LBJ.

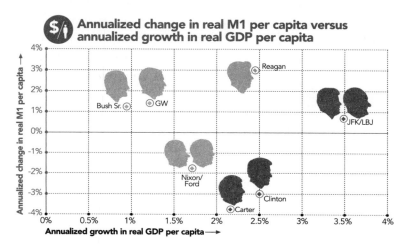

Figure A2-1

At first glance, Figure A2-1 doesn't appear to show a very strong relationship between the money supply and the economic growth rate. However, look what happens when we take out the Republican administrations and look at the Democrats alone (see Figure A2-2).

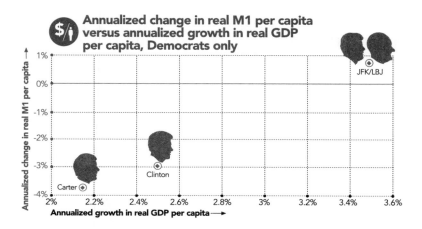

Figure A2-2

Among Democratic administrations, the slowest growth rates in real GDP per capita came under Jimmy Carter; his administration also suffered the biggest decrease in real M1 per capita. Conversely, the only Democratic administration under which real M1 per capita actually increased, that of JFK/LBJ, also produced the fastest increase in real GDP per capita. And then there's Clinton, who came in between Carter and LBJ/JFK on changes to both real M1 per capita and real GDP per capita. Thus, among Democrats, the faster the Fed pumped real M1 per capita into the economy, the faster the economy grew.

What about when we remove the Democratic administrations and just look at the Republicans? (See Figure A2-3.)

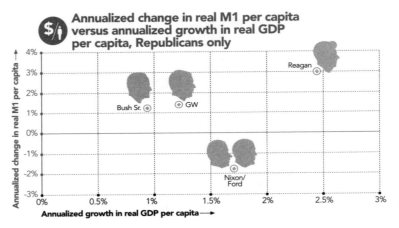

Figure A2-3

Looking at the Republicans alone, the Nixon/Ford administration was the only Republican administration under which the Fed reduced the real money supply per capita. This may have been the result of the Fed operating in uncharted waters during the early 1970s, a period in which inflation was accelerating, the gold standard that had been in place since the 1940s was abandoned, and the Arab oil embargo occurred. Each of these situations was outside the experience of the Federal Reserve.

With Nixon/Ford as an exception, we see the familiar rule among the remaining Republicans: The faster the increase in real M1 per capita, the faster the growth in real GDP per capita.

So it's clear that among Democratic administrations, a faster increase in the real money supply per person tends to mean faster economic growth. That also seems to be the case with Republican administrations.

Another factor that might matter is the tax burden. As we've noted before, Republicans feel that cutting taxes leads to faster economic growth. We examined that claim in some detail in the Interlude Chapter, and it does seem that tax cuts make a difference, albeit not necessarily in the way that Republicans believe it does. Regardless, the tax burden will join real M1 per capita in our little model.

Common sense also argues for considering the degree to which *the previous administration* invested in the future. Administrations whose predecessors invested heavily in education, infrastructure, R&D, and energy independence are more likely to have better conditions for growth than administrations whose predecessors put little emphasis on education, starved the country of infrastructure, failed to invest in R&D, and left the country more at the mercy of countries that wish us ill. In Chapter 12, we looked at the degree to which each administration invested in the future and ranked them accordingly. The three biggest investors in the future were the Eisenhower, JFK/LBJ, and Carter administrations. They were followed by a three-way tie for fourth place among Bush Sr., Bill Clinton, and GW. The two last-place slots were occupied by the Reagan and the Nixon/Ford administrations. Figure A2-4 shows the growth in real GDP per capita for each administration and the ranking the previous administration was awarded on investing in the future for all the administrations from JFK/LBJ to GW Bush.[1]

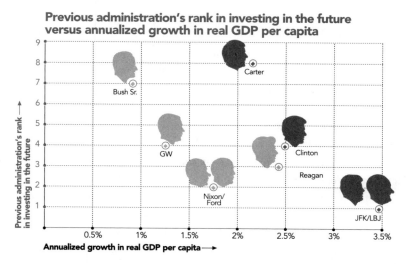

Figure A2-4

As we might expect, Figure A2-4 shows that, in general, the better the previous administration ranked when it came to investing in the future, the faster the growth in real GDP per capita. Granted, it is not a tight fit—otherwise Nixon would have the second-best growth rate and Carter would have the worst. But the figure does give us some support for believing there is a relationship between the previous administration's investments in the future and the current administration's growth rate. The fastest growth in real GDP per capita occurred under the JFK/LBJ administration, which followed Ike, who came in first on investing in the future. The slowest growth in real GDP per capita came under Bush Sr., who succeeded Ronald Reagan, one of the presidents who did the least to invest in the future.

We looked at the tax burden, which Republicans think helps explain growth, so to be fair, let's consider something that Democrats think makes a difference: income inequality. When income gets concentrated at the top, it can become very hard for the majority that is not at the top to afford to buy things, and lackluster consumer spending reduces revenues for many businesses. Economic health depends on a constant, energetic, bottom-up churn of the market.

Increased income concentration can also reduce entrepreneurship in society. Starting a business is risky, and entrepreneurs need to have enough resources not only to get their business afloat, but also to keep body and soul together for however long the business fails to bring in a sufficient profit. The more concentrated income is at the top, the fewer people will have the wherewithal to take the risks needed to start their own business.

There is another potential problem with greater income inequality: Like it or not, money and political power often go hand in hand. When money gets too concentrated in society, power follows. History gives us plenty of examples in which those who happen to have a lot of political power use it to benefit themselves by closing off opportunities to others. Some established businesses will even lobby the government for additional regulations in their own industries, if only to raise the costs for potential competitors.[2] Just or unjust, legal or illegal, that makes the economy less efficient and less vibrant.

So the concentration of income is something we should examine. However, just as investment in the future takes time to have an effect, we'd expect the same of changes in income inequality. After all, it takes a while before people build up enough equity to buy a refrigerator or a home or to start a business. The longer that takes, the slower their contribution to the economy. As a result, if Democrats are right and income inequality matters, the change in income inequality *during the previous administration* should be related to growth in real GDP per capita.

In Chapter 7, we measured income inequality using the Gini coefficient (a.k.a. the Gini ratio). As we noted at the time, that coefficient ranges from 0 to 100 percent. The closer it gets to 100 percent, the more unequal income is; conversely, the closer the Gini coefficient gets to 0, the less income inequality there is in society. So the Democratic assumption would be that increasing the Gini coefficient will translate to less growth sooner or later. Assuming *sooner or later* translates to "during the next administration," Democrats would expect that growth would be faster during administrations under whose predecessors the Gini ratio shrank. It's not clear from Figure A2-5 that this is the case.

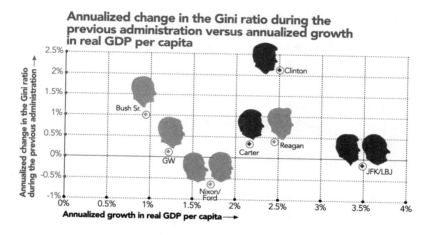

Figure A2-5

However, even though this measure is clearly no slam dunk, Figure A2-5 does seem to indicate at least a possibility that the variable is worth investigating further, so don't wipe it from your mind just yet. In a moment we'll be approaching things from another perspective to see whether the Gini coefficient matters or not.

Before we do that, however, there is one more variable we'd like to consider because it's gotten a lot of attention right about the time we've been writing these words. Rising health care costs burden the economy for a number of reasons. For example, high health care costs chain many people to their health insurance, which typically means they are tied to the job that provides that coverage. As a result, they may forgo moving to better jobs or shy away from starting their own companies. Thus, we might expect that when health care costs rise faster, growth would slow.

Let's have a look (see Figure A2-6).

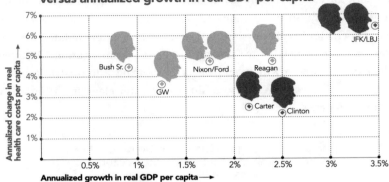

Figure A2-6

As with the situation we just looked at concerning the Gini ratio, the numbers do not unambiguously support the conclusion we proposed—in this case that rising health care costs necessarily reduce growth. What seems to call this notion into question, based on the data in Figure A2-6, is the performance of the JFK/LBJ administration, which posted both the fastest increases in real health care costs and the fastest increases in real GDP per capita. Still, common sense says that rapidly increasing health care costs are an economic problem, so we aren't willing to abandon this factor quite yet.

Now we'll take one more pass at explaining real GDP per capita, this time using all the variables we have mentioned in this section so far. That would encompass the following: the change in real M1 per capita, the change in the tax burden, the rank of the previous administration at investing in the future, the change in the Gini coefficient over the span of the previous administration, and the change in real health care costs per capita.

# Building a Model to Explain Economic Growth

Before we start modeling economic growth, let us consider a simpler situation. Say we want to model umbrella sales by a street vendor. Among the many factors that might help explain the sale of umbrellas are how many people walk by, whether it's raining, and what price the vendor is charging per umbrella. But no matter how many people walk past the vendor, there will be very few umbrella sales on a balmy afternoon. Similarly, it could be raining cats and dogs but if nobody passes by, there will also be no umbrella sales. And no matter how many people are walking past, and no matter what the weather is, the vendor won't sell many umbrellas if the price he is charging is exorbitant. So to model umbrella sales we have to take into account the number of potential customers, bearing in mind the weather and the price of umbrellas. Similarly, we have to see how the weather affects sales, taking into account the number of customers and the price of umbrellas. In other words, all the factors that affect the sale of umbrellas affect those sales simultaneously, so to explain umbrella sales we should consider all those factors simultaneously.

Similarly, if the factors we looked at earlier in the chapter are occurring simultaneously, their effect on real GDP per capita also has to be taken into account simultaneously. For instance, real M1 per capita grew faster under GW than under his predecessor, Bill Clinton, which would tend to give GW an advantage with respect to producing faster growth in real GDP per capita. However, at the same time, health care costs grew more slowly under Clinton than under GW, which on its own would make Clinton more likely to enjoy faster growth in real GDP per capita. Does the effect of the growth in the real money supply outweigh the effect of rising health care costs, and if so, by how much? Plus, how do we take all the other factors (e.g., the previous administration's investments in the future) into account?

To understand economic growth, we have to look at all these factors at the same time. To do that, we're going to use a statistical tool called *regression analysis*. Regression analysis is useful for explaining the behavior of one variable using several other variables. The variable being explained is known as the *dependent variable*—its value depends on the *explanatory variables* in the model. Regressions don't just take into account the effect each explanatory variable has on the dependent variable. Instead, regressions account for the fact that the effects of the explanatory variables on the thing being explained can overlap.

We could use regression analysis to help us model umbrella sales, taking into account multiple effects, but if we did that, we might be muscling in on someone else's book. We will, however, use regression analysis to help us explain real GDP per capita, simultaneously accounting for the effect of several different variables. The regression we ran used data from the JFK/LBJ administration to GW Bush[3] and produced the results shown in Figure A2-7.[4,5]

**Annualized Change in Real GDP per Capita over the Span of each Administration**

| | Coefficient | Standard Deviation | t Statistic | P Value |
|---|---|---|---|---|
| $R^2$ | 0.9997 | | | |
| Adjusted $R^2$ | 0.9982 | | | |
| Observations | 7 | | | |
| Constant | 0.0374 | 0.0013 | 28.5154 | 0.0223 |
| Annualized change in real M1 per capita | 0.4026 | 0.0163 | 24.7411 | 0.0257 |
| Annualized change in the tax burden | 0.7090 | 0.0170 | 41.7567 | 0.0152 |
| Rank, investing in the future, previous administration | −0.0015 | 0.0001 | −19.9150 | 0.0319 |
| Annualized change in the Gini coefficient, previous administration | −0.6162 | 0.0339 | −18.1558 | 0.0350 |
| Real health care costs per capita | −0.1999 | 0.0243 | −8.2294 | 0.0770 |

Figure A2-7

The results can be written as an equation:

> Annual percentage change in real GDP per capita =
> **0.0374 + 0.4026** × annualized change in real M1 per capita
> + **0.7090** × annualized change in the tax burden
> − **0.0015** × previous administration's rank at investing in the future
> − **0.6162** × annualized percentage change in the Gini coefficient during the previous administration
> − **0.1999** × annualized percentage increase in real health care costs per capita

A detailed discussion of the regression and its results are outside the scope of this book, but results are summarized as follows. All else being equal:[6]

- The faster the Fed increased real M1 per capita, the faster real GDP per capita grew.
- The more the tax burden increased while an administration was in office, the faster real GDP per capita increased. Conversely, for those administrations that cut taxes, the bigger the tax cut, the bigger the drag on the economy.
- The higher the rank of the previous administration at investing in the future, the faster real GDP per capita grew.

- The bigger the increase in income inequality (as measured by the Gini coefficient) during the previous administration, the slower real GDP per capita grew.
- The faster real health care costs per capita increased, the slower real GDP per capita increased.
- The growth rate of the real money supply, the change in the tax burden, the previous administration's rank at investing in the future, and the change in inequality over the span of the previous administration were all significant at the 5 percent level. That is, there seems to be less than a 5 percent probability that the above-described relationships observed between these variables and the growth in real GDP per capita occurred by chance.
- Real health care costs per capita are significant at the 10 percent level. That is, there is less than a 10 percent probability that the relationship between the growth in real health care costs per capita and the growth in real GDP per capita are not as described above.[7]
- The model explains most of the variation we've observed in the annualized growth rate of real GDP per capita from administration to administration.

Admittedly, the regression was run on a small number of observations, and therefore, its results should be taken with a grain of salt. That is to say, if the regression tells us something that contradicts what we have already seen, we should discard it. However, each of the findings of the regression either match results we have already seen or confirm intuition we have already described. None of this makes all these results definitively true, but it makes it harder to argue against the findings of the model, at least for the period for which we had data.

For example, the model confirms what we've seen earlier about the relationship between the money supply and economic growth: All else being equal, faster growth in real M1 per capita is associated with faster growth in real GDP per capita. This result also fits perfectly with our intuition and even with textbook descriptions of monetary policy.

Similarly, while Republicans might insist that cutting taxes leads to more growth, we've seen time and again throughout the book that it simply did not happen during our sample. This counterintuitive result is probably due to a combination of factors. One such factor is that the tax burden—despite all the complaining—has not been high enough to dissuade people from working. Furthermore, a focus on tax cutting could have diverted energy and effort away from measures that would have been more helpful. Cutting taxes may even have directly harmed the economy by making funding for growth-related projects harder to obtain.

Additionally, as we have seen, despite a few well-publicized new laws, most changes to the tax burden fly below the radar. That is, they occur because the IRS becomes more—or less—focused on tax collections. Administrations that collect more in revenues do so by writing tighter regulations and pushing enforcement. Conversely, administrations that cut tax burdens do so in part by being more lax on enforcement of existing tax laws. And frankly there is a fine line between an antitax political appointee interpreting regulations broadly and one who simply ignores violations of the law. When the latter occurs, it tends to have a pernicious effect: Those who break one law with impunity, if not the approval of the regulators, can usually justify (in their own minds, at least) breaking other laws. We don't think a nonchalant IRS turns America into the Wild West, but we also don't think that any good can come from an administration encouraging people to cheat on their taxes.

It bears repeating—we have come to the issue of taxes numerous times throughout this book, and we have looked at the effect of taxes on growth several different ways. Nevertheless, we have seen no evidence that cutting the tax burden increases growth rates, at least for the levels of taxation that we observed in the United States from 1953 to 2008. Quite the opposite, in fact.

The third factor in the regression is the degree to which the previous administration invested in the future—no surprise there. Investments intended to pay off in the future, if they pay off at all, pay off in the future. The fourth factor, a reduction in income inequality, also takes time to have an effect.[8] A society with serious inequities in income starts to choke off opportunities for most citizens and thus becomes dependent on a smaller and smaller fraction of its population for ideas, investments, drive, and even purchases needed to fuel economic growth.

The final influence on growth rates for real GDP per capita used by the model is health care costs. The faster health care costs increase, the more drag there is on growth rates from direct effects (i.e., resources being wasted on health care that could be used elsewhere) and indirect effects (e.g., people staying in the wrong jobs in order to keep their health insurance).[9]

# Using the Economic Growth Model to Explain What We've Seen

This small group of variables explains most of the variation in the growth rate of real GDP per capita from JFK/LBJ to GW, so it is worth looking at growth rates by administration again, this time taking into account the model.

The first administration that the model can analyze, that of JFK/LBJ, happens to be the administration that produced the fastest growth rates in real GDP per capita. Real M1 per capita growth was positive while the JFK/LBJ administration was in office, but slower than under Reagan or either Bush. JFK/LBJ also increased the tax burden, unlike any of the Republican administrations, but the increase was less than that under the other Democrats. The JFK/LBJ administration also benefited from actions taken by Ike, who ranked first on investing in the future and second on decreasing income inequality. On the other hand, they hurt their own cause by allowing the cost of health care to explode on their watch.

The Nixon/Ford administration was the only Republican administration to fare less well at the hands of the Federal Reserve than JFK/LBJ; real M1 per capita contracted during the Nixon/Ford years. On the other hand, like all other Republican administrations in our sample, the Nixon/Ford administration reduced the tax burden, which did not help produce economic growth. The Nixon/Ford administration also didn't help itself much when it came to health care costs, allowing those costs to increase at a rate of 4.9 percent a year (tied for second to last with the Reagan administration). Where Nixon/Ford fared well was in following the JFK/LBJ administration, which came in second at investing in the future and did the best job of reducing income inequality.

The next administration, that of Jimmy Carter, got no help from the Fed; real M1 per capita contracted at an annualized rate of 3.7 percent a year. This is the equivalent of subtracting 1.5 percent off the annualized growth of real GDP per capita! Carter also was penalized by following the Nixon/Ford administration—they did the least amount of investing in the future in the sample and did not do much to reduce income inequality either. Where Carter excelled was on items under his control: He produced the second-fastest increase in the tax burden and the second-slowest increase in real health care costs per capita, following Clinton on both measures.

Reagan came next. His Fed story was dramatically different than Carter's. Real M1 per capita rose faster while Reagan was in office than during any other administration. However, Reagan got only middling help from the previous administration; Carter came in third at investing in the future, while finishing an unimpressive sixth on the Gini coefficient. What really hurt Reagan, however, were the factors that *were* under his own control: Reagan produced the second-largest reduction in the tax burden and allowed relatively rapid increases in real health care costs per capita as well.

If Reagan did not help his own cause all that much, he certainly didn't help his successor, George Bush Sr. Reagan came in second to last on both investing in the future and reducing income inequality, both of which weighed heavily on Bush Sr. Together these factors subtracted 1.7 percent a year off the real GDP per capita while Bush Sr. was in office. Bush Sr. fared better at the hands of the Fed, trailing only Reagan and his own son, GW, in terms of real M1 per capita increases. However, despite the "Read my lips" brouhaha, Bush Sr. decreased the tax burden and did little to keep health care costs in check, neither of which helped produce growth.

Bill Clinton followed Bush Sr. and, like Bush Sr., got very little help from his predecessor: Bush Sr. tied for fourth at investing in the future but produced the biggest increase in income inequality of any administration since 1953. Clinton also got no help from the Fed: Despite Greenspan's recent words of praise for Bill Clinton, Greenspan's Fed reduced real M1 per capita at an annual rate of 2.9 percent while Clinton was in office. As a result, the rapid growth in real GDP per capita during the Clinton administration came from his first-place spot at raising the tax burden and from his first-place finish at keeping real health care costs per capita in check.

Which leaves us with GW. George W. Bush got a lot of help from the Fed—only Reagan benefited more from the Fed's largesse. GW also produced the biggest cut in the tax burden of any president, but came in third in terms of keeping health care costs in line. In terms of Bill Clinton's effect on GW's performance—Clinton came in fourth both on investing in the future (tied with Bush Sr.) and on income inequality.

# How Much Did Each President Contribute to Economic Growth?

To compare the performance of each administration in the fairest way possible, we have to remove the effect of those factors that are out of that administration's control; namely, the model's constant term, the change in the real money supply per capita, how much the previous administration invested in the future, and the change in income inequality during the term of the previous administration. Put another way, we want to separate out the piece of economic growth that occurred during each administration that was "unearned" and rank how each administration stacked up when it came to "earned" real GDP per capita growth.

Based on the model we estimated earlier in this chapter, here is how we arrive at the figures:

"Unearned" annual percentage change in real GDP per capita =

$0.0374 + 0.4026 \times$ annualized change in real M1 per capita

$- 0.0015 \times$ previous administration's rank at investing in the future

$- 0.6162 \times$ annualized percent change in the Gini coefficient during the previous administration

Figure A2-8 shows the growth in unearned real GDP per capita, by administration.

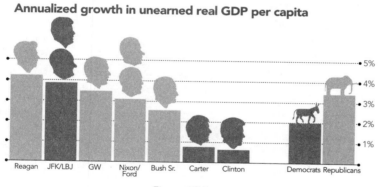

**Annualized growth in unearned real GDP per capita**

Reagan | JFK/LBJ | GW | Nixon/Ford | Bush Sr. | Carter | Clinton | Democrats | Republicans

Figure A2-8

Reagan had the greatest amount of unearned economic growth, largely as a result of the Federal Reserve's massive expansion of real M1 per capita during his administration. He also benefited from Carter's third-place finish at investing in the future.

The JFK/LBJ administration was the second-biggest beneficiary of unearned economic growth; the Eisenhower administration invested in the future more than any other administration since 1952, and did the second-best job of keeping income inequality in line. The third-biggest increase in unearned economic growth came under GW; GW benefited from a fairly generous Federal Reserve, as well as from following Bill Clinton, who did a relatively good job of keeping income inequality in check.

GW was followed by Nixon/Ford and Bush Sr. The two presidents who got the least amount of unearned economic growth were Carter and Clinton; under both, the Federal Reserve kept a tight rein on the real supply per capita, and neither got any favors from their predecessors when it came to investing in the future or preventing economic inequality from escalating rapidly. Overall Democrats fared somewhat worse than Republicans in terms of unearned economic growth; Republicans were far more likely to benefit from a friendly Federal Reserve or the actions of their predecessors than their Democratic counterparts.

Subtracting the unearned growth in real GDP per capita for each administration from the actual growth in real GDP per capita per administration we first computed in Chapter 1 gives us the growth in "earned" real GDP per capita by administration, as shown in Figure A2-9.

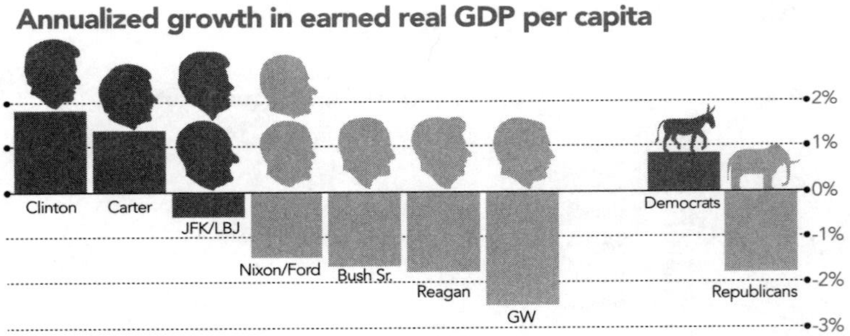

**Annualized growth in earned real GDP per capita**

Figure A2-9

Figure A2-9 shows that "earned" growth in real GDP per capita looks very different from the garden variety of real GDP per capita growth rates. Clinton and Carter have moved up to first and second place; they were the two administrations most penalized by the Fed, so removing that anchor from around their collective necks helped them a lot in these rankings. These administrations were also the two best at growth-related issues under the control of a sitting president, namely keeping health care costs under control and avoiding growth-strangling tax policies.

The other administrations contributed negatively to economic growth while they were in office, paying excessive attention to tax policies that did not work or doing little or nothing useful to contain health care costs. The best of these negative producers was the JFK/LBJ administration, which leaves Republicans in the remaining spots. The two Republicans that did best on an apples-to-apples comparison of real GDP per capita growth were Nixon/Ford and Bush Sr., which leaves Reagan and GW at the bottom. Both Reagan and GW benefited tremendously from the Fed's help; removing that crutch makes them look quite a bit worse.

Which leads to an interesting irony: Clinton, who got very little real cooperation from Alan Greenspan's Fed (which means slower growth for all of us!) would reappoint Greenspan to the role of Federal Reserve chair. Conversely, Reagan benefited tremendously from Paul Volcker's leadership at the Federal Reserve; Volcker strangled inflation and, once inflation was safely dead, pumped up the real M1 per capita growth at a very rapid rate. While that produced rapid growth, benefiting many Americans, members of the Reagan administration repeatedly criticized Volcker for keeping the money supply too tight. (No, we're not kidding.) Reagan would also stack the Fed with members who fought Volcker at every turn. Volcker, responsible for much of the economic growth during the Reagan administration, eventually gave up; he resigned and was replaced by Alan Greenspan. As unhelpful as Greenspan's Fed was to Bill Clinton, it did everything possible to help GW; as we showed earlier, GW benefited from the second most favorable monetary policy of all the administrations in our sample. And yet it wasn't enough; his administration criticized Greenspan unmercifully at times, and GW would eventually appoint a new Fed chair (Ben Bernanke).

Thus Reagan and GW penalized Fed chairmen who helped them out (Volcker and Greenspan, respectively), and Clinton reappointed a Fed chairman (Greenspan) whose actions applied the brakes to growth during his term. Clearly, even presidents, with all their myriad advisors and access to more data than anyone else, have not demonstrated much understanding of what the Federal Reserve is doing or what its actions mean.

## What Does This Model Mean about the Economy Going Forward?

The model we presented earlier implies that presidents should focus less on cutting taxes and more on keeping health care costs under control. It also indicates that presidents should keep a closer eye on the Federal Reserve. That doesn't mean compromising the Fed's independence, as some administrations have reputedly attempted, but it does mean paying enough attention to ask whether the Fed is behaving logically. For example, perhaps the 2001 recession might have been averted if Bill Clinton had mused to reporters about what possible reasons the Fed might have for reducing real M1 per capita during the year 2000. After all, that was a year in which the stock market crashed and the economy was slowing noticeably in the third and fourth quarters, making it a textbook case for looser monetary policy. However, it's unlikely that Bill Clinton had any idea of what the Fed was doing and we have seen no evidence other presidents were any better informed.

Presidents should also pay attention to the future. Policies that increase income inequality, such as "flatter" taxes and cuts in antipoverty programs, tend to rob the country of growth in later years. Similarly, underinvesting in the future leaves behind a poor legacy.

But is this model likely to remain useful in the future? Economists, political scientists, and pundits have a long history of explaining the economy in ways that soon become inapplicable. This model was estimated using data from 1960 to 2008, and the world can change. After all, that was a time of relative stability and prosperity, a time without a Great Depression or world wars. As we write this, on the other hand, the world is struggling to emerge from what is being called the Great Recession in many quarters.

However, it wouldn't take a cataclysm for the model to run into trouble. For example, the model indicates that higher (not lower) tax burdens are associated with faster economic growth. That might not apply if the tax burden became too onerous, and the model doesn't tell us what constitutes "too onerous," merely that as of 2008 we weren't there.

So the model, like the presidents, should be judged by history.

# The Budget of the Executive Office of the President

★ ★ ★

All the data we've looked at so far deal with issues that touch the lives of many Americans. In this appendix, we're going to look at a measure that touches primarily the life of one—the president. We're going to look at the budget for the Executive Office of the President (EOP)—the amount the president gets Congress to give him to spend pretty much as he chooses. We think that figure says something about the character of the president.

The budget of the EOP includes the president's salary, as well as the cost of upkeep at the executive residence in the White House. It also pays for some of the president's advisory councils, such as the Office of National Drug Control Policy and the Office of Management and Budget, from which we've obtained some data used in this book.

But not all the president's expenses show up there. For instance, the president's travel budget for fiscal year 2008 was listed as $100,000[1]—which might cover firing up Air Force One and getting it from here to there once, as long as we're talking about heres and theres that are pretty close together. After one of the planes used as Air Force One made a flyover of New York City in April 2009 for a poorly thought-out photo op, the Air Force claimed the whole affair (including two fighter escorts) cost the taxpayers $328,835.[2] And presidents travel a lot, often flying overseas. But just about all the expenses involved in presidential travel get billed to other sources, from the Air Force to the State Department.

The budget of the EOP also generally contains a sum ($1 million in fiscal 2008)[3] to deal with unanticipated needs. This makes sense—after all, things happen and we want the president to have the resources to react immediately, even before Congress has the opportunity to approve more funding, should that be necessary.

As Figure A3-1 shows, the amount of money that goes into the EOP tends to be very small relative to total government spending.

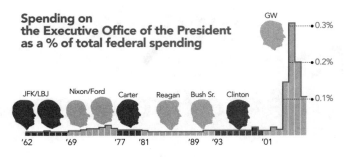

Figure A3-1

The numbers, as we said, are all very small—the amount of spending by the Executive Office of the President never came to as much as a third of 1 percent of total federal spending, and most years it was less than one-fifteenth even of that small figure. Still, one thing stands out. If you look at Figure A3-1 very carefully, you may notice that something changed while GW was president.

What happened during GW's term was the war in Iraq. While just about everyone except Saddam and Baghdad Bob realized that the war was inevitable in the weeks (if not months) leading up to it, technically, in its first year, it could have been considered an unanticipated expense. Thus, the costs associated with the first year of the war were left off the federal budget.

However, as we noted in Chapter 2, the government has a process in place specifically to provide funding for large, unexpected expenses; the president sends Congress a request for "supplemental appropriations" and Congress votes on it, approving it (or not) just as it does the budget. In the case of the second Gulf War, the supplemental appropriations were overwhelmingly approved by Congress.

Nevertheless, by year two of the war, the fact that the United States was fighting a war in Iraq was no longer a surprise even to Saddam and Baghdad Bob, neither of whom, incidentally, was still in the fight. Nevertheless, funding for the war in Iraq was still left off the budget. After the budget passed, the Bush administration requested supplemental funding for the continued operations in Iraq (and the war in Afghanistan).

GW had apparently discovered a few benefits to using the supplemental appropriations process to fund his wars. One was that it made his budgets look better. Not that the spending didn't take place if it was left off the budget, mind you, but it was easier to claim that the budget deficit was under control if big items weren't counted. Another advantage of using the supplemental appropriations process was that Congress was unlikely to balk at expenditures that supposedly were intended specifically for the war effort. Who wanted to be accused of voting against the troops, after all? Given these advantages, GW continued to use the supplemental appropriations process to fund the wars in Iraq and Afghanistan for the rest of his time in office.

However, GW and his people were firm proponents of executive power, and the supplemental appropriations process still allowed for what they felt was too much oversight from Congress. The result was a new item in the budget of the president's office, the Iraq Relief and Reconstruction Fund. That item quickly became the largest piece in the budget of the EOP, though it stayed tucked away, way in the back. By keeping these expenditures under the president's direct control, it provided the administration with a few billion dollars a year to use as it saw fit, virtually free of checks and balances.

Since GW was such a large outlier, let us redo the graph, looking at the series from 1962 to 2000 (see Figure A3-2).

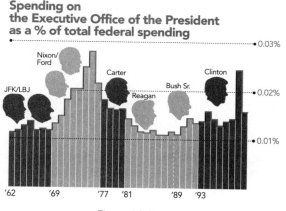

Figure A3-2

Before GW, er, went off the charts, the peak in spending by the Executive Office of the President occurred under Nixon/Ford. There was also a big spike in 1999, which may have been largely due to supplementals related to the war in Kosovo, in which the United States (through NATO) got involved from March to June of that year. (We have not, as of this writing, confirmed that the spike in 1999 was due to the war in Kosovo.) A smaller but similar spike occurred in 1990 and 1991, during the buildup to and the fighting of Gulf War I.

Figure A3-3 shows the annualized percentage change in spending by the Executive Office of the President, by administration.

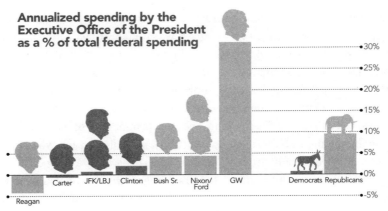

**Annualized spending by the Executive Office of the President as a % of total federal spending**

Figure A3-3

The biggest increases occurred under GW (no surprise); in a very, very distant second was Nixon/Ford. Both GW and Nixon had reputations for secrecy, and one way to pacify a president's penchant for secrecy is to move money into the budget for the Executive Office of the President. Bush Sr., a former director of the CIA, was almost tied with Nixon/Ford at increasing the EOP's share of the budget.

The three Democratic administrations came next: Clinton and JFK/LBJ increased the budget share of the EOP by small amounts, and Carter actually shrank it. However, the biggest decrease in the EOP's budget occurred under Ronald Reagan. Does this mean that Reagan was the least secretive president in our sample? Perhaps. Or perhaps he found other ways of funding causes with no oversight. The Iran-Contra affair, for instance, is a sign that at least some members of his administration were creative in raising money, even if it meant providing advanced weaponry to a country with which we had no diplomatic ties and whose leadership referred to the United States as the Great Satan. Which only goes to show that there are many ways for a president to hide what he is doing from the American public.

# Try This at Home

We're nearing the end of the book. We hope you've had fun reading it. We had a lot of fun writing it. But guess what? Everything you've read is already outdated—well, a little. It may not be old news but it's aging—at least at the fringes. New data has come out. For some series, that includes more data—months or years of data. For other series, data has been revised and results are now a little different. For example, we are writing this just weeks before the Bureau of Economic Analysis (BEA) is slated to release a major revision of nominal GDP figures and to change the base year it uses from 2000 to 2005 at the same time.

Now you are not likely to find a burst of new data about, say, the Nixon-era economy. But you might get some more precise information about the past couple years. And as the months pass, you can start forming a more complete statistical picture of the current administration.

Since most people like to be up on the latest trends—be it news about the crime rate or salacious gossip about the national debt—we suggest that you take a look at late-breaking data yourself. Or at least learn to do it should the need arise. Being familiar with the data and being able to analyze it yourself can be very helpful. One benefit to having these skills is that it will help you stay well-informed. Being well-informed keeps you from sounding like an idiot when you talk to other people who are also informed, and hopefully helps you make better decisions about who to vote for and—just as important—who not to vote for.

Another advantage—perhaps more important—of being able to check things out yourself is that you are less likely to be bamboozled by the huge number of charlatans, political hacks, and plain old ignoramuses who are always eager to say (or imply) things that simply are not true. As Ronald Reagan used to say, "Trust, but verify."

There are a lot of sources of data out there, and we think it's useful to be familiar with many of them. Here are some of the sources of the data we've consulted in writing this book:

- The Bureau of Economic Analysis' National Income and Product Accounts (NIPA) tables. These are the nation's income statements and balance sheets, and they contain detailed information on GDP and its components. NIPA Table 7.1 is particularly helpful—it contains among other things, figures for GDP per capita, real GDP per capita, and the population. The NIPA tables also have a lot of information on aggregate income and savings rates.
- The Bureau of Labor Statistics (BLS), which keeps track of employment issues, and the Consumer Price Index (CPI), which is used to compute inflation.
- The White House's Office of Management and Budget, which compiles data on the federal government's spending patterns and on its tax receipts.
- The FBI, which compiles crime statistics.
- Many health statistics are available from the Centers for Disease Control and the National Institutes of Health.
- The Federal Reserve keeps track of the money supply and interest rates, as well as information about the banking sector and people's wealth. Additionally, the Federal Reserve's St. Louis Branch has a cool tool called the Federal Reserve Economic Database (FRED), which contains data from a lot of other government sources. FRED will also graph the data for you in some nifty ways.
- The Census has all sorts of information on population and demographics, as well as on income, housing, and health care, among other things. In addition, the Census publishes the Statistical Abstract of the United States (both in hard copy and online), which compiles a lot of information from many different government agencies. Want to know how much uranium was produced in 1980? What about the average wind speed in Reno? Or how much military assistance the United States sent to sub-Saharan Africa? You'll find all that and a lot more (including a lot of the data that went into this book!) in the Statistical Abstract of the United States.

All these sources produce or store a lot of data. Most of that data is useful to someone, somewhere, at some point. But *you* have to decide which data is useful to you when you're trying to understand something. And you have to figure out what to do with the data so it will help answer your questions. You have to recognize that most of the time, if you want to understand the size of the economy, looking at GDP is useful, real GDP is more useful, and real GDP per capita is more useful still. You have to realize that if you want to examine growth rates, you may even want to look at net real GDP per capita, which you then have to create yourself by transforming some of the data the government makes available.

Another useful skill is to be able to adjust for inflation. Adjusting for inflation requires, first of all, having a base year. The Bureau of Labor Statistics has a nifty inflation calculator on its Web site (http://data.bls.gov/cgi-bin/cpicalc.pl) that will convert values from one year to values of another (such as your base year), adjusted for inflation. Or you can do it yourself—the process requires a few steps.

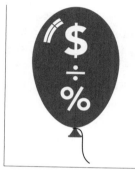

For example, nominal debt per capita in 1992 was $16,164. The average of the monthly CPI in 1992 was 140.3, and the average of the monthly CPI for the year 2008 was 215.3. (Note—for simplicity, in this appendix, we will round to no more than one significant digit past the decimal point. This may cause results to be slightly different from those shown elsewhere in the book. Similarly, in some instances, our results differ marginally from those obtained using the BLS calculator because we round to a larger number of significant digits.) Therefore, the CPI in 2008 was (215.3/140.3) = 153.5 percent higher than in 1992. Therefore, the real debt per capita for 1992, in 2008 dollars, was $16,164 x 153.5 percent = $24,812.

It is worth noting that this method of adjusting for inflation is the one most commonly used by both government sources and the private sector. However, the BEA uses a slightly different method, though it produced similar results.

There is one more "secret" to give away: how to compute the annualized percentage change in a series over the span of a president's term. The formula for computing the annualized percentage change for a series from year X to year Y is this:

$$\{(\text{Year Y value} / \text{Year X value})^{(1/(Y-X))} - 1\} \times 100$$

The formula has a wide range of applications. For example, this is the formula used by the bank to determine how much you should pay on your monthly mortgage.

Consider again real debt per capita in 2008 dollars. In 1988, the year before Bush Sr. took office, it was about $19,862. In 1992, Bush Sr.'s last year in office, it was $24,812. Finally, in the year 2000, Clinton's final year in office, the real debt per capita in 2008 dollars was approximately $24,956.

The annualized percentage change in real debt per capita over the four years of the Bush Sr. administration was $\{(24{,}812/19{,}862)^{(1/4)}-1\} \times 100$, or 5.72 percent. That is, increasing $19,862 each year for four years by about 5.72 percent gives us $24,812. Similarly, the annualized percentage change in real debt per capita over the eight years of the Clinton administration was $\{(24{,}956/24{,}812)^{(1/8)}-1\} \times 100 = 0.07$ percent.

And there it is. Those are our secrets. Simple stuff, but it's all you need to reproduce just about everything you've read in this book. And if you do that, you will get slightly different results than we did on some series—as we noted, the data gets revised on a regular basis, sometimes for several years after it originally comes out. And perhaps you'll round to a different number of significant digits than we do. But for the most part your answers should be very similar to ours.

And that brings us back to the topic of charlatans, political hacks, and plain old ignoramuses. By now you must have noticed that much of what we showed in this book doesn't bear a lot of resemblance to what you've heard from many often highly respected members of the community—politicians,

professors, and personalities in the media. Stated plainly, what many politicians, professors, and personalities in the media tell you is at odds with what the data actually says. Everyone makes mistakes, but some mistakes are more than just mistakes, especially if they're repeated again and again. If such people are lying to you, distorting the facts, or simply mistaken on things that you can easily check, you can bet they are lying to you, distorting the facts, or mistaken on other things as well. That is their fault. But if you choose to believe them when you know (or should know) that they're wrong, well, that is your fault.

And that matters because when some of us allow ourselves to be misled, all of us pay a price. Our politicians—including our presidents and their advisors and their apologists—lie, obfuscate, and disguise the truth because they can. And they can do it only because we allow it, because we don't pay attention, and because, even in those cases where we know they are lying, we don't call them on it, but instead continue to treat them with respect despite the contempt they show for the truth—and for us.

Our simple plea: pay attention to the data. Please.

# Obama

This book has focused on the presidents who served from 1953 to 2008. But now there is a new president, Barack Obama, and he should be judged as the other presidents have been—by how much better (or worse) the country is at the end of his administration than it was when he came into office. And he should be judged objectively—by looking at facts, rather than opinions.

At this writing, data for a few of the issues that we covered elsewhere in this book is starting to trickle in for the first year of President Obama's term. There is no doubt that Obama's first year in office has been tough. He inherited an economic disaster, and economic disasters usually take a while to fix. The Great Recession has been compared to the Great Depression, which Franklin Roosevelt inherited from Herbert Hoover. As we saw in Chapter 1, Figure 1-9, Roosevelt went on to post the fastest economic growth rate ever measured in this country, and that remains true even leaving out the World War II years. However, Roosevelt's first year in office was challenging, and real GDP per capita shrank by 1.9 percent. JFK and Reagan, to cite more recent examples, also inherited poor eco-

nomic conditions (though not as poor as Obama, and much less poor than those faced by FDR) and went on to preside over relatively rapid recoveries.

Therefore, being saddled with a challenging economic environment does not guarantee poor performance by a president, even if it might excuse slow growth for a year or so while he is attempting to right the ship. Let's look at the data available to us from Obama's first year and see what it might tell us about what he has done well, what he hasn't, and where we are likely to go from here.

Real GDP per capita decreased by almost 3.3 percent during 2009, Obama's first year in office, according to preliminary figures from the BEA.[1] If that rate of growth, er, shrinkage, continues throughout his term, Barack

Obama will rank only above Herbert Hoover, among all presidents since 1929, the first year for which for which this data is available. Yet, even including Obama's first-year statistics, growth during years in which the president is a Democrat is still much higher than growth during years in which a Republican is a president, both from 1929 to 2009 and from 1953 to 2009.

The current economic disaster began well before Obama took office, and perhaps it was inevitable that growth would be, if not negative, at least very slow during his first year.

The trajectory of the economy does appear to have improved during Obama's first year in office, as we can see in Figure A5-1.[2]

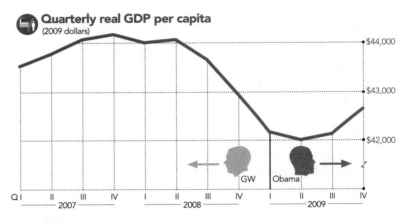

Figure A5-1

Whether the economy will continue to improve, or whether further deterioration is in store, we cannot say with certainty. But we can look at what Obama has done and see whether those policies are similar to those that have worked in the past.

If there is one policy we have looked at over and over in this book, it's tax policy. We did so mostly by looking at the tax burden—the government's current receipts as a percentage of GDP. Put another way, this figure reflects the percentage of the country's total income paid to the government. Figure A5-2 shows what that looks like, on a quarterly basis, going back to the beginning of 2007.[3]

Regardless of rhetoric (whether by Obama's supporters or detractors), the tax burden seems to have followed the same trajectory during the first three quarters of the Obama administration as it did during the last two years of GW's term: It plummeted like Alan Greenspan's reputation. Cuts came in all

**Quarterly federal government revenue as a % of GDP**

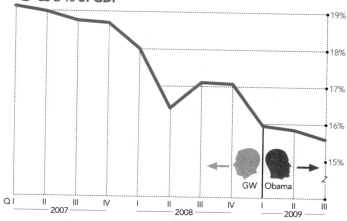

Figure A5-2

forms, from giveaways to home and car buyers, to stimulus money and other incentives for corporations. While it is true that many of those cuts began before Obama took office, his administration made every effort to maintain them.

We hasten to note that a recession does not automatically decrease the tax burden. The amount people pay in taxes might shrink, but then so does their income (and so does GDP). Consider FDR, who took office during the Great Depression. He also increased the tax burden quite a bit—it tripled from 1932 to 1940. In fact, the tax burden nearly doubled just during FDR's first two years in office. But in his second year in office, 1934, real GDP per capita grew by 10.2 percent. And, as a testatment to the strength of FDR's economic policies, real GDP per capita would grow even faster than that in four other years of his administration. No other president came close to producing even a single year with double-digit growth in real GDP per capita.

As we saw in Chapter 2, Figure 2-6, since 1953, every Democratic administration increased the share of GDP that went to the government, and every Republican administration decreased it. Thus, if Obama were to maintain his first-year tax policy for the rest of his term, his presidency would end up looking more like a Republican administration than a Democratic administration.

What about the flip side of the equation—government spending? See Figure A5-3 for a look at government spending, on a quarterly basis, since 2007.[4]

Obama's approach to spending in his first year also seems to owe a lot to policies from his predecessor's final two years. When it finally became obvious

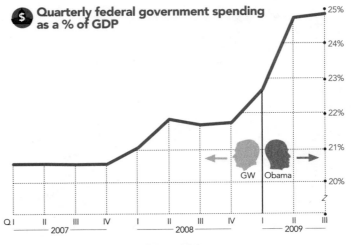

Figure A5-3

to GW that the economy was in recession (around the second quarter of 2008), spending first increased dramatically, but soon leveled off. Only when it became apparent that the problem was of a much larger magnitude than originally feared did the administration seek approval for more spending, mostly through a program called the Troubled Asset Relief Program (TARP). TARP was intended to fund the federal government's purchase or insurance of financial instruments held by financial firms, in order to prevent financial markets from seizing up. TARP supporters felt this was about to happen because nobody knew whether the assets any given firm was holding had value. In layman's terms, nobody on Wall Street wanted to do business with anyone else on Wall Street because nobody knew whose holdings had any value and who was about to be unmasked as a deadbeat.

TARP was one of two means Obama employed to fix the economy in the early days of the crisis. Before we go on, it is important to note that the TARP bailout of the financial companies should not be confused with the stimulus package. And confused with one another they often are—for both good reasons and bad. Some of that is deliberate: Pundits and politicians purposely conflate the two so that one will be tainted by association with the other. The bailout is unpopular and packs added emotional punch since it involves delivering huge payoffs to the bankers who crashed the economy in the first place.

Another reason these policies are confused with each other is that the figures associated with them are similarly incomprehensible in their magnitude. It used to be said in Washington: "A billion here, a billion there, and pretty soon you're dealing with real money." These days, it's "$700 billion here and $700 billion there," and it's very easy to lose perspective. And, as it happens, both TARP and the stimulus package were of nearly the same magnitude.

But the TARP billions were meant to keep the credit markets from failing, while the stimulus package was intended to directly stir demand, fuel growth, and create jobs. The TARP money was not necessarily spent, since much of it was given out in the form of guarantees. And much of what *was* spent was paid back (which freed the banks from restraints on the bonuses they paid).

TARP was inherited from the Bush administration and largely adopted by the Obama administration. The stimulus package, on the other hand, was an Obama administration response to the clearly worsening conditions that Obama faced when he took office and to the rising fear that the economy was sliding toward catastrophe. Partly for political reasons, partly due to the advice of the economists he was listening to, Obama obtained a spending package from Congress that put a lot of money into the economy immediately at the end of 2009 when the economy desperately needed it. But with so much of that package in the form of tax cuts and longer-range projects, it should be noted that the package turned out to be a lot smaller than the big number scrawled on the wrapping. That package is smaller still when we take into consideration that much of the federal spending increase took place just as state and local governments were cutting back by (cumulatively) more or less the same amount, making the net change in total government spending (federal, state and local) relatively small.[5]

Nevertheless, Obama certainly gets credit, or blame, for the stimulus package; it is his plan, however it was tempered by political realities. It was shaped and passed on his watch, and he attached some fairly large promises to it. However, when it comes to TARP, most of the wheels were put in motion before Obama became president. Most, but not all. Which means that Obama does bear some responsibility for TARP. He voted for the program as a senator, did nothing to turn down the funds that had not yet been allocated by the time he became president, and, once he became president, went out looking for more funds for more handouts.

By way of comparison, during his first two years in office, FDR also increased the federal government's spending as a percentage of GDP. However, the focus of the spending in FDR's term was very different from the direction in which Obama appears to be heading. Whereas FDR's spending (the New Deal) was geared toward putting the proverbial little guy back to work through "pump-priming" and keeping close tabs on the financial sector (through the creation of the Securities and Exchange Commission and other agencies), Obama's stimulus was a faint echo of the New Deal, while his approach with TARP was primarily to funnel funding to financial firms.

In essence, by giving money to the entities whose bad bets exacerbated (if not created) the Great Recession, Obama has continued the very "trickle-down" version of government spending practiced by his predecessor. More worrisome still, in his first year Obama failed to take steps to ensure that the calamities that brought about the Great Recession won't happen again.

Fortunately, the stimulus package did aim at putting more money directly into the economy to make up for lost demand. Unfortunately, it was a very fractured effort that was somewhat misnamed, incorporating large pieces of not-so-stimulating tax breaks and whole rafts of spending that were not likely to provide bang for the buck at the moment when things were bleakest.

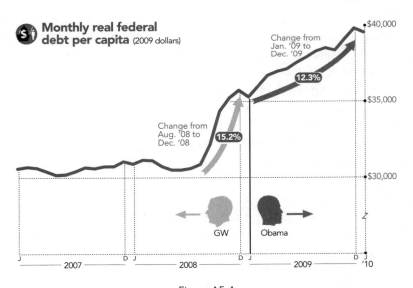

Figure A5-4

Government debt under Obama has not been growing as quickly as it was in the final months of GW's administration, and on the surface, this is probably a good thing (see Figure A5-4). But when private demand is falling badly, adding government demand—without paying for it immediately (i.e., incurring debt)—can fill the gap and get the economy growing again.

Done right, deficit spending—which is what the stimulus package amounts to—softens pain in the near term and lays the groundwork for the growth the nation needs. It begets investment, promotes efficiency, and bolsters the economy in the long term. And if it succeeds at doing all that, a healthier, more productive economy will eventually be able to pay off the debt without substantial pain. But if such a stimulus does not spark productive growth, it will simply become an added burden to an already long-suffering economy. The result is not stimulus but a weak economy and lots of crushing debt.

History does provide some guidance when it comes to evaluating overall policies. In this book, we have shown repeatedly, and in a number of different ways, that administrations that cut taxes and provided more incentives to the rich than to the poor have tended to produce slower economic growth than administrations that did just the opposite. If we cannot put a value on TARP (and similar programs) and the stimulus package, we can at least state with some certainty: Though they did some good, the choices made by GW and Obama do not seem to have produced substantial relief, given their costs, for the American public.

Still, the worst of the crisis seemed to have passed even as the future looked uncertain. The number of monthly job losses ebbed and then some halting job growth began. Several housing market reports hinted at having hit bottom or even of a modest improvement. Even the S&P 500 index of stocks had climbed to a 19-month high by late April 2010.

So, while the administration's first-year effort seemed to fall short of what the crisis might have demanded, it was apparently enough to shove the economy out of the ditch. But as we write, it is too early to tell if that momentum can be sustained. With more than eight million jobs lost in the Great Recession, there will be a lot of ground to make up.

# Notes

## CHAPTER 1

1 Accessed March 2009 from the University of California at Santa Barbara's *The American Presidency Project* archives, available at: http://www.presidency.ucsb.edu/ws/index.php?pid=20544.

2 All data on GDP used in the book comes from the BEA's National Income and Product Accounts (NIPA) tables located here: http://www.bea.gov/national/nipaweb/SelectTable.asp?Selected=Y. GDP figures for 2008 can be found in NIPA Table 1.1.5: http://www.bea.gov/national/nipaweb/TableView .asp?SelectedTable=5&ViewSeries=NO&Java=no&Request3Place=N&3Place=N&FromView=YES& Freq=Year&FirstYear=2008&LastYear=2008&3Place=N&Update=Update&JavaBox=no#Mid. Data accessed March 26, 2009.

3 GDP per capita can be found in line 1 in the BEA's NIPA Table 7.1 (http://www.bea.gov/national/ nipaweb/TableView.asp?SelectedTable=253&ViewSeries=NO&Java=no&Request3Place=N&3Place =N&FromView=YES&Freq=Year&FirstYear=1929&LastYear=2008&3Place=N&Update=Update&Jav aBox=no#Mid). Data accessed March 29, 2009.

4 Estimates from the CIA's World Factbook ranking of countries by GDP, which is published exclusively on the Web (https://www.cia.gov/library/publications/the-world-factbook/rankorder/2001rank .html). Figures used here were from the addition last updated March 5, 2009, accessed March 26, 2009. Note that the CIA's estimates are adjusted by Purchasing Power Parity (PPP)—that is, they attempt to take into account differences in the cost of living in each country.

5 Estimates for GDP per capita from the CIA's World Factbook ranking of countries by GDP per capita (https://www.cia.gov/library/publications/the-world-factbook/rankorder/2004rank.html), last updated March 5, 2009, accessed March 27, 2009.

6 To be precise, we use the "CPI-U"—that is, the CPI for "all urban consumers." The data is available from the BLS directly at this site: ftp://ftp.bls.gov/pub/special.requests/cpi/cpiai.txt. It is also reproduced in an easier-to-use format in the Federal Reserve Bank of St. Louis's Federal Reserve Economic Database (FRED) at this site: http://research.stlouisfed.org/fred2/series/CPIAUCNS?cid=9. Note that to convert GDP figures, the BEA uses an alternative tool called the "GDP deflator," which produces very similar results. Because we want most readers to be able to easily replicate our results, we opted to use the simpler approach, which is also more commonly used on the other series.

7 The BLS inflation calculator is located at this site: http://data.bls.gov/cgi-bin/cpicalc.pl.

8 Data on real GDP per capita in 2000 dollars was obtained in March of 2009 from line 9 of the BEA's NIPA Table 7.1, and converted to 2008 dollars using a factor based on the CPI.

9 In other words, instead of using the year before an administration took office as the "baseline" year, we use the president's first year in office as the baseline.

10 From the NBER's Web site, on the page on business cycle expansions and contractions, accessed March 27, 2009: http://www.nber.org/cycles.html.

11 Ibid.

12 The correlation between real GDP per capita growth over the span of an administration from 1952 to 2008 and the time spent in recession by that administration is –77 percent.

13 GDP, incidentally, was created in the early 1930s when "The Department of Commerce commissioned Nobel laureate Simon Kuznets of the aforementioned NBER to develop a set of national economic accounts" (http://www.bea.gov/scb/account_articles/general/0100od/maintext.htm).

14 A recent, oft-cited example of that line of thought appears in Amity Shlaes, *The Forgotten Man: A New History of the Great Depression* (New York: HarperCollins Publishing, 2007).

15 Leaving out FDR, the best-performing Democrat, and Hoover, the worst-performing Republican, still leaves Democrats outperforming Republicans, with average annualized growth rates of 1.9 percent and 1.5 percent, respectively.

16 Some of you may be wondering why we are discussing real M1 per capita and not interest rates. After all, the Fed generates a lot of hoopla making announcements about interest rates (or rather, one specific interest rate—the Fed funds rate), but the Fed commissioners don't say much about money supply, much less real M1 per capita. The way we see it, though, when you want to figure out a magic trick, you watch the magician's hand and not his mouth. Consider that every year, in December, people like to spend money, and the magician, er, the Fed, generally tries to encourage them. It does this by increasing the real M1 per capita. And we see a clear seasonal pattern in December. In the months between September and March, the high-water mark for real M1 per capita was in December 78 per- cent of the time from 1959 to 2008. Other measures of the money supply did not move to the same extent around December. There also does not appear to be much of a pattern to the Fed funds' behavior in December either. So regardless of the magician's patter, his hand is firmly on real M1 per capita.

17 M1 (for December of each year) was obtained from FRED (http://research.stlouisfed.org/fred2/series/M1NS?cid=25, accessed March 26, 2009). It was multiplied by the CPI conversion factor described earlier in this chapter and divided by population, which also was obtained from FRED (http://research.stlouisfed.org/fred2/series/POP).

18 Alan Greenspan, *The Age of Turbulence,* 1st ed. (New York: Penguin Press, 2007), p. 48.

19 Ibid., p. 208.

20 Ibid., p. 88.

21 Ibid., p. 93.

22 Ibid., p. 217.

## CHAPTER 2

1 Current expenditures were obtained from the BEA's NIPA Table 3.2, line 19, updated on March 26, 2009, accessed April 2009.

2 An example of this comparison can be seen in Benjamin A. Mandel and Andrew E. Vargo, "NIPA Translation of the Fiscal Year 2009 Federal Budget," *Bureau of Economic Analysis Survey of Current Business* (March 2008): 19, Table 1 Budget Receipts and Outlays and NIPA Federal Government Current Receipts and Expenditures (http://www.bea.gov/scb/pdf/2008/03%20March/0308_fedbudget.pdf, accessed April 2009). Note that, for the most part, we do not use the federal budget itself because it is based on fiscal, not calendar, years. The exception occurs when we are comparing it to other data that is only available by fiscal year.

3 GDP was obtained from the BEA's NIPA Table 1.1.5, line 1, updated on March 26, 2009. Real expenditures per capita were calculated using expenditures as well as population and the CPI. Population was obtained from the BEA's NIPA Table 7.1, line 16, updated on March 26, 2009. CPI was obtained from FRED (http://research.stlouisfed.org/fred2/series/CPIAUCNS?cid=9, accessed April 2009).

4 While the State of the Union Address is given in January, LBJ was referring to the fiscal year, which had begun six months earlier in July.

5 See the White House's OMB Historical Table 3.2 "Outlays by Function and Subfunction: 1962–2015." (www.whitehouse.gov/omb/fy2011/assets/hist03Z2.xls) Interest on Treasury Debt is line item 901. total outlays are shown at the bottom of the spreadsheet.

6    Data on the number of federal employees is available from the White House's Office of Management and Budget Table 17.1 (http://www.gpoaccess.gov/usbudget/fy09/sheets/hist17z1.xls, accessed April 2009).

7    The growth rate of measures covered in this chapter, namely government spending, government revenue, and the surplus (or deficit) as a percentage of GDP, are treated differently than measures discussed in other chapters. Whereas the growth rate for issues described in other chapters are generally obtained by annualizing the data, in this chapter, annual averages are used instead. This is because some administrations that inherited deficits left behind surpluses, and vice versa, and it is mathematically impossible to calculate the annualized growth rate for a series that changes signs.

8    IRS publication *Personal Exemptions and Individual Income Tax Rates: 1913–2002*, p. 1. (Document found here: http://www.irs.gov/pub/irs-soi/02inpetr.pdf, accessed April 2009.) Marginal tax rates through 2002 from the same document. Rates from 2003 to 2008 noted from a number of sources, including federal tax forms and the Tax Foundation's *U.S. Federal Individual Income Tax Rates History: 1913–2009*, located here: http://www.taxfoundation.org/publications/show/151.html.

9    Current tax revenues were obtained from the BEA's NIPA Table 3.2, line 1, updated on March 26, 2009, and accessed April 14, 2009. We have chosen to use current receipts rather than total receipts to maintain consistency with our previous choice of using current expenditures rather than total expenditures.

10   All major accounting firms and many top law firms have departments to serve "high-net-worth" individuals; the service these departments provide is generally very expensive.

11   Data on the employment-to-population ratio can be obtained from the Bureau of Labor Statistics: http://www.bls.gov/webapps/legacy/cpsatab1.htm.

12   Ruminating upon receiving the Nobel Prize many years later, Mundell would insist that "[t]here's been no downside to the tax cuts." See Suzanne Trimel, *Columbia University Record*, Vol. 25, No. 07, Oct. 29, 1999, accessed December 17, 2009, at http://www.columbia.edu/cu/record/archives/vol25/07/2507_Mundell_Nobel.html.

13   For reasons we cannot understand, there seems to be a distinct failure among certain circles to grasp that tax cuts that occurred in 1964 simply could not have had an effect on growth before Kennedy was assassinated. For instance, Alan Greenspan (*The Age of Turbulence*, pp. 54–55) insists that "The economy was growing too sluggishly" by January of 1963 and only began to thrive after the tax cuts. We invite you to look once more at Figure 1-9 in Chapter 1 and determine if you are able to reach the same conclusion about the Kennedy years as the Maestro.

14   Current tax revenues were obtained from the BEA's NIPA Table 3.2, line 33, updated on March 26, 2009, accessed April 14, 2009.

15   For readers who are interested in the numbers, we repeat that this is not the annualized change. Because the surplus went from positive to negative (and vice versa) during some administrations, computing the annualized change makes no sense in mathematical terms. Instead, the total percentage change was computed and divided by the number of years.


## CHAPTER 3

1    Accessed December 2009 from the University of California at Santa Barbara's *The American Presidency Project* archives, available at: http://www.presidency.ucsb.edu/ws/index.php?pid=43130.

2    As of December 2008, the Social Security Administration had $2.4 trillion in assets. Those assets were held in the form of U.S. Treasury Bonds, which in effect means that in December 2008, the U.S. government owed the Social Security Administration $2.4 trillion. Data accessed from http://www.ssa.gov/OACT/ProgData/assets.html on April 1, 2009.

3    Data on Social Security's historical income and expenditures is available here: http://www.ssa.gov/history/trustfunds.html.

4 Reducing the money supply is done the opposite way—the Fed just sells bonds it owns and makes the money it was given in payment disappear into the ether.

5 In this chapter, we will be using data for total government debt held on December 31 of each year. Data from 1993 to the present can be found on a nifty application on the Treasury's Web site located here: http://www.treasurydirect.gov/NP/BPDLogin?application=np. Data for earlier years was obtained from the "Monthly Statement of the Public Debt," prepared by the Treasury every month and accessible online here: http://www.treasurydirect.gov/govt/reports/pd/mspd/mspd.htm. Statements are available going back to 1953. The statement for December 1953 also contains data for December 1952. Note that the monthly statements from 1973 to 1988 only contain data in dollars. Data on foreign holdings comes from the Treasury Department's "TIC" (i.e., Treasury International Capital System) data: http://treasury.tpaq.treasury.gov/tic/mfh.txt, accessed on July 26, 2009.

6 We have combined debt owed to Hong Kong with debt owed to China; the Treasury breaks these out into separate accounts.

7 Debt as a percentage of GDP by fiscal year—not calendar year—is available from the White House Office of Management Budget's Historical Table 7.1 (http://www.gpoaccess.gov/usbudget/fy09/sheets/hist07z1.xls), going back to 1940.

8 Address before a Joint Session of the Congress on the Program for Economic Recovery, February 18, 1981, accessed in April 2009 from the University of California at Santa Barbara's *The American Presidency Project* archives, available at: http://www.presidency.ucsb.edu/ws/index.php?pid=43425.

9 BEA NIPA Table 3.2, line 28, accessed April 2009.

10 Alan Greenspan, *The Age of Turbulence,* (New York: Penguin Press, 2007), p. 147.

11 Because debt is best measured by the end of the year, to be as consistent as possible we will use real GDP per capita from the fourth quarter of every year.


## CHAPTER 4

1 Press conference by George W. Bush in St. Petersburg, Florida, accessed in December 2009 from the University of California at Santa Barbara's *The American Presidency Project* archives, available at http://www.presidency.ucsb.edu/ws/index.php?pid=72948.

2 Not surprisingly, the employment-to-population ratio is closely related to the state of the economy at large. The correlation between the annual average employment rate and the annual real GDP per capita is above 90 percent.

3 The employment-to-population ratio is among the data presented in the BLS's Table A-1, titled "Employment Status of the Civilian Population by Sex and Age (Numbers in Thousands)." That table is located at: http://www.bls.gov/webapps/legacy/cpsatab1.htm. Data accessed April 4, 2009. While unemployment data is typically analyzed monthly, we have opted to use the annual average employment-to-population ratio. Monthly employment data fluctuates a lot, and the business "Birth-Death" model that feeds into it often produces results that seem somewhat unrealistic, especially in periods of transition. Thus we felt the smoothing effect obtained from using average annual data made annual averages a better choice than monthly data.

4 Jimmy Carter, Economic Recovery Program: Message to the Congress, January 31, 1977, available at University of California at Santa Barbara's *The American Presidency Project* archives, accessed in April 2009 from: http://www.presidency.ucsb.edu/ws/index.php?pid=7344.

5 Jimmy Carter, Report to the American People: Remarks from the White House Library, February 2, 1977, accessed in April 2009 from the University of California at Santa Barbara's *The American Presidency Project* archives at: http://www.presidency.ucsb.edu/ws/index.php?pid=7455.

6 Jimmy Carter, News Conference, July 12, 1977, Old Executive Building, accessed in April 2009 from the University of California at Santa Barbara's *The American Presidency Project* archives at: http://www.presidency.ucsb.edu/ws/index.php?pid=7786.

7   BLS Table B-3, available at: http://www.bls.gov/webapps/legacy/cesbtab3.htm. Data accessed April 4, 2009.

8   Jobs data originates with the BLS, but was accessed from FRED (in April 2009) for convenience (http://research.stlouisfed.org/fred2/categories/11).

9   Data from 1999 to 2007 available at http://www.census.gov/hhes/www/hlthins/historic/hihistt1.xls. Data from 1987 to 2005 available at http://www.census.gov/hhes/www/hlthins/historic/hlthin05/hihistt1.html. Data accessed April 4, 2009. Note that the two series are computed differently. As a result, for Figure 4-5, we use figures from 1987 to 1998 from the second series, and data from 1999 to 2007 from the first series. However, to compute the percentage change in people with employer-based health insurance over the span of each administration (Figure 4-6), we use data from the same series for each administration. Thus, for Bush Sr. and Bill Clinton we use data from the series available from 1987 to 2005, but for GW, we use data from the series available from 1999 forward.

## CHAPTER 5

1   Accessed from the University of California at Santa Barbara's *The American Presidency Project* archives in May 2009, available at http://www.presidency.ucsb.edu/ws/index.php?pid=163&st=ownership+society&st1=.

2   Data from the BLS's 2007 American Time Use Survey (http://www.bls.gov/news.release/atus.t01.htm, accessed in July 2009).

3   Data from 1974 to 2007 is available from the Census' Historical Tables on Income, "P-7. Regions of People (Both Sexes Combined—All Races) by Median and Mean Income: 1974 to 2007" (http://www.census.gov/hhes/www/income/histinc/p07AR.html, accessed October 2008). Data from earlier years going back to 1947 was obtained from a Census Bureau report titled "Measuring 50 Years of Economic Change," Current Population Reports P60-203, Table C-2. Note that the data was inflation-adjusted, but the CPI used at the time was calculated differently than the CPI used today. However, the CPI used in that report was provided in Table C-1 of the report; we used that to convert the income to nominal data, and then used the current iteration of CPI to adjust for inflation as in earlier chapters.

4   Thomas R. Barnes, George R. Chastain, and Don C. Wetzel, Credit Card Automatic Currency Dispenser, Patent Number, 3,761,682, September 1973.

5   Personal income data comes from NIPA Table 2.1, "Personal Income and Its Disposition" (http://www.bea.gov/national/nipaweb/TableView.asp?SelectedTable=58&ViewSeries=NO&Java=no&Request3Place=N&3Place=N&FromView=YES&Freq=Qtr&FirstYear=1947&LastYear=2008&3Place=N&Update=Update&JavaBox=no#Mid), accessed April 7, 2009. Population comes from FRED. Debt figures were obtained from multiple sources, as described in notes to Chapter 3.

6   Series FL152090005.A. We used data accessed on April 8, 2009, updated through March 12, 2009.

7   Data from: Current Population Survey/Housing Vacancy Survey, Series H-111 Reports, Table 14 (http://www.census.gov/hhes/www/housing/hvs/historic/files/histtab14.xls, accessed April 2009). Data presented is for the fourth quarter of the year. However, when computing the change in home ownership by administration, to avoid wasting sparse data, we computed the change over the span of the JFK/LBJ administration as if it ran from the first quarter of 1965 to the last quarter of 1968, and annualized it over 4.75 years.

8   "White House Fact Sheet: New Steps to Help Homeowners Avoid Foreclosure," August 31, 2007.

9   If you'd like to try it yourself, the law can be found here: http://frwebgate.access.gpo.gov/cgi-bin/getdoc.cgi?dbname=110_cong_public_laws&docid=f:publ289.110.

10  Series FL155035015.Q and FL155035065.Q. We used data accessed on April 12, 2009, updated through March 12, 2009.

11  Ben Conery, "Mortgage Fraud Cases Swamp FBI," *Washington Times* (March 26, 2009)

## CHAPTER 6

1  http://www.reagan.utexas.edu/archives/speeches/1982/61782e.htm

2  Data on the end-of-year number of active-duty military personnel for 2008 comes from the Department of Defense's Active Duty Military Strength Report for February 28, 2009, accessed
on August 23, 2009 (http://siadapp.dmdc.osd.mil/personnel/MILITARY/ms1.pdf). Active-duty
figures for 1960 to 2007 come from the 2009 Statistical Abstract of the United States, Table 494
(http://www.census.gov/compendia/statab/tables/09s0494.xls, accessed April 2009). Figures
for 1957 to 1959, and for 1952 to 1956, come from the 1963 Statistical Abstract of the United
States, Table 344, and the 1957 Statistical Abstract of the United States, Table 289, respectively.
Versions of the Statistical Abstract of the United States from 1953 to 1994 can be accessed from:
http://www.census.gov/prod/www/abs/statab1951-1994.htm. This section also uses data on the
U.S. population, which is obtained from NIPA Table 7.1 (http://www.bea.gov/national/nipaweb/
TableView.asp?SelectedTable=253&Freq=Year&FirstYear=1929&LastYear=2008).

3  Julian E. Barnes, "Military Recruiters Are Seeing Better Days," *Los Angeles Times* (October 11,
2008). The article was accessed in April 2009 at http://articles.latimes.com/2008/oct/11/nation/
na-recruit11.

4  The Stockholm International Peace Research Institute 2007 Yearbook (http://yearbook2007
.sipri.org/files/YB0708.pdf) places the figure at 46 percent. The document was accessed
in April 2009. However, if you aren't the sort of person to consider a bunch of Swedish
pacifists as particularly credible, note that figures from other sources tend to come up with
similar estimates.

5  Data on defense spending was obtained from the BEA's NIPA Table 3.9.5, Government Consumption Expenditures and Gross Investment (http://www.bea.gov/national/nipaweb/TableView.asp
?SelectedTable=96&ViewSeries=NO&Java=no&Request3Place=N&3Place=N&FromView=YES&
Freq=Year&FirstYear=1947&LastYear=2008&3Place=N&Update=Update&JavaBox=no#Mid),
accessed April 26, 2009, and updated March 26, 2009.

6  Data on total expenditures, which is used less often as a measure of government spending, goes
back only to 1960, and also includes expenditures by government-owned corporations that have
their own revenue streams and are usually kept off the government books.

7  As noted in Chapter 2, the correlation between current and total expenditures was 99.98 percent.

8  These were the first major wars for the United States since before World War II in which the
enemy was not a major power or at least a proxy for a major power. They could be described as
guerrilla conflicts, occupations, or both.

9  White House OMB Historical Table 17.5, Government Employment and Population, 1962–2007
(http://www.gpoaccess.gov/usbudget/fy09/sheets/hist17z5.xls). The data employed was reported
for the 2009 budget year, and was accessed April 24, 2009. The equivalent table in the 2010 budget (http://www.gpoaccess.gov/usbudget/fy10/sheets/hist17z1.xls) no longer reports employees,
but rather full-time-equivalent employees, which is not directly comparable. However, the first
year for which that series is reported is 1981. Given a choice between using employees (data from
1962 to 2007) and full-time-equivalent employees (data from 1981 to 2008), we elected to go
with the longer series.

10  The annualized reduction in the size of the federal executive branch workforce as a percentage of
the population from the end of 1992, a month before Clinton took office, to December 31, 1994,
just before the Republican Revolution, was 3.1 percent a year. From the end of 1994 to the end
of 2000, the last full month that saw both Clinton in the White House and the Republicans controlling Congress, the reduction was 2.7 percent a year.

11  IRS Updates Tax Gap Estimates, IR-2006-28, Feb. 14, 2006 (http://www.irs.gov/newsroom/
article/0,,id=154496,00.html). Page last reviewed or updated: Nov. 2, 2007, accessed April 2009.

12  Understanding the Tax Gap, FS-2005-14, March 2005 (http://www.irs.gov/newsroom/ article/0,,id=137246,00.html). Page last reviewed or updated: Nov. 2, 2007, accessed April 2009.

13  Data from the BEA's NIPA Table 2.1, Personal Income and Its Disposition (http://www.bea.gov/ national/nipaweb/TableView.asp?SelectedTable=58&ViewSeries=NO&Java=no&Request3Place= N&3Place=N&FromView=YES&Freq=Year&FirstYear=1929&LastYear=2008&3Place=N&Update= Update&JavaBox=no#Mid), accessed on March 26, 2009. Personal income was obtained from line 1; personal current taxes came from line 25.

14  Special Message to the Congress on Taxation, April 20, 1961. Accessed from the University of California at Santa Barbara's *The American Presidency Project* archives in April 2009, and available at: http://www.presidency.ucsb.edu/ws/index.php?pid=8074&st=&st1=.

15  BEA's NIPA Table 3.2, Federal Government Current Receipts and Expenditures, line 26: Grants-in-aid to state and local governments (http://www.bea.gov/national/nipaweb/TableView.asp ?SelectedTable=85&ViewSeries=NO&Java=no&Request3Place=N&3Place=N&FromView= YES&Freq=Year&FirstYear=1929&LastYear=2008&3Place=N&Update=Update&JavaBox=no#Mi d). Data accessed March 26, 2009.

16  General Explanation of the State and Local Fiscal Assistance Act and the Federal-State Tax Collection Act of 1972, H.R. 14370, 92d Congress, Public Law 92-512 Prepared by the Staff of the Joint Committee on Internal Revenue Taxation, February 12, 1973 (Washington, D.C.: U.S. Government Printing Office, 1973) JCS-1-73, p. 1 (http://ia331418.us.archive.org/3/items/gener-alexplanati00 jcs173/generalexplanati00jcs173.pdf, accessed March 2009).

17  Ibid., p. 2.

18  Richard Nixon, Statement on Signing a Bill to Facilitate the Preservation of Historic Structures Donated to State and Local Governments, August 4, 1972 (http://www.presidency.ucsb.edu/ws/ index.php?pid=3518&st=&st1=, accessed March 2009).

19  Data on social spending by the federal government from line 3 of NIPA Table 3.12, Government Social Benefits. (http://www.bea.gov/national/nipaweb/TableView.asp?Selected Table=108&ViewSeries=NO&Java=no&Request3Place=N&3Place=N&FromView=YES&Freq= Year&FirstYear=1929&LastYear=2007&3Place=N&Update=Update&JavaBox=no#Mid). Data accessed April 19, 2009, updated through August 6, 2008. GDP was obtained from the BEA's NIPA Table 1.1.5, line 1, updated on March 26, 2009. Real expenditures by the federal government per capita were calculated using expenditures as well as population and the CPI. Population was pulled from the BEA's NIPA Table 7.1, line 16, updated on March 26, 2009. CPI was obtained from FRED (http://research.stlouisfed.org/fred2/series/CPIAUCNS?cid=9, accessed April 2009).

20  Special Message to the Congress Transmitting Reorganization Plan of 1953 Creating the Department of Health, Education, and Welfare, March 12, 1953. Accessed in April 2009 from the University of California at Santa Barbara's *The American Presidency Project* archives, available at: http://www.presidency.ucsb.edu/ws/index.php?pid=9794&st=&st1=.

21  Data on spending by the NEA comes from the NEA's Appropriations History (http://www.nea.gov/ about/Budget/AppropriationsHistory.html, accessed April 2009). The data is collected by fiscal year. Given the way the data was reported, we assumed that expenditures for 1976, including the orphan quarter, were the amount reported as being spent through the third quarter of 1976, and adjusted the Nixon/Ford figures to reflect that orphaned quarter. Additionally, because the NEA budget is by calendar year, federal expenditure data used in this section is also by calendar year and was collected from the White House's OMB Historical Table 1.3—Summary of Receipts, Outlays, and Surpluses or Deficits (−) in Current Dollars, Constant (FY 2000) Dollars, and as Percentages of GDP: 1940–2013 (http://www.gpoaccess.gov/usbudget/fy09/sheets/hist01z3.xls), accessed April 16, 2009.)

1   Accessed from the University of California at Santa Barbara's *The American Presidency Project* archives, available at: http://www.presidency.ucsb.edu/ws/index.php?pid=42687, accessed April 2009.

2   The government does receive small amounts of revenue from other sources, such as customs duties (which differ from taxes how?), donations from the public (for example, civic-minded Americans donate to national parks and museums, and even to reduce the national debt), sales of government property, and interest on deposits made by the Federal Reserve or by trust funds run by the federal government (such as Social Security or Medicare). However, these tend to be much smaller than the take from taxes.

3   All data used in this chapter has been cited in earlier chapters.

4   All population data for Rondônia comes from the Brazilian Institute for Geography and Statistics (Instituto Brasileiro de Geografia e Estatística), 2007 Census (Contagem da População), Table 1.1.1 (ftp://ftp.ibge.gov.br/Contagem_da_Populacao_2007/Agregado_por_Setores_Censitarios_2007/, accessed April 2009).

5   Ohio population data from the state government of Ohio (http://www.odod.state.oh.us/Research/files/p103000006.xls, accessed April 2009).

6   The average tax burden is computed only for the years an administration was in office. Thus, for Ike, the average tax burden was the average of the tax burdens from 1953 to 1960. The annualized change in real GDP per capita over the span of each administration was taken from Chapter 1.

7   Greenspan, *The Age of Turbulence*, p. 147.

8   T. Tamkins, "Study: Job Loss Associated with Health Problems," CNN, May 8, 2009 (http://www.cnn.com/2009/HEALTH/05/08/job.loss.hypertension/, accessed April 2009).

## CHAPTER 7

1   Accessed May 2009, from the University of California at Santa Barbara's *The American Presidency Project* archives, available at http://www.presidency.ucsb.edu/ws/index.php?pid=78283.

2   Data on social spending by the federal government from line 3 of NIPA Table 3.12, Government Social Benefits (http://www.bea.gov/national/nipaweb/TableView.asp?SelectedTable=108&ViewSeries=NO&Java=no&Request3Place=N&3Place=N&FromView=YES&Freq=Year&FirstYear=1929&LastYear=2007&3Place=N&Update=Update&JavaBox=no#Mid). Data accessed April 19, 2009, updated through August 6, 2008. GDP was obtained from the BEA's NIPA Table 1.1.5, line 1, updated on March 26, 2009. Real expenditures by the federal government per capita were calculated using expenditures as well as population and the CPI. Population figures were drawn from the BEA's NIPA Table 7.1, line 16, updated on March 26, 2009. CPI was obtained from FRED (http://research.stlouisfed.org/fred2/series/CPIAUCNS?cid=9, accessed May 2009).

3   It should be noted that many people seem to feel that FDR's policies made the Great Depression worse. This theory fails to take into account one key detail: The Great Depression affected countries around the world and its effects lasted the longest in countries where the government did not intervene in the market.

4   Data is available from 1959 to 2007 from the Census Bureau's Historical Poverty Table 2, Poverty Status of People by Family Relationship, Race, and Hispanic Origin: 1959 to 2007 (http://www.census.gov/hhes/www/poverty/histpov/hstpov2.xls, accessed May 2009).

5   Ronald Reagan, Address before a Joint Session of Congress on the State of the Union, January 25, 1988. Accessed from the University of California at Santa Barbara's *The American Presidency Project* archives at (http://www.presidency.ucsb.edu/ws/index.php?pid=36035. Accessed April 2009

6   Data is available from the Census Bureau's "Historical Income Tables—Families," *Gini Ratios for Families, by Race and Hispanic Origin of Householder: 1947 to 2007* (http://www.census.gov/hhes/

www/income/histinc/f04.html), accessed April 23, 2009. Note that data for the Gini ratio applied to individuals is also available (http://www.census.gov/hhes/www/income/histinc/ie2.html), but it only goes back to 1967, so we opted to use family-level data, since it goes back further. However, the correlation between the Gini ratio calculated using family-level data and the Gini ratio calculated using individual-level data is 98 percent, so we believe our results would be similar had we been able to use data for individuals going back to 1952.

7   Carmen DeNavas-Walt, Bernadette D. Proctor, and Jessica C. Smith, "Income, Poverty, and Health Insurance Coverage in the United States: 2007," U.S. Department of Commerce, Economics and Statistics Administration, U.S. Census Bureau, p. 9, Footnote 14 (http://www.census.gov/prod/2008pubs/p60-235.pdf, accessed April 2009).

8   http://research.stlouisfed.org/fred2/series/HOUST. Accessed April 2009.

9   Brian Riedl, "Another Year at the Federal Trough: Farm Subsidies for the Rich, Famous, and Elected Jumped Again in 2002," Heritage Foundation Backgrounder #1763 (http://www.heritage.org/Research/Budget/bg1763.cfm, accessed April 2009).

10  Adam Smith and Germain Garnier, *An Inquiry Into the Nature and Causes of the Wealth of Nations: . . . with a Life of the Author. Also, A View of the Doctrine of Smith Compared with That of the French Economists . . . from the French of M. Garnier.* Complete in One Volume, T. Nelson, ed., 1852, p. 355 (digitized by Google: http://books.google.com/books?id=70759KjSs0sC). Accessed April 2009.

11  Ibid.

12  "Historical Effective Federal Tax Rates: 1979 to 2006," Congressional Budget Office, table titled: "Effective Federal Tax Rates for All Households, by Comprehensive Household Income Quintile, 1979–2006" (http://cbo.gov/publications/collections/taxdistribution.cfm, accessed April 2009).

13  *IRS Updates Tax Gap Estimates,* IR-2006-28, Feb. 14, 2006 (updated November 2, 2007). Accessed April, 2009, at http://www.irs.gov/newsroom/article/0,,id=154496,00.html.

14  Data is available from the White House Office of Management and Budget Table 3.1, "Outlays by Superfunction and Function: 1940–2013" (http://www.gpoaccess.gov/usbudget/fy09/sheets/hist03z1.xls, accessed April 2009) by fiscal year, through 2007. While forecasts for later years are available, we have not used the forecasts, as OMB forecasts are typically politically motivated and inaccurate. Fiscal years ran from July to June until 1976, and from October to September thereafter. Because the "orphaned" quarter results showed an uncharacteristically large and not credible change, we assumed spending on natural resources in the environment as a share of the budget at the end of the Nixon/Ford term was equal to spending on natural resources and the environment as a share of the budget at the end of the 1976 fiscal year. Because the data is by fiscal year, all other data we used in this section was by fiscal year as well. Additional data employed includes total federal spending by fiscal year, also from OMB Table 3.1, and GDP from OMB Table 1.2, "Summary of Receipts, Outlays, and Surpluses or Deficits (–) as Percentages of GDP: 1930–2013" (http://www.gpoaccess.gov/usbudget/fy09/sheets/hist01z2.xls, accessed April 2009). CPI was obtained from FRED (http://research.stlouisfed.org/fred2/series/CPIAUCNS?cid=9, accessed April 2009), but we deflated by fiscal rather than calendar year. Population figures also came from FRED (http://research.stlouisfed.org/fred2/series/POP?cid=104, accessed April 2009)—end-of-fiscal-year data was used.

15  It's worth noting that the nation "discovered" a number of toxic disasters in the 1970s, perhaps epitomized by Love Canal.

## CHAPTER 8

1   Accessed May 2009, from the University of California at Santa Barbara's *The American Presidency Project* archives, available at: http://www.presidency.ucsb.edu/ws/index.php?pid=9077&st=health&st1=.

2   Data from the World Bank Quick Query tool (http://ddp-ext.worldbank.org/ext/DDPQQ/member .do?method=getMembers&userid=1&queryId=208), accessed on April 11, 2009.

3   OECD member countries are: Australia, Austria, Belgium, Canada, the Czech Republic, Denmark, Finland, France, Germany, Greece, Hungary, Iceland, Ireland, Italy, Japan, Korea, Luxembourg, Mexico, the Netherlands, New Zealand, Norway, Poland, Portugal, the Slovak Republic, Spain, Sweden, Switzerland, Turkey, the United Kingdom, and the United States.

4   Data for 2006, the last year for which data is available, from the OECD Health Data 2008 file (http://www.irdes.fr/EcoSante/DownLoad/OECDHealthData_FrequentlyRequestedData.xls). Data accessed on April 11, 2009.

5   For some reason, a number of defenders of the American health care system attribute the poor U.S. showing to differences in the way different countries compute infant mortality. However, the U.S. Centers for Disease Control states categorically that "It appears unlikely that differences in reporting are the primary explanation for the United States' relatively low international ranking." Quote from Marian F. MacDorman and T. J. Mathews, M.S., "Recent Trends in Infant Mortality in the United States," NCHS Data Brief, Number 6, October 2008 (http://www.cdc.gov/nchs/data/ databriefs/db09.htm#howdoes, accessed May 2009).

6   Centers for Medicare and Medicaid Services, Office of the Actuary: Data from the National Health Statistics Group (http://www.cms.hhs.gov/NationalHealthExpendData/downloads/nhegdp07.zip, accessed May 2009). Data was converted to 2008 dollars using the CPI, as in previous chapters.

7   Ibid.

8   Ibid.

9   "Limiting Tort Liability for Medical Malpractice," Congressional Budget Office, January 8, 2004. (http://www.cbo.gov/doc.cfm?index=4968&type=0, accessed February 2009).

10  Unfortunately, we have not found any easy-to-use repositories of that data. Instead, we collected data from various sources, each of which obtains that data from the CDC. Because the data is revised, on occasion data obtained from the various sources doesn't match precisely. In those instances, we used the data that seemed to have been provided by the CDC most recently. (Note that differences that do exist as a result of revisions are trivial; the CDC does a thorough job.) Data for 2005 through 2007 was obtained from the CDC directly: "Births, Marriages, Divorces, and Deaths: Provisional Data for 2007," National Vital Statistics Reports, vol. 56, no. 21, National Centers for Health Statistics, CDC (http://www.cdc.gov/nchs/data/nvsr/nvsr56/nvsr56_21.htm, accessed May 2009). Data for 1970 and 1980 was obtained from the 2009 Statistical Abstract of the United States, Table 110 (http://www.census.gov/compendia/statab/tables/09s0109.xls, accessed May 2009). Data for 1955, 1957, 1960, and 1971 to 1979 was obtained from the 2007 Statistical Abstract of the United States, Table 75 (http://www.census.gov/compendia/statab/tables/07s0076.xls, accessed May 2009). Data for 1961 to 1969 was obtained from the OECD (http://lysander.sourceoecd.org/ vl=2829650/cl=16/nw=1/rpsv/factbook2009/11/01/02/index.htm, accessed May 2009). Data for 1956, 1958, and 1959 was obtained from the Statistical Abstract of the United States for 1962, Table 66, and data for 1953 through 1954 came from the Statistical Abstract of the United States for 1956, Table 75. PDF versions of the Statistical Abstract of the United States from 1951 to 1994 can be obtained from the Census Bureau: http://www.census.gov/prod/www/abs/statab1951-1994.htm.

11  Note that the OECD does not have this data for South Korea, and data for Mexico is included beginning only in 1970, thus explaining the small spike observed that year.

12  Special Message to the Congress on Problems of Population Growth, July 18, 1969, accessed in May 2009, from the University of California at Santa Barbara's The American Presidency Project archives, available at: http://www.presidency.ucsb.edu/ws/index.php?pid=2132.

13  America's Children in Brief: Key National Indicators of Well-Being, 2008, National Institutes of Health (http://www.nichd.nih.gov/publications/pubs/upload/americas_children_in_brief _report2008.pdf, accessed May 2009).

14  2006 Current Population Survey, Fertility of American Women, Historical Table SF1 (http://www.census.gov/population/socdemo/fertility/cps2006/SupFertTab1.xls, accessed May 2009).

15  Data for health insurance is available from Table HIA-1, Health Insurance Coverage Status and Type of Coverage by Sex, Race and Hispanic Origin: 1999 to 2007 (http://www.census.gov/hhes/www/hlthins/historic/hihistt1.xls, accessed May 2009); as noted by the title, this covers the period from 1999 to 2007. Data for earlier years was obtained from Table HI-1of the same document. Health Insurance Coverage Status and Type of Coverage by Sex, Race and Hispanic Origin: 1987 to 2005 (http://www.census.gov/hhes/www/hlthins/historic/hlthin05/hihistt1.html), accessed April 2009. Unfortunately, the two series were computed differently, and though the numbers during overlapping years are similar, they are not identical. Thus, for graphing purposes, we use figures from 1987 to 1998 from the first series, and from 1999 onward from the second one. However, to be consistent, when computing the growth rate under Clinton, we use data from 1992 and 2000 from the second series, and to compute the growth rate under GW, we use data from 2000 to 2006 from the first series.

16  Figures from "Giving Hillary Credit for SCHIP," FactCheck.org, March 18, 2008. Available at http://www.factcheck.org/elections-2008/giving_hillary_credit_for_schip.html and accessed December 2009.

17  M. E. Rimsza, R. J. Butler, and W. G. Johnson, "Impact of Medicaid Disenrollment on Health Care Use and Cost," *Pediatrics* 119, no. 5 (2007): e1026–e1032. doi:10.1542/peds.2006-2747. PMID 17473075. (http://pediatrics.aappublications.org/cgi/content/full/119/5/e1026, accessed May 2009).

## CHAPTER 9

1  Accessed in December 2009, from the University of California at Santa Barbara's *The American Presidency Project* archives avaiable at http://www.presidency.ucsb.edu.

2  Data on public order and safety is obtained from line 49 of the BEA's NIPA Table 3.16 (http://www.bea.gov/national/nipaweb/TableView.asp?SelectedTable=315&ViewSeries=NO&Java=no&Request3Place=N&3Place=N&FromView=YES&Freq=Year&FirstYear=1959&LastYear=2007&3Place=N&Update=Update&JavaBox=no#Mid, accessed April 2009). In this section, we also use total Federal Expenditures (line 42 of Table 3.16), as well as average annual population (http://research.stlouisfed.org/fred2/series/POP, accessed April 2009) and CPI (http://research.stlouisfed.org/fred2/series/CPIAUCNS?cid=9, accessed April 2009), both of which were obtained from FRED.

3  The data comes from multiple pages on the FBI Web site. As has been our practice throughout this book, when multiple sources provide data for the same year, we have used the most recent source. Data for 2008 comes from Crime in the United States, Preliminary Semiannual Uniform Crime Report, January to June 2008, Table 3, Percent Change for Consecutive Years (http://www.fbi.gov/ucr/2008prelim/table_3.html). Data for 2007 comes from Crime in the United States, 2007, Table 16, Rate: Number of Crimes per 100,000 Inhabitants (http://www.fbi.gov/ucr/cius2007/data/table_16.html). Data for 1987 through 2006 comes from Crime in the United States, 2006, Table 1: Crime in the United States by Volume and Rate per 100,000 Inhabitants, 1987–2006 (http://www.fbi.gov/ucr/cius2006/data/table_01.html). Data for the period from 1950 to 1986 comes from J. A. Fox and M. W. Zawitz, Homicide trends in the US, Bureau of Justice Statistics, table titled: "Long term trends." Last revised July 11, 2007 (http://www.ojp.usdoj.gov/bjs/homicide/tables/totalstab.htm). All series were accessed on April 14, 2009.

4  Steven D. Levitt and Stephen J. Dubner, *Freakonomics*, (New York: Harper Collins, 2005), p. 6.

5  Data on officers from 1982 to 2005 comes from the FBI's Bureau of Justice Statistics (http://bjsdata.ojp.usdoj.gov/dataonline/Search/EandE/state_emp_totals.cfm, accessed April, 2009).

6  P. Shukovsky, "FBI Saw Mortgage Fraud Early," *Seattle Post-Intelligencer* (January 28, 2009) (http://seattlepi.nwsource.com/national/397690_fbiweb28.html, accessed January 28, 2009).

7  Because this is a charged topic, it's worth pointing out right off the bat that one of the authors of

this book owns a few guns.

8   Crime in the United States, 2007, Expanded Homicide Table 6 (http://www.fbi.gov/ucr/cius2007/offenses/expanded_information/data/shrtable_06.html, accessed April 2009).

9   http://www.reuters.com/finance/stocks/companyProfile?symbol=RGR.N&rpc=66, accessed April 16, 2009.

10  Data on the monthly closing price, adjusted for stock splits and dividends, was obtained from Yahoo's Finance page (http://finance.yahoo.com/). The data was accessed on April 16, 2009.

11  http://www.ojp.usdoj.gov/bjs/homicide/tables/oagetab.htm, accessed April 16, 2009.

12  http://www.ojp.usdoj.gov/bjs/homicide/gender.htm, accessed April 16, 2009.

13  Data from 1986 to 2007 was obtained from Report to Congress on the Activities and Operations of the Public Integrity Section for 2007 (http://www.usdoj.gov/criminal/pin/docs/arpt-2007.pdf, accessed April 2009). Data from 1980 to 1985 was obtained from the 1999 version of the same report (http://72.14.253.104/search?q=cache:oRol66AmuSEJ:www.usdoj.gov/criminal/pin/docs/Annual_Report_1999.pdf+%22report+to+congress+on+the+activities+and+operations+of+the+public+integrity+section%22+1990&hl=en&ct=clnk&cd=1&gl=us, accessed April 2009).

14  The conviction rate exceeds 100 percent in some years because defendants might have been arrested years before they were finally convicted.

15  Ike was included even though there was only enough data to give him a score on one issue—the murder rate—because only two issues were involved in producing the ranking on crime.

## CHAPTER 10

1   Accessed in December 2009, from the University of California at Santa Barbara's *The American Presidency Project* archives, available at: http://www.presidency.ucsb.edu/ws/index.php?pid=25954.

2   Until 1976, the survey was only conducted every four months.

3   Consumer confidence is available from FRED. Data through 1977 is available at http://research.stlouisfed.org/fred2/series/UMCSENT1?cid=98. Data beginning in 1978 is available at http://research.stlouisfed.org/fred2/series/UMCSENT?cid=98.

4   A. J. Kposowa, "Unemployment and Suicide: A Cohort Analysis of Social Factors Predicting Suicide in the US—National Longitudinal Mortality Study," *Psychological Medicine* 31, no. 1 (2001): 127–138 (http://journals.cambridge.org/action/displayAbstract?fromPage=online&aid=64005, accessed December 2008).

5   M. Berk, S. Dodd, and M. Henry, "The Effect of Macroeconomic Variables on Suicide," *Psychological Medicine* 36, no. 2 (2006): 181–189 (http://journals.cambridge.org/action/displayAbstract?fromPage=online&aid=379660, accessed December 2008).

6   A. Fleischmann et al., "Effectiveness of Brief Intervention and Contact for Suicide Attempters: A Randomized Controlled Trial in Five Countries," *Bulletin of the World Health Organization* 86, no. 9 (September 2008): 657–736. (http://www.who.int/bulletin/volumes/86/9/07-046995/en/index.html, accessed December, 2008.). We use age-adjusted data to account for the fact that suicide is more prevalent among certain age groups.

7   Data from 1952 to 1959 from the CDC's National Center for Health Statistics, HIST293. Age-Adjusted Death Rates, Suicide, 1950–59 (http://www.cdc.gov/nchs/data/dvs/hist293_1950_59.pdf, accessed December 2008). Data from 1960 to 2005 comes from the Statistical Abstract of the United States, 2009, Table 112 (http://www.census.gov/compendia/statab/tables/09s0112.xls, accessed December 2008.). Data for 2006 comes from line 11 of Table B from M. Heron et al., "Deaths: Preliminary Data for 2006," *National Vital Statistics Reports* 56, no. 16 (June 11, 2008): p. 5. (http://www.cdc.gov/nchs/data/nvsr/nvsr56/nvsr56_16.pdf, accessed December 2008).

8   BEA, U.S. International Transactions Accounts Data, Table 1, "U.S. International Transactions" (http://www.bea.gov/international/xls/table1.xls), accessed July 20, 2009.

9    Data obtained from FRED: http://research.stlouisfed.org/fred2/series/DTWEXM/
     downloaddata?cid=94, accessed January 2009.

10   *The Onion*, "Bush: 'Our Long National Nightmare Of Peace And Prosperity Is Finally Over,'"
     January 17, 2001, available at http://www.theonion.com/content/node/28784, accessed
     January 2009.


## CHAPTER 11

1    Accessed in December 2009 from the University of California at Santa Barbara's *The American
     Presidency Project* archives, available at http://www.presidency.ucsb.edu.

2    All data on abortions used in this chapter comes from S. Gamble et al., "Abortion Surveillance:
     United States, 2005," *Surveillance Summaries*, Division of Reproductive Health, National Center
     for Chronic Disease Prevention and Health Promotion (Washington, D.C.: Centers for Disease
     Control, November 28, 2008). The document was accessed in February 2009, at http://www.
     cdc.gov/mmwr/preview/mmwrhtml/ss5713a1.htm.

3    Data from the U.S. Census. Figures from after 1980: http://www.census.gov/compendia/statab/
     tables/07s0011.xls, accessed in February 2009. Figures from before 1980: http://www.census.
     gov/opes/archives/pre=1980/PE=11.html, accessed in February 2009. Update, December 2009:
     the first website has become inactive since this footnote was originally written; however, the
     Census currently maintains a portal from which all population data is available at http://www.
     census.gov/popest/national/asrh/.

4    Data for states in which abortion data is missing for a given year also do not include figures for
     live births in those states during those years.

5    Gary L. Bauer, "Illegitimate Rhetoric: Clinton Administration's Policies toward Sex Education,"
     *National Review* (August 15, 1994): 59 (http://findarticles.com/p/articles/mi_m1282/is_n15_v46/
     ai_15729654/). Accessed February 2009.

6    Data through 1967 comes from "100 Years of Marriage and Divorce Statistics, United States,
     1867–1967" (http://www.cdc.gov/nchs/data/series/sr_21/sr21_024.pdf, accessed February 2009.)
     and data for 1968 and 1969 comes from the 1971 Statistical Abstract of the United States (http://
     www2.census.gov/prod2/statcomp/documents/1970-01.pdf, accessed February 2009). Data
     for 1970 through 2005 comes from the 2009 Statistical Abstract of the United States, Table 77
     (http://www.census.gov/compendia/statab/tables/09s0077.xls, accessed February 2009).
     Data for 2005 through 2007 comes from the 2009 Statistical Abstract of the United States,
     Table 123 (http://www.census.gov/compendia/statab/tables/09s0123.xls, accessed February
     2009). Note that data for some years excludes some states. However, when marriage data is
     missing for a given state, divorce data is also excluded for that state, and vice versa.

7    The conference was chaired by then–U.S. Representative Jim Guy Tucker (D-Ark.), who would
     later be convicted of conspiracy and mail fraud.

8    Inner-city men who become fathers are more likely to marry the mother of their children if they
     have a job. Inner-city women are more likely to marry when they are high school graduates, who
     have better earning prospects than their dropout counterparts. (Mark Testa, Nan Marie Astone,
     Marilyn Krogh, and Kathryn M. Neckerman, "Employment and Marriage among Inner-City
     Fathers," *Annals of the American Academy of Political and Social Science*, Vol. 501, The Ghetto
     Underclass: Social Science Perspectives (Jan. 1989), pp. 79–91.)

9    Data on births to unwed mothers is collected by the CDC. Data from 1986 to 2006 was
     obtained from J. Martin et al., "Births: Final Data for 2006," *National Vital Statistics Reports* 57,
     no. 7 (January 7, 2009): 11, Table D (http://www.cdc.gov/nchs/data/nvsr/nvsr57/nvsr57_07.pdf,
     accessed February 2009). Data for years prior to 1986 was obtained from a CDC document,
     Table 1-17, Number and Percent of Births to Unmarried Women, by Race and Hispanic

Origin: United States, 1940–94 (http://www.cdc.gov/nchs/data/statab/t941x17.pdf, accessed February 2009).

10  The reduction in some STDs was so strong that under Clinton, the Centers for Disease Control felt confident enough to launch a program intended to completely eradicate syphilis.

## CHAPTER 12

1   Accessed on December 10, 2009, from the University of California at Santa Barbara's *The American Presidency Project* (http://www.presidency.ucsb.edu/ws/index.php?pid=34162&st=highways&st1=).

2   Thomas Jefferson to John Adams, 1813. ME 13:399. This particular quote is noted at: http://etext.virginia.edu/jefferson/quotations/jeff1370.htm, accessed May 2009.

3   *The Works of John Adams, Second President of the United States*, Volume 4, by John Adams and Charles Francis Adams, p. 199. (The book is accessible via Google Books: http://books .google.com/books?id=QZw8AAAAIAAJ&printsec=frontcover&source=gbs_v2_summary_r&cad =0#v=onepage&q=&f=false.)

4   Data on educational spending from the National Center for Education Statistics. Data for the 2005–2006 school year from: http://nces.ed.gov/pubs2008/expenditures/xls/table_01.xls. Data for earlier school years from: http://nces.ed.gov/programs/digest/d07/tables/dt07_162.asp, accessed April 2009. Note that from 1952 to 1970 data is only available every two years.

5   The list of prestigious schools attended by this very well-educated president includes the Kinkaid Academy in Houston; the Phillips Academy in Andover, Massachusetts; Yale University; and Harvard Business School.

6   When it comes to rankings, we're giving Nixon/Ford a tie with Bush Sr.

7   Terrel H. Bell, *The Thirteenth Man: A Reagan Cabinet Memoir* (New York: The Free Press, 1988), p. 30.

8   "A Nation at Risk," April 1983, http://www.ed.gov/pubs/NatAtRisk/recomm.html, accessed April 2009.

9   E. B. Fiske, "A Nation at a Loss," *New York Times* (April 25, 2008), http://www.nytimes.com/2008/04/25/opinion/25fiske.html, accessed April 2009.

10  Remarks at a White House ceremony marking the first anniversary of the Report of the National Commission on Excellence in Education, May 11, 1984 (accessed in April 2009, from the University of California at Santa Barbara's *The American Presidency Project* archives, available at: http://www.presidency.ucsb.edu/ws/index.php?pid=39915&st=education&st1= federal+government).

11  For example, see Reagan's remarks on receiving another Department of Education report. "Remarks on Receiving the Department of Education Report on Improving Education," March 4, 1986 (accessed in April 2009, from the University of California at Santa Barbara's *The American Presidency Project* archives, available at: http://www.presidency.ucsb.edu/ws/index.php?pid=369 44&st=What+works&st1=).

12  National Patterns of R&D Resources: 2007 Data Update, NSF 08-318, National Science Foundation, Division of Science Resources Statistics, Table 13, Gross Domestic Product and Research and Development (accessed in April 2009 from: http://www.nsf.gov/statistics/nsf08318/ tables/tab13.xls in April 2009).

13  The growth rate for the Eisenhower administration is computed for the seven years from 1953 to 1960, since data for 1952 is not available.

14  For the rankings, we consider JFK/LBJ to be tied with Clinton on this measure.

15  Data on federal infrastructure spending is available from the White House's Office of Management and Budget Table 9.3. Total nondefense infrastructure spending as a share of the budget was computed as the total infrastructure as a share of the budget less defense infrastructure as

a share of the budget. Note that because the data is from the OMB, it is in fiscal years rather than calendar years. As noted earlier, the fiscal year ran from July to June prior to 1976, and has run from October to September since then. Thus, to calculate the annualized change during the Nixon/Ford administration, to account for the added quarter (which occurred while they were in office), the Nixon/Ford administration was assumed to last 8.25 years.

16  R. Weingroff, "In Memory of Ronald Reagan," U.S. Department of Transportation, Federal Highway Administration, Highway History (accessed April 2009 at: http://www.fhwa.dot.gov/infrastructure/reagan.htm).

17  Data from the Energy Information Administration's (EIA) Short-Term Energy Outlook Table 4a, updated April 14, 2009. (http://tonto.eia.doe.gov/cfapps/STEO_Query/steotables.cfm?periodType=Annual&startYear=2004&startQuarter=1&startMonth=1&endYear=2008&endQuarter=4&endMonth=12&tableNumber=9&noScroll=false), accessed April 2009.

18  Data on imports from the EIA's table titled "Crude Oil and Total Petroleum Imports Top 15 Countries," updated April 14, 2009, accessed April 17, 2009 (http://www.eia.doe.gov/pub/oil_gas/petroleum/data_publications/company_level_imports/current/import.html).

19  Data for 2007. Source: Annual Energy Review 2007, Energy Information Administration, Table 1.3, "Energy Consumption by Source, 1949–2007," updated June 23, 2008 (http://www.eia.doe.gov/aer/txt/stb0103.xls), accessed April 2009.

20  Ibid.

21  Full disclosure: One of the authors of this book works for a power company that operates both a pump storage facility and several nuclear power plants. The pump storage facility uses electricity to pump water up a hill to a reservoir at times when demand for power is low and lets the water run downhill through turbines to generate more electricity when demand is greater.

22  Imagine the outcry if someone who wasn't an attorney was nominated for a seat on the Supreme Court or for the position of attorney general.

23  Data from Annual Energy Review 2007, Energy Information Administration, "Table 1.1 Primary Energy Overview, 1949–2007" (http://www.eia.doe.gov/emeu/aer/txt/stb0101.xls), accessed April 2007.

24  FRED, Consumer Price Index for All Urban Consumers: Energy (http://research.stlouisfed.org/fred2/series/CPIENGNS?cid=9), accessed April 2009. Note that the data originates with the Bureau of Labor Statistics.

25  Special Message to the Congress: Program for Economic Recovery and Growth, February 2, 1961 (accessed in April 2009, from the University of California at Santa Barbara's *The American Presidency Project* archives, available at: http://www.presidency.ucsb.edu/ws/?pid=8111.).

26  FRED, Consumer Price Index for All Urban Consumers: Energy (http://research.stlouisfed.org/fred2/series/CPIENGNS?cid=9), accessed April 2009.

27  More oil and gas can be withdrawn from wells if certain chemicals are pumped into those wells. The precise ingredients used in this process—called hydraulic fracturing—vary by company, but suffice it to say it usually isn't stuff you want coming out of your tap.

28  Jim VandeHei and Justin Blum, "Bush Signs Energy Bill, Cheers Steps Toward Self-Sufficiency. Measure Includes Billions in Tax Breaks for Industry," *The Washington Post* (August 9, 2005): A3.

## CONCLUSION

1  Greenspan, *The Age of Turbulence*, p. 122.

2  Ibid., p. 217.

3  Ibid., p. 208.

## APPENDIX 2

1  Ike's administration is not included because we do not have a ranking for the Truman administration that preceded it.

2  A recent example is the Consumer Products Safety Improvement Act of 2008. Large toymakers such as Mattel and Hasbro lobbied heavily to require all toys to undergo third-party testing for lead. Why would a company like Mattel, which had been forced to conduct three recalls (of toys made in China) for that very reason in the years leading up to the passage of that bill, push for such legislation? Large companies can afford that kind of testing, while artisanal toymakers and small competitors cannot. (Timothy P. Carney, "Washington Toy Story Shows Why Regulation Helps the Big Guys," *Washington Examiner,* January 30, 2009, accessed May 3, 2009, at: http://www.washingtonexaminer.com/opinion/columns/TimothyCarney/Washington-toy-story-shows-why-regulation-helps-the-big-guys38690727.html).

3  The model was not applied to Ike because three of the variables are not available for the Ike administration—the previous administration's rank at investing in the future, the change in the Gini coefficient over the span of the previous administration, and the annualized growth in real health care costs per capita.

4  This regression is an ordinary least squares regression, easily replicable using most spreadsheet programs.

5  Because the "investing in future" variable we constructed in Chapter 12 is computed from the rankings of its components (e.g., spending per pupil, energy independence, spending on infrastructure, and spending on R&D), its numerical value does not necessarily have much meaning to most people. Hence, we opted to use rankings for how well each administration performed on that issue, which is an easier concept for most people to understand. However, a regression does not differentiate between ordinal and cardinal values. Thus, using rankings means that for the purpose of the regression, the difference between the first and second ranked administrations is 100% (i.e. "2" is 100% more than "1"), the difference between the second and third ranked administrations is 50% (i.e., "3" is 50% more than "2"), and so on. Differences between administrations at the top of the rankings are magnified, and differences (in terms of the effect on the dependent variable) between administrations at the bottom of the rankings are diminished.

6  Based on the assumptions typically made when running ordinary least squares regressions.

7  Interestingly, while the growth rate in real health care costs per capita is significant at explaining real GDP per capita, it is not significant at explaining real net GDP per capita.

8  Additionally—when looking at the graphs and the regression together, we can conclude that the effect of this variable is clear only when the effect of other variables—like the growth in real M1 per capita, the change in the tax burden, and the previous administration's investments in the future—are taken into account.

9  As with the Gini coefficient, the effect of this variable on real GDP per capita growth rates is only clear when the effect of other variables is taken into account.

## APPENDIX 3

1  Office of Management and Budget, *Budget of the United States* (2008), p. 963 (http://www.whitehouse.gov/omb/budget/fy2008/pdf/appendix/eop.pdf). Accessed May 18, 2009.

2  E. Chen and R. Runningen, "Obama Aide Who Authorized New York Air Force One Flight Quits," Bloomberg, updated May 9, 2009 (http://www.bloomberg.com/apps/news?pid=20601087&sid=aQTmGTV_jBkU&refer=home). Accessed May 9, 2009.

3  Office of Management and Budget, *Budget of the United States* (2008), p. 970 (http://www.whitehouse.gov/omb/budget/fy2008/pdf/appendix/eop.pdf). Accessed May 2009.

## APPENDIX 5

1    Data from NIPA Table 7.1a, accessed February 20, 2010. (http://www.bea.gov/national/nipaweb/
     TableView.asp?SelectedTable=264&ViewSeries=NO&Java=no&Request3Place=N&3Place=N&
     FromView=YES&Freq=Year&FirstYear=1929&LastYear=2009&3Place=N&Update=Update&JavaBox
     =no#Mid).

2    Data from NIPA Table 7.1q, accessed February 20, 2010. As of this writing, data is available through
     the fourth quarter of 2009. (http://www.bea.gov/national/nipaweb/TableView.asp?SelectedTable=
     264&Freq=Qtr&FirstYear=2007&LastYear=2009).

3    Data on revenues is available from NIPA Table 3.2q, accessed February 20, 2010. As of this writ-
     ing, data is available through the third quarter of 2009. (http://www.bea.gov/national/nipaweb/
     TableView.asp?SelectedTable=87&ViewSeries=NO&Java=no&Request3Place=N&3Place=N&
     FromView=YES&Freq=Qtr&FirstYear=1952&LastYear=2009&3Place=N&Update=Update&
     JavaBox=no#Mid). Data on GDP is available from NIPA Table 1.1.5q, accessed February 20, 2010.
     (http://www.bea.gov/national/nipaweb/TableView.asp?SelectedTable=5&ViewSeries=NO&Java=no
     &Request3Place=N&3Place=N&FromView=YES&Freq=Qtr&FirstYear=1947&LastYear=2009&3Plac
     e=N&Update=Update&JavaBox=no#Mid).

4    Data on revenues is available from NIPA Table 3.2q, accessed February 20, 2010. As of this writ-
     ing, data is available through the third quarter of 2009. (http://www.bea.gov/national/nipaweb/
     TableView.asp?SelectedTable=87&ViewSeries=NO&Java=no&Request3Place=N&3Place=N&
     FromView=YES&Freq=Qtr&FirstYear=1952&LastYear=2009&3Place=N&Update=Update&Ja
     vaBox=no#Mid). Data on GDP is available from NIPA Table 1.1.5q, accessed February 20, 2010.
     (http://www.bea.gov/national/nipaweb/TableView.asp?SelectedTable=5&ViewSeries=NO&Java=no
     &Request3Place=N&3Place=N&FromView=YES&Freq=Qtr&FirstYear=1947&LastYear=2009&3Plac
     e=N&Update=Update&JavaBox=no#Mid).

5    Joshua Aizenman and Gurnain Kaur Pasricha, "On the ease of overstating the fiscal stimulus in the
     US, 2008-9," NBER Working paper 15784 (2010).

# Acknowledgments

★ ★ ★

This book is a collaboration between the two authors. While we worked together, each of us also brought his own support system to the project, and the book has benefited tremendously not just from the melding of the authors' writing, but also from the merging of the help and support provided to each of the authors separately and together.

## ACKNOWLEDGMENTS BY MIKE KIMEL

I would like to thank, first and foremost, my wife Heather. She read every word of every draft, and eviscerated what we wrote when it needed eviscerating. She not only tolerated all the time and energy and effort I had to dedicate to this book, but encouraged me to go forward as well. It is no exaggeration to say that this book would not exist at all without her active help and support.

I also would like to thank my parents Isidoro and Deanna, my sister Laura, and my stepmother Suzy for providing encouragement and suggestions beginning when this book was only a vague idea. Lee Fischman also provided thoughts on how to bring a loose collection of ideas and concepts together into a book.

Another source of encouragement and assistance came from the crew at the Angry Bear blog (http://www.angrybear.blogspot.com) Many of the ideas and explanations from early drafts of the book were posted on the blog and shaped by feedback from the readers. Special thanks are owed to Dan Crawford, for encouraging me to test-drive some concepts for the book on the blog, and Daniel Becker, who read several early drafts and made extremely detailed comments and suggestions. Other writers and readers who were especially helpful with comments include Tom Bozzo, Dale Coberly, Spencer England, Laurent Guerby, Ken Houghton, Mike Johnson, Holly Nelson, Robert Waldmann, and Bruce Webb; incisive points made by each of them are a part of this book. Don Black and Doug Fuller often disagreed with me and frequently forced me back to the drawing board, and yet continued to encourage this project throughout.

The Angry Bear influence on this book also comes by way of Donald Trader, perhaps the first person outside my circle of immediate family and lifelong friends to believe in the project. Don thought this book could have a big impact, and I am so very sorry he did not live see to it completed. I can only hope the book lives up to his expectations. I would also like to thank Emily Trader for sparing kind words for this project at a time of great loss.

Since some of the spirit of the book first appeared in blog posts, commentary from other bloggers also formed feedback. Having a post "linked to" approvingly by a respected writer provides a reality check when one is working on a topic that can be controversial. Posts by Steve Benen, Hilary Bok, Brad DeLong, Kevin Drum, Ezra Klein, Bill McBride, Yves Smith, Mark Thoma, Andrew Sullivan, and Matthew Yglesias commenting on one or another topic all helped to propel the book forward, whether these bloggers know it or not. Alex Tabarrok provided some advice via email on writing a book. While help and positive comments are encouraging, being disparaged can also be useful, as it can point to changes that must be made. Megan McArdle and James Pethokoukis will probably be horrified to be mentioned here, but they did make the book much stronger, however inadvertently.

Several colleagues read early drafts and provided comments, including Larry Dent, Robert Skupinski, Craig Truesdell, and Jim Webb. Encouragement was also provided by Alin Baciu, Marty Bolan, Marie Savula-Smith, and James Vrbanic. Outside the workplace, Tom Salk and Mario de Souza also provided feedback at different points during the project. Xie Shiqiang also helped by checking some of the numbers.

Finally, I would be derelict if I did not thank my coauthor, Michael E. Kanell, who was willing to put so much time, effort, and frustration into working on this vision. Prior to his involvement, the book was not just a shapeless blob; it was an unreadable shapeless blob with no focus. Together we wrote and rewrote and rewrote and rewrote and rewrote, and then rewrote some more until the book took the form you see before you.

## ACKNOWLEDGMENTS BY MICHAEL E. KANELL

My wife, Gillian F. Gansler, deserves my never-ending gratefulness and thanks for so many reasons. I want to thank her now for her patience, encouragement, and willingness to share childcare during the long and late hours that went into this project. Without her help and support, my participation would have been impossible. To my children, Jenna and Vance, I also owe thanks, for tolerating a sometimes distracted, often sleep-deprived father, of course. But by making my home life so rich, they afforded me the luxury of using so much energy for this project.

To my mother, Sylvia, and my late father, Martin, I owe a set of values that include a willingness to work hard, determination to complete what you start, and an openness to all sides of an argument that has served me well as a journalist. My family had a devotion to both education and practicality, as well as a certain argumentative streak that also led to the understanding that sometimes only one side is right.

I would like to thank the *Atlanta Journal-Constitution* for its support. The paper has been one of the premier journalistic institutions in the country with a proud history. I very much appreciate the AJC providing me the opportunity to study and report on the economy these years.

Among the many excellent editors I have worked with during my career, I want to thank Jennifer Hill, Donna Lorenz, Dean Anason, and Paige Oliver Taylor. They pushed me to do my best work and I am grateful.

To my colleagues, here and at other newspapers, I give thanks for frequent debates over the economy, as well as for the shared expectation that whatever the odds, we all strive for excellence.

Long ago, when I was covering government in Massachusetts, my editor suggested I shift to covering business and the economy: "No night meetings," he said. That turned out to be an excellent move. Thank you, Ken Hartnett.

I also want to thank some of the economists to whom I spoke frequently and who influenced my judgment and analysis along the way: Talking with Rajeev Dhawan, Roger Tutterow, Mark Vitner, and Adrian Cronje has been like taking a series of seminars with a set of patient, smart, and well-informed mentors.

I also want to thank my coauthor, Mike Kimel, who was a terrific partner throughout this project, tirelessly crunching numbers and following the facts wherever they led. Despite the similarities in our names, we were clearly of different minds on many questions. But if we had disagreements, there was never a hint that his views were anything but a devotion to the hard kernels of truth beneath the sifted data. This book was his vision and the lion's share of the data was always in his hands, but he let me join him in the enterprise and treated me as an equal. I owe him thanks for all of that.

## JOINT ACKNOWLEDGMENTS

Two individuals who did a lot to make this book into what it is are our agent David Fugate of Launch Books and our editor Becky Koh of Black Dog & Leventhal Publishers. Each of them tore to shreds manuscripts we honestly thought were done (and they did it so nicely!!!), and then forced us to rewrite them over again. It was painful at times, but the difference between then and now is huge. We cannot thank either of them enough.

We also owe a debt of gratitude to Nigel Holmes, who took the graphs we created in Excel and made them look book-worthy. Nigel also created a number of diagrams and illustrations clarify concepts mentioned in the text, making the book more readable.

Finally, we are, no doubt, forgetting someone's help and contributions, and for that we apologize.

# Index

★ ★ ★